Proceedings in Technology Transfer

Series Editors

The book series "Proceedings in Technology Transfer" provides a valuable platform for researchers, practitioners, and policymakers to share their experiences and insights related to technology transfer. Our aim is to facilitate knowledge exchange between academic researchers and industry professionals, accelerating the introduction of new technologies and driving economic growth.

Our series publishes books and conference proceedings that focus on original research findings, best practice recommendations, emerging trends, and technology evaluations. The series covers all topics which explore the transfer of technology in various industry sectors that require innovations and economic growth.

Join us in advancing the technology transfer and its impact on innovation. Publish your proceedings with us and offer insights and expertise to professionals in your field.

Lukas Bechtel · Tobias Heer
Editors

Computation and Communication for Smart Systems Symposium

Proceedings of the C2S3, April 9–11, 2025, Esslingen, Germany

Springer

Editors
Lukas Bechtel
Computer Science and Engineering
Esslingen University of Applied Sciences
Esslingen, Germany

Tobias Heer
Informatik und Informationstechnik
Hochschule Esslingen
Esslingen, Deutschland

ISSN 2948-2321 ISSN 2948-233X (electronic)
Proceedings in Technology Transfer
ISBN 978-3-032-10568-4 ISBN 978-3-032-10569-1 (eBook)
https://doi.org/10.1007/978-3-032-10569-1

This Springer imprint is published by the registered company Springer Nature Switzerland AG
The registered company address is: Gewerbestrasse 11, 6330 Cham, Switzerland

Foreword

"Smart" is the magic word of our time. Hardly any area of computer science or engineering gets by without this label: smart homes and smart buildings, smartphones, smartwatches, smart production. But what actually makes these systems truly smart? It's not just the technology itself, but above all their ability to respond flexibly, provide new functions, deliver real benefits for users while lowering costs. Often there's also interoperability with other systems—that is, the use of standards and open interfaces. If they deserve the name, smart systems are always designed with the future in mind: updatable, extensible, and thus capable of reinventing themselves again and again.

Yet "smart" is a moving target. What was considered innovative yesterday seems self-evident today. New technologies, methods, and ways of thinking continually shift the benchmark—toward more powerful, more ingenious, and more flexible solutions. Artificial intelligence now often solves problems more naturally and efficiently than its classical, programmed predecessors. User interactions via speech and multimodal input are seen today as the epitome of "smart." But does that automatically make tomorrow's devices even smarter—or is the benchmark simply shifting again? This constant change turns "smart" into a promise that is never definitively fulfilled, but continually reformulated.

The Computation and Communication for Smart Systems Symposium (C2S3 2025) takes up precisely this idea. On April 9, 2025, the Faculty of Computer Science and Engineering at Esslingen University, together with the projects DFG FIP: Smart Factory Grids and HE-Personal, invited doctoral candidates and researchers to present and discuss their work on smart production systems, IT and network security, artificial intelligence, simulation and modeling, digital twins and Asset Administration Shells (AAS), as well as industrial regulations and trends in critical infrastructures.

The contributions presented here reflect the diversity and dynamism of these topics. They show that "smart" is not a static attribute but a process: the continuous effort to make technology not only more powerful, but also more useful, sustainable, and future-proof.

Contents

Predicting Blood Glucose Levels with Advanced Time Series Models 1
Tolgahan Kandemir, Maike Knauer, Enes Coskunyürek, and Markus Enzweiler

Security Analysis of Hardware Electric Vehicle Charging Infrastructure 13
Nils Lohmiller, Henning Weise, and Tobias Heer

Data-Driven Approaches to Micromobility Demand Modeling 37
Ruben Röhner, Damir Ravlija, Ingo Trautwein, and Mirko Sonntag

How to Tame GeNESIS: A Tutorial for Utilizing GeNESIS to Simulate Realistic Industrial Evaluation Scenarios 53
Samuel Müller, Lukas Popperl, Lukas Bechtel, and Tobias Heer

I Still Know Who You Scanned Last Summer: An Update on the Landscape of Internet Scanners 74
Markus Schramm, Nils Lohmiller, Sabrina Kaniewski, and Tobias Heer

A Performance Comparison of the Homomorphic Encryption Schemes CKKS and TFHE 92
Clemens Krüger, Bhavinkumar Moriya, and Dominik Schoop

Tracking Micromobility-Battery-SOC-Levels with 3D-SUMO-Simulations Based on Real World Ride-Data 109
Emanuel Reichsöllner, Damir Ravlija, Andreas Freymann, and Mirko Sonntag

Unmasking SSH Attackers: A Study on Brute-Force Attempts and Cryptographic Usage 125
Bastian Buck and Tobias Heer

Network Automation with Flow-Based Programming: A Case Study with Node-RED 140
Lukas Bechtel, Julius Ruppert, René Hummen, and Tobias Heer

Weight Initialization of Ensemble Forecast Output Statistics Models for Probabilistic Wind-Speed Forecasting 155
Götz Grimmer, Steffen Schober, and Corinna Möhrlen

Improving Anonymization of Mobility Trajectories with Map-Matching 171
Di Hu and Gabriele Gühring

Author Index 183

Predicting Blood Glucose Levels with Advanced Time Series Models

Tolgahan Kandemir, Maike Knauer, Enes Coskunyürek, and Markus Enzweiler(✉)

Institute for Intelligent Systems, Esslingen University, 73728 Esslingen, Germany
markus.enzweiler@hs-esslingen.de
https://www.hs-esslingen.de/iis

Abstract. Diabetes mellitus is a widespread metabolic disease that requires continuous monitoring of blood glucose levels to prevent life-threatening complications such as hypoglycemia and hyperglycemia. Accurate prediction of blood glucose levels is crucial for improving diabetes management and patient outcomes. This research explores the application of deep learning models to forecast blood glucose levels using the OhioT1DM dataset. A key focus of this study is the optimization of data preprocessing, feature engineering, and hyperparameter tuning to enhance prediction accuracy. Various advanced time series models, including LightTS, Pyraformer, and Crossformer, are evaluated for their ability to predict glucose trends. Our results indicate that LightTS, when trained with a diverse set of additional features besides blood glucose, e.g. air temperature, heart rate, and physical activity, yields the lowest root mean square error (RMSE), surpassing previous state-of-the-art in the public Blood Glucose Level Prediction (BGLP) Challenge. By leveraging attention mechanisms and time-series forecasting techniques, this research demonstrates the potential of these models in medical applications beyond natural language processing. Our findings contribute to the ongoing effort to integrate artificial intelligence into healthcare, providing a foundation for real-time, personalized diabetes management.

Keywords: Blood Glucose Prediction · Time Series Analysis · Medical AI

1 Introduction

1.1 Background

Diabetes mellitus refers to a group of chronic metabolic disorders that affect a significant proportion of the global population. These disorders are primarily classified into two main types. Type 1 diabetes mellitus (insulin-dependent) is typically caused by an autoimmune-mediated destruction of pancreatic β-cells, resulting in insufficient insulin production. In contrast, Type 2 diabetes mellitus is characterized by a combination of insulin resistance - a reduced sensitivity of body cells to insulin - and a compensatory overproduction of insulin, which over

L. Bechtel and T. Heer (Eds.): CCSSS 2025 PTT, pp. 1–12, 2026.
https://doi.org/10.1007/978-3-032-10569-1_1

time leads to functional exhaustion of insulin-producing β-cells. This progressive dysfunction ultimately results in inadequate insulin levels to meet the body's metabolic demands. Type 2 diabetes accounts for the vast majority of diabetes cases worldwide.

Individuals with Type 1 diabetes require lifelong insulin therapy, typically administered via daily injections or insulin pumps, to regulate their blood glucose levels. Maintaining the correct insulin dosage is critical: insufficient insulin can lead to hyperglycaemia, a condition characterized by abnormally high blood glucose levels, which over time increases the risk of long-term complications such as cardiovascular disease, neuropathy, and retinopathy. Conversely, excess insulin may cause hypoglycaemia, defined as abnormally low blood glucose levels, which can result in acute symptoms such as confusion, loss of consciousness, seizures, and, in severe cases, death. Both conditions can have such life-threatening consequences if not promptly detected and managed. Autonomous insulin injection systems integrate real-time glucose monitoring with predictive algorithms to automatically adjust insulin delivery, reducing the risk of dangerous fluctuations and minimizing patient intervention. Accurate blood glucose prediction remains challenging due to the influence of multiple factors such as food intake, activity, and stress.

Ongoing research investigates the integration of artificial intelligence (AI) into medical technology. The potential of AI applications lies in their ability to enhance the health of individuals with diabetes by providing early warnings of dangerous glucose levels and facilitating prevention strategies. However, the research endeavor is substantially hindered by the scarcity of real patient data, a challenge that is further compounded by concerns regarding data protection. Nonetheless, the SmartHealth Lab at Ohio University initiated the BGLP Challenge in 2018 [1]. The BGLP Challenge is a competition for researchers in the field of machine learning to obtain results for 30- and 60-minute prediction horizons of blood glucose levels. The challenge adopts a methodological approach that regards the prediction of blood glucose levels as a time series forecasting problem, investigated through the utilization of batch and incremental time series regression models. Transformer models [2] or efficient sampling-based models [10], widely used for time series forecasting, offer a promising approach by efficiently processing sequential data [2]. Their application in diabetes management could lead to more precise and adaptive glucose prediction, improving automated insulin delivery and patient outcomes.

1.2 Research Question

This study aims to investigate the suitability of advanced time series models, including Transformers, for predicting blood glucose levels. Given their success in various fields, particularly in time series forecasting, the central research question is: *"To what extent are recent advanced time series models suitable for the prediction of blood glucose levels?"* This research explores the effectiveness, accuracy, and potential limitations of such approaches in handling sequential glucose data. By evaluating their ability to capture complex temporal dependencies, we assess their viability for real-world applications in diabetes management and predictive healthcare.

Our research aims to advance blood glucose level prediction using recent models for time series forecasting, comparing their performance against previously published models, which are primarily neural network-based, e.g. [3,4] and [5]. To ensure a rigorous evaluation, we use the public BGLP Challenge as a benchmark. Our goal is to achieve results that comply with the benchmark regulations while being competitive versus the published state-of-the-art in terms of prediction error.

2 Related Work

Despite significant advancements in blood glucose prediction, prior research has predominantly relied on traditional machine learning and deep learning models, such as recurrent neural networks (RNNs) [4] and [6], long short-term memory networks (LSTMs) [7], and convolutional neural networks (CNNs) [3] and [8]. These models have been effective in capturing glucose trends, yet they exhibit limitations in handling long-term dependencies and computational efficiency. To date, no study has systematically explored recent advanced time series models, including Transformer-based architectures, for blood glucose prediction. The best reported results in the BGLP Challenge were achieved using conventional deep learning methods, with an RMSE of 17.45 for a 30-minute prediction window using a convolutional recurrent neural network [3]. While these methods provide reasonable accuracy, their performance is constrained by their sequential processing nature, which limits scalability and the ability to efficiently model long-range dependencies in time series data. Our research addresses this gap by evaluating Transformer models and efficient sampling-based multilayer perceptron (MLP) models as an alternative approach to capture complex temporal relationships more effectively than previous models.

Our contributions are as follows. We evaluate the superiority of advanced time series models for blood glucose level prediction by systematically comparing them against previously published approaches using the BGLP Challenge as a benchmark. Additionally, we enhance predictive accuracy by integrating physiological and contextual features such as air temperature, heart rate, and physical activity, improving the model's adaptability to glucose fluctuations. Our best-performing model overall, LightTS [10], achieved an RMSE of 16.14 for a 30-min prediction window, surpassing the previous state-of-the-art (RMSE of 17.45) on this benchmark. The best-performing transformer-based model is Pyraformer, achieving an RMSE of 19.34 for a 30-min prediction horizon.

These results establish light sampling-based MLP and transformer models as a robust alternative to traditional deep learning methods for personalized diabetes management. Furthermore, this study reinforces the potential of modern architectures for time series forecasting, demonstrating their applicability beyond natural language processing to real-world medical and healthcare applications.

3 Methodology

3.1 Overall Approach

In this study, we employ advanced time series models for blood glucose level prediction, focusing on architectures specifically designed for time series forecasting. Among the available models, we utilize and compare the following: LightTS [10], Crossformer [11], DLinear [12], FiLM [13], Informer [14], iTransformer [15], PatchTST [16], Pyraformer [17], and Transformer [2].

These models differ substantially in their architectural designs and inductive biases. Transformer-based models such as Informer, Pyraformer, and Crossformer employ various attention mechanisms to capture temporal dependencies, with Pyraformer using a pyramid attention structure for multi-scale processing and Crossformer introducing cross-dimension interactions for enhanced temporal representation. PatchTST adopts a patch-based representation tailored for long-horizon forecasting, while iTransformer introduces structured decomposition of temporal features within a Transformer-based framework. FiLM leverages feature-wise linear modulation, providing flexible, context-aware adaptations of intermediate representations. DLinear, in contrast, is a non-attention-based model that assumes linearity and excels in efficient trend modeling.

LightTS is not Transformer-based but rather a lightweight MLP architecture. It applies downsampling strategies to efficiently capture both short- and long-term dependencies. Despite its simplicity, LightTS has shown competitive performance in several time series forecasting benchmarks and is included here to benchmark against Transformer-based approaches.

To ensure a structured evaluation, we use the publicly available Time-Series-Library (TSLib) [9] as our implementation framework. TSLib provides standardized implementations and evaluation pipelines for a broad range of time series models, enabling reproducibility and consistent comparison across model types.

Our methodology consists of the following key steps: First, we preprocess the dataset by integrating additional physiological and contextual features next to the actual blood glucose level measurements, such as air temperature, heart rate, and physical activity, to enhance predictive accuracy. Next, we conduct an extensive model selection process, evaluating multiple Transformer-based architectures within the TSLib framework to determine the most suitable approach for blood glucose level prediction. Following model selection, we perform hyperparameter tuning using grid search and Bayesian optimization to maximize predictive performance. The primary evaluation metric is RMSE, ensuring comparability with the BGLP Challenge benchmark.

3.2 Data Description

In this study, we incorporate multiple contextual signals beyond the raw blood glucose measurements that are continuously measured every five minutes to improve predictive performance. Two key additional modalities are considered: *insulin administration* and *physical activity*, both of which have a direct and physiologically well-established influence on glucose metabolism.

The *insulin* signal is decomposed into three sub-components that differ in temporal structure and physiological effect: *bolus insulin*, which is administered as discrete doses typically around meals; *temporary basal rate* adjustments, which are used to temporarily override the standard background insulin rate; and the continuous *basal rate* itself, which maintains a steady background level. Since these sub-components may overlap in time, we implement a priority-based merging strategy to create a unified insulin time series. At any given time point t, if bolus insulin is present, it is considered the most critical signal and takes precedence. If no bolus dose is recorded, a temporary basal adjustment is used. If neither is present, the basal rate is taken as the default. This prioritization ensures that high-impact, short-term interventions like bolus injections are not obscured by background insulin values.

Similarly, the *activity* signal is composed of overlapping physical and physiological states. We consider three categories: *exercise*, *work-related activity*, and *sleep*. These states are also combined into a single time series using a priority hierarchy, where structured *exercise* takes precedence, followed by *work*, and then *sleep*. This ensures that active and glucose-relevant states such as physical exertion are correctly emphasized over more passive states like sleep when they co-occur or are recorded simultaneously in the dataset.

This priority-based fusion approach preserves semantically relevant temporal information while preventing conflicting or overlapping inputs from degrading signal quality. The resulting structured time series features for insulin and activity are then fed into the forecasting models, providing a richer context for accurate glucose level prediction.

3.3 Full Set of Additional Features

The OhioT1DM dataset [1] that we use provides a diverse set of physiological, behavioral, and environmental features relevant to blood glucose level prediction. These features include direct glucose measurements, insulin administration data, physical activity information, and additional physiological signals such as heart rate and skin temperature. By incorporating these features into our predictive models, we aim to analyze their individual and combined contributions to blood glucose forecasting.

Among these, some features-such as *insulin* and *activity*-are composed of multiple sub-features and require preprocessing before being used as model inputs, as discussed before. These features are merged using a priority-based scheme to ensure a structured representation of their temporal variations. Other features are directly provided as independent time series variables.

Table 1 summarizes the full set of features available in the OhioT1DM dataset. These features can be utilized individually or in combination to assess their impact on prediction performance.

Table 1. Overview of all physiological, behavioral, and environmental features available in the OhioT1DM dataset [1]. The *insulin* and *activity* features are derived from multiple sub-components using priority-based merging, while the remaining features are directly extracted from the dataset and used as individual time series inputs. These features can be flexibly combined to assess their impact on blood glucose level prediction. Note that *glucose_level* is always used as model input.

Feature	Description
glucose_level	Continuous blood glucose measurements (always used)
insulin	Insulin level, merged with other sub-features
activity	Physical activity, merged with other sub-features
finger_stick	Blood glucose measurement via finger stick test
basal_rate	Constant insulin delivery rate
temp_basal_rate	Temporary constant insulin delivery rate
GSR	Galvanic skin response, measures stress
air_temp	Air temperature
heart_rate	Heart rate
skin_temp	Skin temperature
sleep	Sleep quality
work	Work intensity
exercise	Physical exercise
meal	Meal size

3.4 Data-Driven Feature Selection

To identify the optimal combination of features for each model, we determine which feature set yields the best performance for an individual model. A brute-force approach would involve training all possible feature combinations for each model and selecting the set with the lowest RMSE on a validation set. However, this process is computationally prohibitive when applied to all models in the pipeline. To address this, a more efficient strategy is employed. Initially, a single model, LightTS, is used to evaluate all possible feature combinations. The top 10 feature sets, ranked by RMSE, are then identified and subsequently applied to all other models in the pipeline. We assume the selected optimal feature sets to be largely independent from the particular choice of model instance.

This approach significantly reduces the number of training runs while ensuring an informed selection of the most effective feature combinations. By applying the pre-optimized feature sets to all models, the process achieves efficient and effective optimization across the entire model set. Table 2 presents the four best-performing feature sets for LightTS, ranked by RMSE and mean absolute error (MAE).

An interesting observation from Table 2 is that the merged feature *activity*, which consists of the individual sub-features *sleep*, *work*, and *exercise*, does not

Table 2. Top four feature combinations for the LightTS model, ranked by validation RMSE. Each combination is evaluated using both RMSE and mean absolute error (MAE).

Feature Combination	RMSE	MAE
finger_stick, basal_rate, temp_basal_rate, bolus, GSR, air_temp	17.41	12.93
bolus, GSR	17.59	12.69
air_temp, heart_rate, skin_temp, sleep, work, exercise, meal	17.62	12.99
sleep, work	18.35	13.36

yield superior performance compared to the use of its individual sub-features. This is evident from the fact that *activity* is absent from the top-performing feature combinations. If the merged representation had provided a predictive advantage, it would have been ranked among the best-performing feature sets. These findings suggest that preserving individual sub-features instead of merging them may enhance model performance.

4 Experiments and Results

4.1 Experimental Setup

The OhioT1DM dataset [1] consists of continuous glucose monitoring (CGM) readings, insulin administration records, meal consumption details, sleep patterns, and physical activity metrics for individuals with Type 1 diabetes. To ensure the reproducibility of our findings, we follow the dataset partitioning provided by the BGLP Challenge, which had already pre-split the data into training, validation and test sets. Thus, no additional partitioning has been performed in our study.

Our experimental approach follows a structured pipeline, as follows. Data preprocessing involves handling missing values, normalizing time series data, and generating features based on past glucose trends and external influences, such as meal intake and heart rate fluctuations. Training methodologies are explored across three settings: single-patient training, where models were trained on data from an individual patient; cross-patient training, in which models were trained using multiple patients while validating on a separate individual; and generalized model training, where a global model was trained on all available patients and evaluated on a test subset. For details, please refer to the BGLP Challenge description [1].

Model evaluation is based on both the RMSE and MAE metrics. The experiments are conducted on a high-performance computing cluster utilizing GPU-accelerated training in PyTorch using the Time-Series-Library (TSLib) [9] for reproducibility.

4.2 Results

In this section, we present the results of our study, in which we first optimize the hyperparameters of the models under consideration. To this end, we initially select the hyperparameters using brute force sampling (`BruteForceSampler` in the Optuna library) on a validation set. This approach allows to identify the five models with the most promising results in terms of the lowest RMSE, indicating a low model error and thus more precise predictions. By methodically testing all possible hyperparameter combinations, we identify the optimal configuration for each model. As shown in Table 3, LightTS achieves an RMSE of 15.35, while all other models have an RMSE of above 16 on our validation set.

Table 3. Top five results for BruteForceSampler on the validation set. For the Transformer-based models, the following model hyperparameters were optimized: `e_layers` (number of encoder layers), `d_layers` (number of decoder layers), `factor` (attention factor for context selection), `n_heads` (number of attention heads), `d_model` (model dimensionality), `d_ff` (dimension of the feed-forward network), and `top_k` (number of top attention scores retained).

Model	RMSE	Parameter						
		`e_layers`	`d_layers`	`factor`	`n_heads`	`d_model`	`d_ff`	`top_k`
LightTS	15.35	n/a	n/a	n/a	n/a	n/a	n/a	n/a
Transformer	16.18	2	1	2	9	64	3	7
Dlinear	16.34	2	2	1	7	192	2	7
FiLM	16.44	3	1	2	8	384	3	5
Pyraformer	16.49	1	3	3	9	64	3	7

Table 4. Top five results for TPESampler on the validation set. For the Transformer-based models, the following model hyperparameters were optimized: `e_layers` (number of encoder layers), `d_layers` (number of decoder layers), `factor` (attention factor for context selection), `n_heads` (number of attention heads), `d_model` (model dimensionality), `d_ff` (dimension of the feed-forward network), and `top_k` (number of top attention scores retained).

Model	RMSE	Parameter						
		`e_layers`	`d_layers`	`factor`	`n_heads`	`d_model`	`d_ff`	`top_k`
LightTS	15.82	n/a	n/a	n/a	n/a	n/a	n/a	n/a
Pyraformer	15.97	1	1	1	7	64	3	3
Transformer	16.00	3	2	2	9	64	2	5
Dlinear	16.26	1	2	1	8	320	4	3
FiLM	16.47	3	1	2	8	64	3	7

In order to verify the accuracy and robustness of the obtained results, we conducted a comparative study using the same models and hyperparameters to be optimized by a Tree-structured Parzen Estimator (`TPESampler` in the Optuna library). As shown in Table 4, the RMSE values determined by both optimization methods are found to be highly similar, with LightTS still performing best at an RMSE of 15.82 after optimization. The consistency between these approaches provides confidence in our findings. Consequently, the model with the lowest overall RMSE, LightTS with parameters optimized through the brute force sampling, is selected for subsequent analysis and evaluation on the test set.

Table 5. Test set performance of all models and selected BGLP Challenge baselines, evaluated using RMSE and MAE. For each model, the best-performing feature combination (identified during validation) is listed.

Model	Additional Features	RMSE	MAE
LightTS	air_temp, heart_rate, skin_temp, sleep, work, exercise, meal	16.14	11.44
Pyraformer	finger_stick, basal_rate, temp_basal_rate, bolus, GSR, air_temp	19.34	14.28
Crossformer	bolus, GSR	19.91	14.53
PatchTST	bolus, GSR	27.76	20.26
iTransformer	sleep, work	26.35	20.68
Transformer	sleep, work	28.23	21.04
FiLM	sleep, work	30.40	24.83
DLinear	sleep, work	37.21	30.81
Informer	finger_stick, basal_rate, temp_basal_rate, bolus, GSR, air_temp	45.46	36.63
Baseline [3]	no additional features besides glucose_level	17.45	11.22
Baseline [4]	bolus, time_of_day, meal	18.22	12.83
Baseline [21]	no additional features besides glucose_level	18.23	14.37
Baseline [19]	bolus, meal	18.34	13.37
Baseline [20]	basal_rate, temp_basal_rate, bolus, meal, time_of_day	19.05	13.50
Baseline [18]	no additional features besides glucose_level	19.21	13.08

Table 5 presents the final performance of our models and their used features versus state-of-the-art baselines. The models are evaluated based on their RMSE and MAE on the test set, showcasing the impact of different input features on model performance. LightTS achieves an RMSE of 16.14 and a MAE of 11.44, outperforming state-of-the-art. Figure 1 shows qualitative results of LightTS, illustrating the predicted vs. actual blood glucose levels. This visualization demonstrates the model's ability to predict blood glucose levels over time. We observe, that LightTS effectively tracks overall glucose trends, including peaks and drops. However, slight deviations occur, particularly in regions

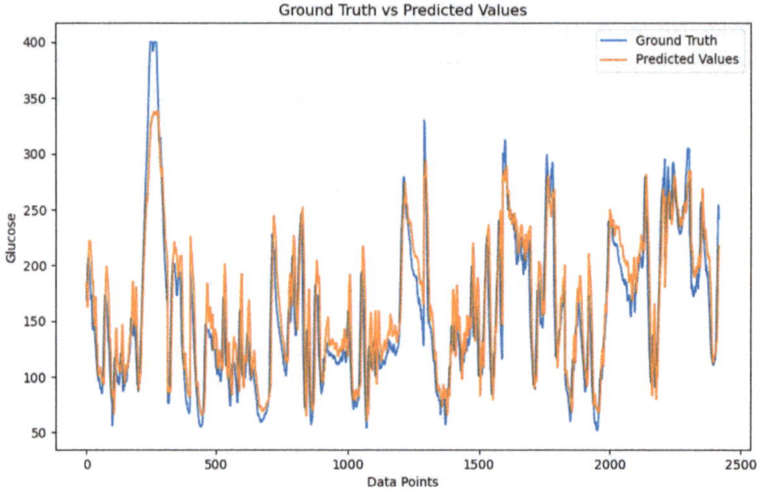

Fig. 1. Ground truth vs. predicted glucose values (mg/dL) for the final LightTS model. The plot illustrates the model's ability to closely track real glucose variations over time. Blue represents the actual blood glucose levels, while the orange curve indicates the predicted values.

with sharp fluctuations, which may be attributed to noise in the input features or the model's response time to rapid changes.

Our results also suggest that incorporating additional physiological and contextual features, such as air temperature, heart rate, skin temperature, sleep, work, exercise, and meal intake, significantly improves glucose prediction accuracy when a model is able to capture the underlying relations properly. Among the evaluated advanced time series models, LightTS demonstrated the best predictive performance, while Transformer-based models showed slightly higher, but still competitive, errors. This suggests that alternative architectures beyond transformers may offer advantages in time series forecasting for blood glucose prediction, providing valuable insights for proactive diabetes management.

5 Discussion

Results indicate that recent advanced time series models, particularly LightTS, outperform traditional methods for blood glucose prediction. LightTS, the best-performing model, demonstrated its capability to capture glucose fluctuations effectively by integrating diverse physiological and contextual features. Transformer architectures have shown to be competitive but have been outperformed by LightTS.

Despite promising results, several challenges remain. The accuracy of all models is influenced by the quality of input data. Missing or inconsistent measurements that are present in the OhioT1DM dataset can further impact prediction quality. Additionally, while advanced models excel in handling temporal dependencies, they require substantial computational resources, which may pose challenges for real-time deployment on low-power devices.

Our study highlights both strengths and limitations of the evaluated models. On the positive side, the results suggest that incorporating external physiological signals enhances prediction accuracy compared to relying solely on glucose history. However, limitations include the need for extensive hyperparameter tuning and the potential risk of overfitting to specific patient characteristics, which may reduce generalizability across broader populations. We take this to be an artifact of the limited OhioT1DM dataset that we used. However, this dataset was chosen to ensure comparability with the BGLP Challenge results. Furthermore, medical data is inherently critical, and as a result, publicly available datasets for blood glucose prediction are scarce. This poses a challenge for developing models that generalize well across diverse populations and clinical scenarios.

Our findings can have important implications for personalized diabetes management. By leveraging advanced time series models, future glucose monitoring systems can provide more accurate and adaptive predictions, helping individuals make informed decisions about insulin administration, meal planning, and physical activity.

6 Conclusion and Future Work

While advanced time series models, including Transformer-based architectures, have been widely applied in various domains, relatively few studies have explored their effectiveness for medical time series data, particularly in the context of diabetes management. This work confirmed their potential for AI-driven blood glucose monitoring and prediction, where accurate forecasting is critical for proactive intervention and personalized healthcare.

Our study demonstrated that incorporating external physiological and contextual features significantly improves blood glucose level prediction compared to relying solely on glucose history. LightTS in particular effectively captures complex temporal dependencies and essential patterns, even in small datasets, highlighting its robustness and adaptability.

Future research should focus on improving generalizability by addressing overfitting risks and dataset limitations. The scarcity of publicly available medical data remains a major challenge, necessitating collaborations with research institutions, healthcare organizations, and industry partners to facilitate access to larger and more diverse datasets. By advancing these models toward practical deployment, AI-driven solutions could contribute to more effective, personalized diabetes management and predictive healthcare technologies.

References

1. Marling, C., Bunescu, R.: The OhioT1DM dataset for blood glucose level prediction. In: CEUR Workshop Proceedings (2020)

2. Vaswani, A., et al.: Attention is all you need. In: Advances in Neural Information Processing Systems (NeurIPS 2017), vol. 30 (2017)
3. Freiburghaus, J., et al.: A deep learning approach for blood glucose prediction and monitoring of type 1 diabetes patients. In: KDH@ECAI (2020)
4. Rubin-Falcone, H. et al.: Deep residual time-series forecasting: application to blood glucose prediction. In: KDH@ECAI (2020)
5. Hameed, H., et al.: Investigating potentials and pitfalls of knowledge distillation across datasets for blood glucose forecasting. In: KDH@ECAI (2020)
6. Daniels, J., et al.: Personalised glucose prediction via deep multitask networks. In: KDH@ECAI (2020)
7. Cappon, G., et al.: A personalized and interpretable deep learning based approach to predict blood glucose concentration in type 1 diabetes. In: KDH@ECAI (2020)
8. Hesamian, M., Jia, W., He, X. et al.: Region proposal network for lung nodule detection and segmentation. In: KDH@ECAI (2020)
9. Wu, H., Hu, T., Liu, Y., et al.: TimesNet: temporal 2D-variation modeling for general time series analysis. In: International Conference on Learning Representations (2023)
10. Zhang, T., Zhang, Y., Cao, W., et al.: Less is more: fast multivariate time series forecasting with light sampling-oriented MLP structures (2022). https://arxiv.org/abs/2207.01186
11. Zhang, Y., Yan, J.: Crossformer: transformer utilizing cross-dimension dependency for multivariate time series forecasting (2023)
12. Zeng, A., Chen, M., Zhang, L., et al.: Are transformers effective for time series forecasting? (2022). https://arxiv.org/abs/2205.13504
13. Zhou, T., Ma, Z., Wang, X., et al.: FiLM: frequency improved legendre memory model for long-term time series forecasting (2022)
14. Zhou, H., Zhang, S., Peng, J., et al.: Informer: beyond efficient transformer for long sequence time-series forecasting (2021). https://arxiv.org/abs/2012.07436
15. Liu, Y., Hu, T., Zhang, H., et al.: iTransformer: inverted transformers are effective for time series forecasting (2024). https://arxiv.org/abs/2310.06625
16. Nie, Y., Nguyen, N., Sinthong, P., et al.: a time series is worth 64 words: long-term forecasting with transformers (2023). https://arxiv.org/abs/2211.14730
17. Liu, S., Yu, H., Liao, C., et al.: Pyraformer: low-complexity pyramidal attention for long-range time series modeling and forecasting (2022)
18. Hameed, H., Kleinberg, S.: Investigating potentials and pitfalls of knowledge distillation across datasets for blood glucose forecasting (2020)
19. Zhu, T., Yao, X., Li, K., et al.: Blood Glucose Prediction for Type 1 Diabetes Using Generative Adversarial Networks (2020)
20. Yang, T., Wu, R., Tao, R. et al.: Multi-scale long short-term memory network with multi-lag structure for blood glucose prediction (2020)
21. Bevan, R., Coenen, F.: Experiments in non-personalized future blood glucose level prediction (2020)

Security Analysis of Hardware Electric Vehicle Charging Infrastructure

Nils Lohmiller(✉), Henning Weise, and Tobias Heer

Esslingen University, Esslingen am Neckar, Germany
{nils.lohmiller,heweit01,tobias.heer}@hs-esslingen.de

Abstract. The growing adoption of eletric vehicles (EVs) highlights the need for strong security in the EV infrastructure. As the demand for EV charging facilities increases, ensuring the security of the entire charging ecosystem becomes essential. These security requirements cover various aspects, including hardware security, power grid stability, and compliance with relevant standards and regulations. This work examines the security aspects of EV hardware systems, focusing on current standards and possible threats. We review key standards such as IEC 62196 Type 1, Combined Charging System, ISO 15118, and OCPP to assess their effectiveness in protecting EV communication and charging systems. We also explore various attack vectors targeting EVs, including intercepting communications, using fake RFID cards, and exploiting weaknesses in vehicle networks. Furthermore, we highlight the impact attacks can have on the EV charging infrastructure. This analysis demonstrates the importance of strong security measures and the need to continually improve them as new threats emerge. This research aims to contribute to ongoing efforts to keep EV systems safe and secure.

Keywords: EV Charging · Charging Infrastructure · Vulnerability Scoring · Charging Attacks

1 Introduction

The rapid adoption of EVs is changing the automotive landscape, offering environmentally friendly transport solutions and advanced technological features. In 2022, a total of 14% of all new vehicles sold were EVs compared to 9% in the previous year and less than 5% in 2020 [23]. With the growing number of EVs, it is also necessary to expand the EV charging infrastructure. The EV infrastructure refers to the network of physical and technological elements that support the charging, maintenance, and overall operation of EVs. This includes charging stations, power grids, battery swapping stations, and related technologies necessary to facilitate the use and growth of EVs (Fig. 1).

We structure the EV infrastructure into three key layers, as shown in Fig. 2: 1) charging connector, 2) charging communication, and 3) charging topology. Between the vehicle and the charging station, the charging connector serves as

L. Bechtel and T. Heer (Eds.): CCSSS 2025 PTT, pp. 13–36, 2026.
https://doi.org/10.1007/978-3-032-10569-1_2

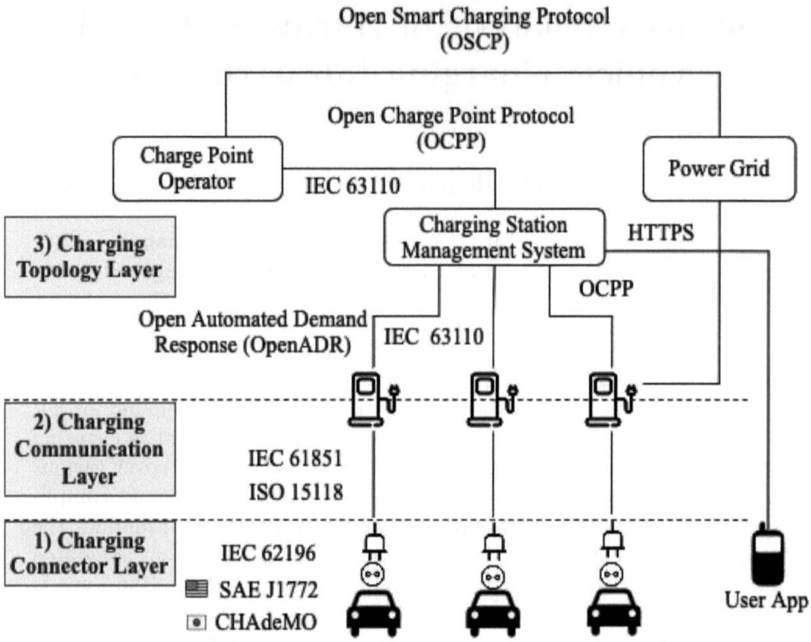

Fig. 1. Overview of electric vehicle infrastructure including standards and norms [35, 41]

the interface. The charging communication layer describes the layer between the charging connector and the eletric vehicle charging station (EVCS). One EVCS can have several Charge Points (CPs). We refer to the layer between the EVCS and the Charging Station Management System (CSMS) as charging topology. Above this is the outer topology that handles the connection to the power grid and to the CP operator. For each layer of the charging infrastructure, there are numerous standards in existence that reflect the intricate web of regulations and specifications that govern various aspects of the system.

The increasing use of EVs poses new challenges, particularly in the area of cyber security, as they become more integrated into the modern transport ecosystem. The software, hardware, and communication systems that power EVs not only improves their efficiency but also exposes them to a wide range of potential cyber threats. The EV charging infrastructure contains multiple communication protocols and network technologies e.g., OCPP, OpenADR, and OSCP [35]. The EV charging infrastructure is vulnerable to a variety of potential cyber threats due to its interconnected nature, which involves interactions with vehicles, charging stations, power grids, and mobile applications [20]. Each manufacturer and operator implements their own system, which increases the complexity and heterogeneity of the environment. This complexity makes it difficult to establish uniform security standards and impedes the implementation of effective security measures. Charging stations are easily accessible to the public, making it easier to exploit vulnerabilities. Rapid growth of charging stations, driven by the urgent need to expand the charging infrastructure, adds to this complexity. The absence of clearly defined standards and protocols makes the EV infrastructure susceptible to vulnerabilities that attackers can exploit. Cyber criminals may attempt to intercept data, disrupt charging station operations, or even interfere with vehicle control systems.

Vehicle security must extend beyond direct attacks on vehicles and target fleets, mobility applications and services, and even electric vehicle charging infrastructure [43]. Given these vulnerabilities, immediate and comprehensive action is necessary. This analysis focuses on detailed examinations of the three layers of the EV charging infrastructure. We examine potential threat scenarios and existing countermeasures. We aim to provide a comprehensive understanding of the current state of security in the EV infrastructure. The development of industry-wide standards, aimed at standardizing various systems and closing security gaps, is imperative. The safety of the increasingly interconnected EV infrastructure can only be guaranteed by a coordinated and concentrated effort.

The remainder of this paper is structured as follows. First, we present related work in Sect. 2. In Sect. 3, we briefly present the fundamentals of charging stations. We discuss the three layers of the EV infrastructure with their vulnerabilities and possible mitigation strategies in Sect. 4. In Sect. 5, we discuss the vulnerabilities found and further steps towards a secure EV charging infrastructure. Finally, Sect. 6 concludes the paper.

2 Related Work

Existing literature examines vulnerabilities and security measures in different areas of the charging infrastructure, such as charging connector, charging communication, and charging topology.

Skarga-Bandurova et al. [41] explored the cyber security of the EV charging infrastructure, highlighting the critical role of secure communication through the charging connector and the potential risks associated with it. However, their work does not provide a detailed analysis of the possible impact of cyber attacks on the EV charging infrastructure.

Johnson et al. [25] reviewed the cyber security of electric vehicle chargers, providing information on potential vulnerabilities and threats within the charging topology. While their work provides a valuable overview of EV cyber security, it lacks integration on in-depth case studies or real-world examples of cyber security incidents.

Fries and Falk [15] provide an overview of the architecture and components of a secure communication system for EVs and the Smart Grid. They also discuss the importance of standardization and interoperability in ensuring the successful integration of EVs into the Smart Grid. Although their work addresses the importance of security in the communication between EVs and the Smart Grid, a more detailed analysis of potential cyber security threats and vulnerabilities specific to EV-to-grid communication could be included. Given the dynamic nature of standards, their work may become outdated as standards continue to evolve. This work extensively examines current cyber security threats and vulnerabilities in the context of EV charging infrastructure.

Automotive standards often apply to specific regions, and depending on the region, the standards cover different aspects. Van Aubel and Poll [44] conducted an extensive analysis of the security of EV charging protocols in the Netherlands. Their work thoroughly explores the security aspects of various charging communication protocols and identifies potential vulnerabilities, with a specific focus on those associated with the charging connector. They show that TLS is not yet mandatory in the charging protocols. For vehicles that do not support ISO 15118 or plug-and-charge, the driver must authenticate using RFID, which according to the authors is a relatively weak authentication method. In contrast to their work, we also consider standards from outside the Netherlands and assess the impact of the vulnerabilities and also show which hardware vulnerabilities exist.

Although numerous studies provide valuable findings in these areas, there is no overview of the state of the art and the impact of existing vulnerabilities. Specifically, this involves a comprehensive examination of each of the three defined layers within the EV infrastructure. The purpose of this work is to assess the impact of vulnerabilities in the individual layers.

3 Background

The EV revolution is transforming our transportation landscape, bringing with it a complex web of technological advancements and potential vulnerabilities. This section provides a comprehensive overview of the key elements shaping the EV charging ecosystem. First, we mention the diverse standards that govern EV charging across different regions, highlighting their crucial role in ensuring compatibility, safety, and regulatory compliance. Next, we present our adapted vulnerability scoring system, which draws inspiration from the DREAD model [30] but incorporates modifications to better assess and prioritize security risks. Finally, we examine common attack vectors that pose significant threats to smart charging systems, including Man-in-the-Middle (MITM) attacks, Denialof- Service (DoS), Denial-of-Charge (DoC), and malware infiltrations.

3.1 Standards

Most vulnerabilities or attacks within the EV infrastructure are associated with specific standards. The prevalence of EV standards around the world is a response to the expanding landscape of EVs. As EVs introduce new security risks and require interoperability with emerging technologies, the definition of standards and norms becomes essential. Standards play a crucial role in ensuring compatibility, safety, and regulatory compliance within the EV infrastructure. By doing so, they not only foster innovation, but also provide a solid foundation for a trustworthy and interconnected network of EV systems worldwide. We present the standards for the EV charging infrastructure in Table 1. Different countries adhere to distinct standards set by organizations such as the International Organization for Standardization (ISO), Society of Automotive Engineers (SAE), the Institute of Electrical and Electronics Engineers (IEEE), the International Electrotechnical Commission (IEC), Guobiao (GB/T) and CHAdeMO. The SAE and IEEE standards are predominantly used in the USA, while IEC is widely employed in Europe. China has their respective EV charging standards, Guobiao (GB/T), issued by the Standardization Administration of China and the Chinese National Committee of ISO and IEC for AC and DC charging. However, the GB/T AC charging standards closely resemble IEC standards [7].

Table 1. EV charging infrastructure standards

Standard	Usage
IEC 61851	Requirements EV charging
ISO 15118-2	Plug-and-Charge protocol for charging and billing of EVs
DIN TS 70121	Charging protocol without security features
SAE J1772/IEC 62196	Type 1 charging connector
IEC 62196 Type 2	Type 2 charging connector
CCS	Charging connector
SAE J3400	North American charging connector
CHAdeMO	Japanese charging connector

The general standards used for charging communication are IEC 61851 [45], ISO 15118 [24], and DIN TS 70121 [9]. The IEC 61851 is an international standard that defines the requirements for conductive charging systems for EVs. It covers the characteristics, operating conditions, and safety requirements for EV supply equipment, ensuring compatibility between charging stations and vehicles. ISO 15118 [24] defines a Plug-and-Charge (PnC) protocol for charging and billing of EVs. For authentication, ISO 15118 specifies Transport Layer Security (TLS) version 1.2 only. As only TLS 1.2 is specified, the use of other cryptographic algorithms is not compatible with the ecosystem. The DIN TS 70121 [9] is a simplified version of the ISO 15118-2 without security or PnC features.

3.2 Vulnerability Scoring

The CVSS model is commonly used for traditional vulnerability assessments; however, we opt for a simpler and more easily extensible approach instead. We have developed a vulnerability scoring system called DREAD-D, inspired by the DREAD model [30] to evaluate and prioritize potential security risks. While this approach uses the core principles of DREAD—assessing factors such as damage potential, reproducibility, exploitability, affected users, and discoverability—it is not an exact replication of the original model. Specifically, we added the "detectability" metric to reflect how easily users can detect or recognize an attack. Our scoring system assesses vulnerabilities based on the following categories: **Damage Potential** (severity of harm if exploited), **Reproducibility** (consistency of attack replication), **Exploitability** (ease of exploitation), **Affected Users** (number of users impacted), **Discoverability** (ease with which attackers can discover the vulnerability), and **Detectability** (added) (ease with which users can detect the attack). For each category, we assign values of 0–3 for low impact, 4–6 for medium impact, and 7 for high impact. The sum of the assign values represents the total score. This adapted DREAD-based approach allows for a more contextually relevant vulnerability assessment, enabling effective risk management strategies.

3.3 Common Attack Vectors

Smart charging systems for EVs enable unprecedented convenience and efficiency to the landscape of sustainable transportation. However, this innovation is not without challenges, particularly in the realm of cyber security. As EVs become more integrated with smart grids and charging infrastructure, the potential for security vulnerabilities increases, requiring a comprehensive understanding of the potential risks and proactive measures to protect these systems. Among the various security concerns associated with smart charging, attacks such as MITM, DoS, DoC, and Malware pose a significant threat.

MITM attacks are the most common threat for the EV infrastructure [4,5, 14,16,20,29]. In this form of active eavesdropping, communication between two authorized parties is monitored and potentially modified by unauthorized entities, all while appearing normal to the transmitting party. The consequences extend beyond the compromised integrity of the data, with the potential to overload distribution transformers and disrupt the frequency and voltage stability of the power grid, possibly leading to power grid failure.

Another notable threat is posed by **DoS** attacks. DoS attacks can be used to prevent legitimate users from accessing essential services, such as depriving EV owners of the ability to charge their vehicles [2,5,16,25,29,41]. In a specific variation known as **DoC**, exemplified by the Brokenwire attack, wireless termination of vehicle charging from a considerable distance introduces a new dimension of vulnerability. This could have cascading effects, especially if the charging of critical vehicles, such as those used for emergency or government services, is abruptly stopped.

Malware attacks further compound these security challenges, targeting CSMS networks and Original Equipment Manufacturers (OEMs) [41]. Malware injections through EVs or CSMS can lead to the unauthorized acquisition of sensitive information, including payment details (debit/credit card information), personal data, charging schedules, payment amounts. The compromised EVCS not only impact individual charging stationc network of EVCSs. Sarieddine et al. [39] discovered default configurations in 15 % of the 33,320 EVCSs they analyzed, posing a vulnerability to botnet-like malware attacks that exploit default logins to breach infrastructure security. Furthermore, their research revealed that while

Table 2. Vulnerability scoring in EV infrastructure; D (Damage Potential) severity of harm if exploited, R (Reproducibility) consistency of attack replication, E (Exploitability) ease of exploitation, A (Affected Users) number of users impacted, D (Discoverability) ease with which attackers can detect the vulnerability, D (Detectability) ease with which users can detect the attack. The three major vulnerabilities are highlighted in color.

Vulnerability Name	D	R	E	A	D	D	Score
A1) Small conductor cross-section	8	5	5	1	4	8	**32**
A2) ChargeX	2	4	4	1	4	8	23
A3) BROKENWIRE	4	6	4	6	10	7	**37**
A4) CAN exposure	8	5	2	3	5	8	31
A5) IEC 61851 Authentication	4	3	3	1	3	9	23
A6) ISO 15118 with TLS 1.2	4	2	3	2	3	7	21
A7) Charging Process under False Identity	3	5	4	3	3	6	24
A8) Unauthorized Charging	3	7	4	3	3	6	26
A9) CSMS DoS	4	2	4	7	3	8	28
A10) Legacy OCPP	4	2	7	9	6	8	**36**

instances of malware within EV infrastructure remain relatively scarce, there is evidence of a growing trend in such occurrences. The malware injected into EVCSs has the potential to propagate to EVs and power grids, causing detrimental effects for all stakeholders involved. This type of malware attack not only endangers the security of sensible information but also has the potential to damage the reputation of manufacturers, revealing insights into vehicle charging habits, locations, and other private information [41]. Such breaches not only pose risks to data integrity, but also undermine the reputations of manufacturers and compromise the privacy of EV owners.

Attacks on bidirectional power flows, where electricity is used to charge the battery and feed back into the grid, not only damage the reputation of the manufacturers but also has far-reaching effects on the connected power grids. In such a scenario, compromised vehicles might be programmed to request or send power at the same time, creating a real danger of overloading the power grid. This situation could pose threats to pedestrians, networks, and crucial road safety initiatives. When analyzing the promising but complex landscape of smart charging for EVs, understanding and mitigating these security concerns are paramount.

4 Attacks on Eletric Vehicle Infrastructure

The increasing prevalence of EVs underscores the importance of a secure and reliable charging infrastructure. However, the charging connector and communication layers, while essential for energy transfer, also represent potential attack vectors. In the following, we cover each layer of the EV infrastructure by analyzing the security aspects of different charging connector standards and examining the communication protocols that govern the interaction between EVs and charging stations. The goal is to reveal potential vulnerabilities, rate their DREAD-D score, and provide a foundation for the development of stronger and more secure charging solutions. We present the vulnerabilities found and their score in Table 2. This scoring allows for assessing and prioritizing identified vulnerabilities for possible countermeasures.

4.1 Charging Connector Layer

The Charging Connector Layer represents a critical interface in EV charging infrastructure, encompassing various standards for physical connections between EVs and charging cables, refer to Fig. 2. This diversity of charging connectors, influenced by regional preferences and evolving EV technology, also introduces distinct security vulnerabilities. Understanding the complexities and security implications of these connectors requires a detailed examination of each major standard.

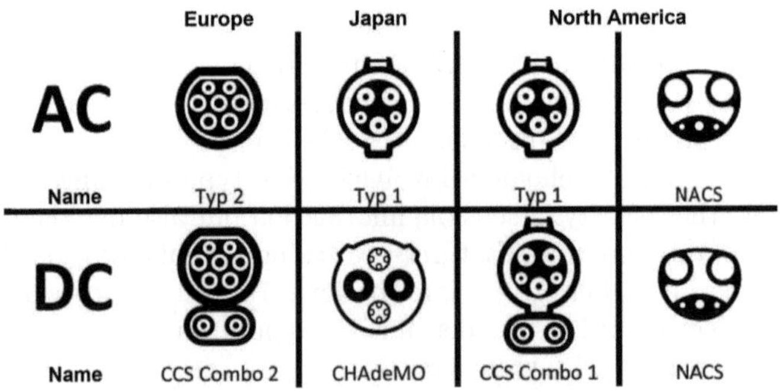

Fig. 2. Overview of connector systems [17,21]

SAE J1772/IEC 62196 Type 1. The SAE J1772/IEC 62196 Type 1 plug system (Type 1), along with the Tesla SAE J3400, serves as the prevailing standard for single-phase AC charging in the United States and Japan [21]. Type 1 features a manual locking mechanism positioned on the top of the plug. A plastic bar located underneath mechanically prevents any twisting during the plugging process. The Type 1 plug comprises five contact pins, with the control pilot and proximity pilot pins facilitating communication between the EVCS and the vehicle [21,25]. The other three pins are used to transmit power. Within the Type 1 standard, the proximity pilot contact conveys information on the position of the mechanical locking mechanism to both the vehicle and the EVCS. The inability

of the proximity pilot pin to monitor the charging cable's conductor cross-section introduces a security limitation. The conductor cross-sectional area refers to the extent of the copper wire within the cable that is responsible for carrying electrical current. A greater conductor cross-section enables the cable to transmit a higher current without the risk of overheating or melting. Using a charging cable with an insufficiently small conductor cross-section could potentially lead to a short circuit or fire. The small conductor cross-section is not visible from the outside. Replicating this attack is complex and requires commonly available tools. We refer to this as vulnerability 1 **(A1)** and classify the following DREAD-D scoring:
D = 8; **R** = 5; **E** = 5; **A** = 1; **D** = 4; **D** = 8

Zhou et al. [46] published another attack called ChargeX in May 2023, which targets IEC 62196 Type 1. ChargeX modifies the communication signals by inserting a hardware attack circuit into the communication line. Due to the small size of the attack circuit, it can easily be built into the cable by the attacker, which is foisted on the victim. The attack circuit can change pin states, where false information can be sent to the EVCS. The authors describe how an attacker can reduce the vehicle charging rate, achieving a degree of DoC. Furthermore, the attack circuit can force a vehicle connected but in standby mode into charging mode. To discover the vulnerability, the attacker must be physically close to the charging station. Instead of simply cutting the cable this attack is more difficult to detect. The reduced charging rate caused by a ChargeX attack limits the number of vehicles that can be charged within a given timeframe. Replicating this attack is possible but complex and requires commonly available tools. In addition, the attack usually goes unnoticed for longer time, increasing the effectiveness of the attack. As a countermeasure, it is recommended that users do not use third-party charging cables or check third-party cables carefully before use. It is crucial that systems relay relevant safety information to users. At this point, Zhou et al. recommend that manufacturers of EVs implement a better pre-testing procedure. Specifically, EVs should always check the state consistency between the EVs and the EVCS. This results in vulnerability 2 **(A2)**:
D = 2; **R** = 4; **E** = 4; **A** = 1; **D** = 4; **D** = 8

IEC 62196 Type 2. The IEC 62196 Type 2 plug system, originated from the German plug manufacturer Mennekes and was officially designated by the European Commission in 2013 as the standardized charging system for EVs in Europe [21]. In Europe, a deliberate choice was made to forego Type 1 due to its support only for single-phase AC charging. In contrast, Type 2 enables both single-phase and three-phase AC charging, thanks to additional pins. Additionally, there are distinctions in the method of securing the charging cable during the charging process: Type 2 has an electromechanical locking mechanism, whereas Type 1 depends on manually unlocking the charging cable [21]. The Type 2 plug is equipped with a total of seven contact pins. The control pilot and proximity pilot, facilitate communication between the vehicle and the EVCS. The remaining five pins are dedicated to transferring energy [21,25].

Our research did not reveal specific vulnerabilities or attacks targeting the IEC 62196 Type 2 standard in EV infrastructure. This absence raises the question of whether previous research overlooks vulnerabilities in this standard, or whether the standard is inherently more robust. Further investigation is needed to understand the reasons for this apparent security and ensure a complete assessment of electric vehicle technology security.

Combined Charging System (CCS). The CCS resulted from a collaborative effort between European and American commissions, giving rise to two variants: CCS Combo 1 and CCS Combo 2. CCS Combo 1 aligns with the American Type 1 standard, while CCS Combo 2 is built upon the European Type 2 standard. AC charging typically employs analog data transmission, while DC fast charging uses digital communication [21]. Modern EVCSs utilize the DIN TS 70121 or ISO 15118 protocol. The ISO 15118 protocol enables data exchange through Power Line Communication (PLC) [21,25]. This enables features such as transmitting the vehicle's state of charge and enabling automatic authorization via PnC.

Köhler et al. [27] introduced a new attack targeting the CCS. Their attack, named BROKENWIRE, disrupts the PLC between the vehicle and the charger, leading to the termination of charging sessions. We refer to this as vulnerability 3 (**A3**). With CCS, an IP connection is established via PLC following initialization to manage the charging process. This connection must be maintained during the entire charging process. The authors managed to disrupt this PLC through electromagnetic interference, which leads to charging processes being interrupted. They also describe how the attack can be carried out using commercially available wireless hardware and minimal technical knowledge. Their wireless attack can be executed remotely without the attacker being present, enabling the stealthy and simultaneous disruption of individual vehicles or entire fleets. They demonstrate that the attack is effective across different floors within a building, such as in a multi-story parking structure, through perimeter fences, and even in 'drive-by' scenarios [27]. In practice, a successful BROKENWIRE attack was carried out up to a distance of 47 m. BROKENWIRE has immediate consequences for the approximately 12 million EVs currently operating around the world using the CCS. It also has significant impacts on the emerging wave of vehicle fleet electrification, affecting both private enterprises and essential public services. It is easy for an attacker to discover the vulnerability, as all they need to do is look for CCS charging stations. Replicating this attack is complex and requires commonly available tools. The authors mention various countermeasures against BROKENWIRE. Electromagnetic shielding can reduce the charging cable's susceptibility to electromagnetic interference. However, additional shielding presents challenges to cable handling. While flexibility is crucial for easy plug-in, charging cables are already heavy and rigid, making them difficult to handle. Adding another layer of shielding exacerbates weight and stiffness, leading to higher costs. In addition, PLC interference only occurs during the transmission of interference signals by the attacker. Although communica-

tion between the EV and EVCS should continue after the jamming signal has ended, this is not often observed in practice. Currently, users need to repeat the authentication process after interruptions. To address this, the proximity pilot can be employed to monitor cable disconnections, eliminating the necessity for re-authentication and allowing seamless continuation of the charging process. Although the literature does not mention any transfer of this attack to other charging connector types, we believe that this type of attack can be transferred to other connector types, as their control signals can also be altered by electromagnetic manipulation.
A3): D = 4; **R** = 6; **E** = 4; **A** = 6; **D** = 8; **D** = 10

SAE J3400. Since November 2022, Tesla has rebranded its proprietary charging system as the SAE J3400. This standardization represents a significant shift in the EV charging landscape. The SAE J3400 connector is characterized by a five-pin configuration, which facilitates both AC and DC charging. For AC charging, communication between the vehicle and EVCS utilizes a modulated signal following IEC 61851-1, while DC charging employs digital communication through PLC as per DIN TS 70121 [21]. Additionally, the SAE J3400 supports PnC functionality in accordance with ISO 15118 [42]. Despite the use of similar communication protocols by SAE J3400 and CCS, our investigation did not identify comparable attacks against SAE J3400. The BROKENWIRE attack, for example, is only described for the CCS standard.

CHAdeMO. CHAdeMO serves as a Japanese standard for DC fast charging in EVs [27]. Data transmission in CHAdeMO is based on the well-established Controller Area Network (CAN) bus technology, widely acknowledged in the automotive sector [25,27]. CHAdeMO uses unencrypted CAN messages, lacking inherent security features [1,5] While safety-critical functions such as brakes on the CAN bus are protected by MACs, the widespread use of electronic control units (ECUs) in modern vehicles together with Internet-enabled telematic control units (TCUs) and the associated high level of message exchange between these devices underscores the need for strong security measures.

According to Sagstetter et al. [37], CHAdeMO poses a potential attack vector on vehicle battery operations if CAN bus messages cannot be filtered on the vehicle side of the connection. They describe how vehicles that use a CHAdeMO charger expose their CAN bus to the charger, creating a potential security vulnerability [37]. Specifically, exposing communication over the CAN protocol without proper message filtering poses significant risks when directly connected to the in-vehicle network, a scenario not uncommon with legacy CAN-CAN gateways in modern vehicles. We identify this as vulnerability 4 **(A4)**. Such vulnerabilities could enable a attacker to program a new key to unlock the car or allow criminals to flash ECUs via the charging plug. This is particularly important because communication via the charging plug is very susceptible to MITM attacks. In such attacks, an attacker could insert a connector between the charging plug and the EVCS, enabling them to eavesdrop on communications or tamper with packages. This attack can be recreated using existing tools, even if it is somewhat complex and easier to recognize using the connector. To protect the vehicle from attacks via the charging plug, it is necessary to have authentication methods for the CAN bus.

A4): **D** = 8; **R** = 5; **E** = 2; **A** = 3; **D** = 5; **D** = 8

The vulnerabilities and attacks observed in the charging connector layer highlight the existence of vulnerabilities in real-world connectors. However, many attacks exploit vulnerabilities not only in the charging connector layer but also in the charging communication layer. Analysis of the charging communication layer is essential to fully understand potential attack scenarios and implement effective countermeasures.

4.2 Charging Communication

The charging communication layer, as depicted in Fig. 2, is central to the connection between the eletric vehicle charging station (EVCS) and the EV. This layer facilitates fault detection, real-time monitoring, and user authentication, all critical for secure and efficient charging. The standardized communication protocols in this layer enable compatibility between different manufacturers and enable the interoperability between current EVs and future developments in electric vehicle technology. In the following, we examine the major standards regarding their security implications.

IEC 61851. Standards ensure equipment compatibility between manufacturers and provide a framework for developing new products. In Europe, all EVs support the IEC 61851 communication standard [12]. This standard outlines three modes that form the basis for communication between EV and EVCS [8,14,15,41]:

- Mode 1: The EV is directly connected to a standard household socket. In this mode, there is no communication support between EV and the charging station [10,41].
- Mode 2: The EV is charged with a standard household socket with an in-cable control and protection device (IC-CPD) that is equipped with the necessary control and safety functions [41]. This mode protects against electric shocks in the event of insulation failures if the customer connects their vehicle to a socket that was not intended to charge EVs when installed [10].
- Mode 3: This mode is used for single-phase or three-phase charging with alternating current at permanently installed charging stations. The plug connectors at both ends of the charging cable are fastened in this charging mode, preventing disconnection when the cable is under load [8,10].
- Mode 4: Fast charging with an external charger. The charging connection remains consistently attached to the station [41].

However, IEC 61851 lacks authentication and authorization functions. In this work, we refer to it as vulnerability 5 **(A5)**. In none of the IEC 61851 modes is

security ensured [15]. If no authentication and authorization functions are available, the vulnerabilities can be exploited without additional tools. The missing security mechanisms are not always recognizable to attackers and users, and all users who use this charging station are affected. Possible effects can be DoS and MITM.
A5) D = 4; **R** = 3; **E** = 3; **A** = 1; **D** = 3; **D** = 9

ISO 15118. [24] defines, among other things, a Plug-and-Charge (PnC) protocol for charging and billing of electric vehicles. PnC is used for the one-time registration of the vehicle and authorization for a payment function, it is sufficient for the user to connect the EV and the charging station with the cable. For authentication, ISO 15118 specifies TLS version 1.2 only. The vehicle automatically transmits the data required to authorize the payment process to the charging station. This eliminates the need for the user to perform the authorization process using a payment card, app, or web interface. Authorization is achieved with a public key infrastructure (PKI) that uniquely identifies each of the vehicles [25]. The transmission of vehicle identities represents a major risk, as the credentials of existing vehicles and new vehicles must be secured throughout their entire lifetime. Vehicles that use authentication via TLS 1.2 are at risk of being broken. A cryptographically relevant quantum computer is capable of cracking the encryption of public keys and digital signatures in a reasonable amount of time [6,28]. This means that the identity of existing vehicles could be decrypted and misused. We derive from this vulnerability 6 (**A6**):
D = 4; **R** = 2; **E** = 3; **A** = 2; **D** = 3; **D** = 7

ISO 15118 utilizes ISO 61851-1, specifically employing the charging point to detect the insertion and removal of the EV. The protocol delineates three usage environments, 1) public environment, 2) private environment, and 3) trusted environment. The public environment pertains to unrestricted access to the EVCSs, where individuals can freely utilize the charging facilities. Such locations include charging stations in supermarkets, gas stations, or other public areas. Each user is required to authenticate individually, typically by using methods such as RFID tags, mobile apps, or QR code scanners. Given its widespread accessibility, this setting requires rigorous security protocols.

The private environment denotes EVCSs that are privately owned and are not accessible to the public. This environment encompasses EVCSs located on company premises or within residential complex garages, among other locations. Authentication methods in this setting can be more stringent, often employing special access cards or authorized vehicle lists.

The recommended use of the trusted environment arises in situations where access to EVCSs requires even greater restrictions or enhanced control. This may involve additional security zones or access controls. Examples include applications in closed user groups, such as a taxi company, as described by Berg and Svantesson [5]. In this context, individual users, such as taxi drivers, may not necessitate individual identification for charging; instead, a shared token is adequate within this environment.

ISO 15118-2 requires TLS only in public and private environments. In the trusted environment, TLS is categorized as optional, as long as the specific requirements of the trusted environment are met [40]. However, when RFID tags are used for authentication, Unique Identifiers (UIDs) are transmitted in plain text through RFID tags, making them susceptible to interception by potential attackers. In such scenarios, Van Aubel and Poll [44] describe how all communication between the charging station and the RFID tag could be compromised. They explain that the UIDs can be easily read using a standard NFC-enabled phone. An attacker could easily attach their eavesdropping device to the charging station. With physical access and specialized equipment, an eavesdropper could intercept communication between the RFID tag and an EVCS, even from a distance of several meters [11,19]. Once they've gained access, if the attacker possesses a valid UID, they can effortlessly program it onto a card with a configurable UID or fabricate it using an NFC-enabled phone, for instance [13]. The lack of RFID tag security results in several vulnerabilities. Weak authentication methods can cause unauthorized individuals to gain access to charging services, creating possibilities for misuse or security breaches. Furthermore, the transmission of UID plain text raises concerns about the privacy of EV drivers, as sensitive information could be intercepted and exploited [44].

In a trusted environment, it is assumed that there are no attackers, but there is no specification for checking whether the trusted environment is applied correctly. In this environment is TLS omitted, leading to unencrypted communication, an attacker can intercept and manipulate transmitted information at the interface between the vehicle and the EVCS. For example, the mobility provider sends their tariff options to the vehicle via the EVCS. Using a modified charging cable or strategically placing a counterfeit EVCS between the EV and the supply equipment, an attacker could modify this information [4,14]. Such compromises could disrupt the normal operation of the charging infrastructure, lead to financial losses and affect the service availability and reliability [41]. There might be EVCSs that technically fulfill the criteria for the public or private environment, yet manufacturers opt for the trusted environment due to its simpler implementation and may overlook crucial security measures like TLS. Consequently, this could render easily accessible EVCSs outside the trusted environment vulnerable.

Bao et al. describe an attack targeting the charging communication level to enable the continuation of an EV charging process under false identity [4]. This attack is based on the trusted environment established by ISO 15118 and External Identification Mean (EIM) as an authentication mechanism. EIM refers to the process or mechanism by which an external entity, such as a EVCS, identifies and authenticates an EV or its user. This identification can involve various methods such as RFID tags, mobile apps, or QR code scanners. Before the attack itself, a MITM attack must have been executed to acquire relevant parameters during communication. The MITM attack is feasible within the trusted environment when TLS is absent. Figure 3 shows the timeline of the attack. Once the attacker successfully intercepts the communication, they wait until the vic-

tim initiates an authenticated charging session. Once the victim completes the charging process, the attacker intervenes to prevent its completion by deliberately interrupting it. This interruption requires ensuring that the control pilot pin does not recognize the unplugging of the victim's EV. This is achieved by the control pin remaining in state B, even if the person concerned disconnects the plug, which is facilitated by the use of a modified cable. Consequently, the victim believes that their charging process is finished and departs. At this point, the attacker resumes the charging process with their vehicle, necessitating the session ID and billing parameters acquired through the previous MITM attack. To prevent this attack, TLS should always be used, regardless of the ISO 15118 environment used. In addition, victims should consistently utilize their own cables for charging to prevent manipulation by potential attackers. We characterize this as vulnerability 7 (**A7**):
D = 3; **R** = 5; **E** = 4; **A** = 3; **D** = 3; **D** = 6

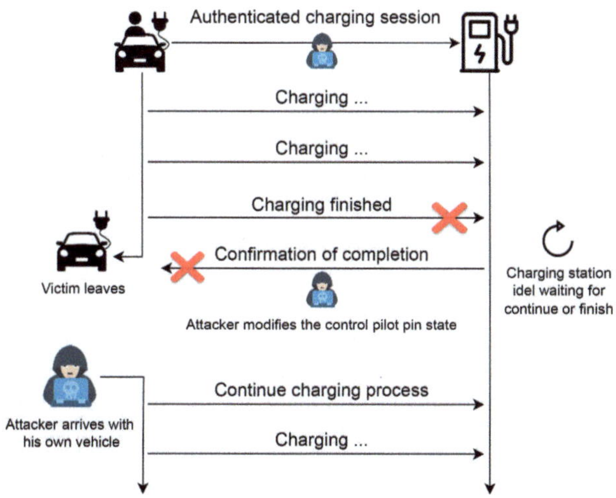

Fig. 3. Procedure of an attack to continue charging under false identity

Bao et al. [4] outline an attack that allows unauthorized charging at the expense of another user. To initiate a fraudulent authenticated charging session, the attacker targets one of the authentication mechanisms, PnC or EIM. PnC relies on contract certificates for EV authentication, comprising an X.509 certificate and a private key stored in the vehicle. The attacker has two options: obtaining a valid certificate and key, or utilizing an expired certificate. The private key is generated online during the first charging process or offline by the e-Mobility Service Provider (eMSP) owner via a provided PKCS#12 file. eMSPs are companies that provide roaming services to enable charging on different charging networks. If the attacker gains access to the OEM provisioning certificate used to encrypt the contract private key, they can initiate an ISO 15118

charging session and request certificate installation. Alternatively, tampering with or stealing the Electric Vehicle Communication Controller (EVCC) could provide access to the private key of the OEM provisioning or contract certificate. We define this as vulnerability 8 **(A8)**:
D = 3; **R** = 7; **E** = 4; **A** = 3; **D** = 3; **D** = 6

In conclusion, the analysis of the charging communication layer, encompassing protocols such as IEC 61851 and ISO 15118, has revealed critical vulnerabilities and potential attacks, such as charging with false identity or using fraudulent certificates, particularly within trusted environments where TLS implementation may be omitted. Additionally, there remains the inquiry into the extent of manufacturers' adherence to standard requirements in their implementations. Investigating potential misconfigurations in manufacturer implementations could provide valuable insights and serve as an intriguing avenue for future research. The identified vulnerabilities underscore the urgent need for robust security measures to safeguard EV infrastructure.

4.3 Charging Topology

The charging topology layer describes the connection between the eletric vehicle charging station (EVCS) and the overarching Charging Station Management System (CSMS). In this layer the Charge Point Operator (CPO) coordinates the operation and management of Charge Points (CPs) [26]. Positioned as a central entity within the EV ecosystem, the CPO has the option to take on the role of CP manufacturer or entrust responsibilities, such as maintenance services, to external entities. This layer is instrumental in orchestrating the operational aspects and logistics of the charging infrastructure. It serves as the interface that allows seamless communication, data exchange and coordination between individual EVCSs and the centralized management system. The EVCSs send their physical configuration, capabilities, and availability through the charging topology layer to the CSMS. This communication is pivotal for the CSMS to efficiently manage and allocate resources, monitor station health, and address any issues. As the demand for electric vehicle charging grows, this layer ensures that new EVCSs can be seamlessly integrated into the existing infrastructure. It contributes to the optimization of EVCS deployment, grid integration, and overall system efficiency.

CSMS. The intricate interplay of hardware and software components extends to other crucial elements in the EV infrastructure, including the Power Grid. The Power Grid sustains the energy demands of EV charging, necessitating effective communication and coordination with EVCS and related systems. Furthermore, the CSMS software, whether based on firmware, web-based (hosted on a cloud server), or mobile-based, serves as a linchpin in overseeing all operations of public EVCS [32]. It directs users to available EVCS, schedules and manages charging sessions, and logs utilization data. Furthermore, the EV management system communicates specific control signals related to charging session duration, charging rate, and initiation and termination commands [40]. In this intricate interplay of charging infrastructure, the CSMS emerges as a central orchestrator, facilitating communication between the EVCS, Electric Vehicle Supply Equipment (EVSE), and various service parameters. These service parameters encompass a wide range of factors that influence the charging process and user experience, ensuring efficient operation and customer satisfaction. These include, for example, the charging rate or payment options. The responsibilities of the CSMS include defining service parameters based on user input, EV and power grid status, collecting and storing data from the charging system, hosting user applications, and maintaining a service registry [16,33].

At the core of EVCS lies the fundamental function of delivering power on demand for charging EV batteries. However, advanced EVCS go beyond their fundamental role, integrating functionalities such as Internet connectivity to enable remote management [32]. This multifaceted functionality is governed by critical components, including EVCS Firmware, EVCS software, and the Open Charge Point Protocol (OCPP). The EVCS firmware, ensures seamless control over CP hardware, remaining unchanged unless explicitly updated by the EVCS Administrator. It typically includes a compact operating system along with peripheral libraries and binary files. CSMS offers a user interface and tools for remote control and management of EVCS operations. It encompasses functions such as planning, fee recording, and user authentication.

Open Charge Point Protocol (OCPP). The communication in the charging topology layer is mostly handled by a protocol called Open Charge Point Protocol (OCPP). This protocol, developed by the Open Charge Alliance, is the international standard protocol for communication between eletric vehicle charging stations (EVCSs) and their Charging Station Management System (CSMS) [3,29,32]. Currently the latest version of OCPP is OCPP 2.1. As shown in Table 3, OCPP 2.1 is compatible with three security profiles, 1) TLS with client-side certificates, 2) TLS with basic authentication, and 3) unsecured transport with basic authentication [2,29,34].

Table 3. OCPP security profiles [29,35]

Profile	**Authentication**		Security
	Charging Station	Charging Station Management System	
Unsecured Transport with Basic Authentication	credentials	trusted	–
TLS with Basic Authentication	credentials	X509 certificate	TLS
TLS with Client-Side Authentication	X509 certificate	X509 certificate	TLS

The first profile secures the communication channel with TLS. Both the EVCS and CSMS authenticate themselves using certificates, with the CSMS authenticating the EVCS via the TLS client certificate.

The second profile, which provides medium security, secures the communication channel with TLS. The CSMS authenticates with a TLS server certificate, and EVCSs authenticate with HTTP Basic Authentication, ensuring encrypted password transmission.

The third profile, which offers a low-security level, relies on a non-secured communication channel. Authentication of the EVCS occurs through a username and password, which is lacking authentication for the CSMS. It is suitable for trusted networks with an activated VPN connection between the CSMS and the EVCS. Whether this profile is only used when the VPN connection is activated is up to the manufacturer. Sayed et al. [40] explain how manufacturers and operators often tend towards simpler implementations to reduce effort and costs. We conclude that certain CSMSs could in practice use the *unsecured transport with basic authentication* profile even without a VPN connection.

Despite the implementation of TLS, OCPP has been shown to remain vulnerable to MITM attacks in specific scenarios and due to misconfigurations [36]. A MITM attack has the potential to expose sensitive user information, which the attacker could subsequently exploit to impersonate the victim [2].

Sarieddine et al. [38] describe a DoS attack scenario in the CSMS. They deploy 10 phantom EVCSs with identical registered device IDs. The OCPP backend system accepts all registration requests, establishing connections with each registered device. Using this method, the adversary can exhaust the backend resources by launching numerous phantom EVCSs, instigating a large-scale Distributed Denial-of-Service (DDoS) attack. This attack exploits the absence of rate limiting and insufficient access control mechanisms within the system. Using these vulnerabilities, an attacker could disable multiple charging stations simultaneously. Although this type of attack requires a higher level of effort to discover and execute, it is challenging for users to detect. From the user's perspective, the unavailability of charging stations may appear as a technical malfunction rather than a deliberate attack. As outlined in the work of Morosan and Pop [31], requests, e.g. Authorize, BootNotification, and DataTransfer, typically initiated by the EVCSs, can be leveraged by adversaries to disrupt the backend availability, potentially leading to a DoS situation. Resulting from this, we derive vulnerability 9 (**A9**):
$\mathbf{D} = 4$; $\mathbf{R} = 2$; $\mathbf{E} = 4$; $\mathbf{A} = 7$; $\mathbf{D} = 3$; $\mathbf{D} = 8$

In Table 4 we show potential threats to OCPP 2.0.1 configuration variables described by Alcaraz et al. [2]. The *HeartBeatInterval* variable determines the frequency with which heartbeats are send from the EVCS to the CSMS. This mechanism is used to verify the accessibility of the EVCS. If the attacker gains access to this variable, they can induce a DoS attack in the CSMS by reducing it to a lower value. A lower value increases the rate of heartbeats, resulting in more messages transmitted within the same timeframe. Without sufficient memory and computational resources, the CSMS may become overloaded by the increased heartbeat frequency, leading to a DoS. The *RetryBackOffWaitMinimum* variable specifies the duration for which a EVCS should wait before attempting to repeat a failed transaction. If the attacker extends this duration,

it causes the EVCS to wait considerably longer following a failed transaction, rendering it unavailable during this period. This unavailability of the EVCS during the extended waiting time creates a scenario where the attacker initiates a DoC situation. Regarding to the authors the OCPP configuration includes options like "SmartChargingEnabled," "SmartChargingAvailable," and "ExternalControlSignalsEnabled," the attacker may effectively impersonate an external entity, such as an external Energy Management System (EMS), to connect with legitimate EVCSs. A manipulated EMS could modify energy profiles, desynchronize, restricting the current/power of EVCSs to destabilize energy resources or consume power beyond the allowed limits through manipulation of charging profiles. We refer to this as vulnerability **(A10)**:
D = 4; **R** = 2; **E** = 7; **A** = 9; **D** = 6; **D** = 8

Table 4. Potential threats to OCPP 2.0.1 configuration variables [2]

Configuration Variable	Attack	Use	Impact
HeartBeatInterval	Set a LOW number	Interval of inactivity after the EVCS sent the last HeartbeatRequest	DoS to CSMS
RetryBackOffWaitMinimum	Set a HIGH number	Minimum time waiting to reconnect after a connection loss	DoS to EVCS
AuthorizeRemoteStart	Set to TRUE and spoof the CSMS	Allow remote transactions by CSMS	Start transactions in an unauthorized manner

As we show, there are numerous vulnerabilities present in OCPP. However, the latest version of the protocol incorporates numerous security features, making it imperative to avoid utilizing versions older than OCPP 2.0. This recommendation underscores the importance of adopting current standards to mitigate potential security risks in the EV infrastructure.

Open Automated Demand Response (OpenADR). OpenADR is a standardized communication protocol designed to facilitate demand response interactions between utilities, aggregators, and end-users [22]. Although its main application has been the management of electricity demand in commercial and industrial settings, OpenADR also plays a significant role in the evolving landscape of EV infrastructure it enables seamless integration between CSMSs and utility demand response programs. By leveraging OpenADR, EVCSs can receive signals from utilities or aggregators to adjust their charging schedules based on grid conditions, electricity prices, or other factors. This functionality allows EV owners to participate in demand response programs, potentially earning incentives for flexible charging behavior while supporting grid stability and reliability. Overall, OpenADR plays a crucial role in enhancing the flexibility, efficiency, and sustainability of EV charging infrastructure, enabling seamless integration with grid operations and demand response initiatives. However, we did not find any vulnerability analysis for OpenADR during our investigation.

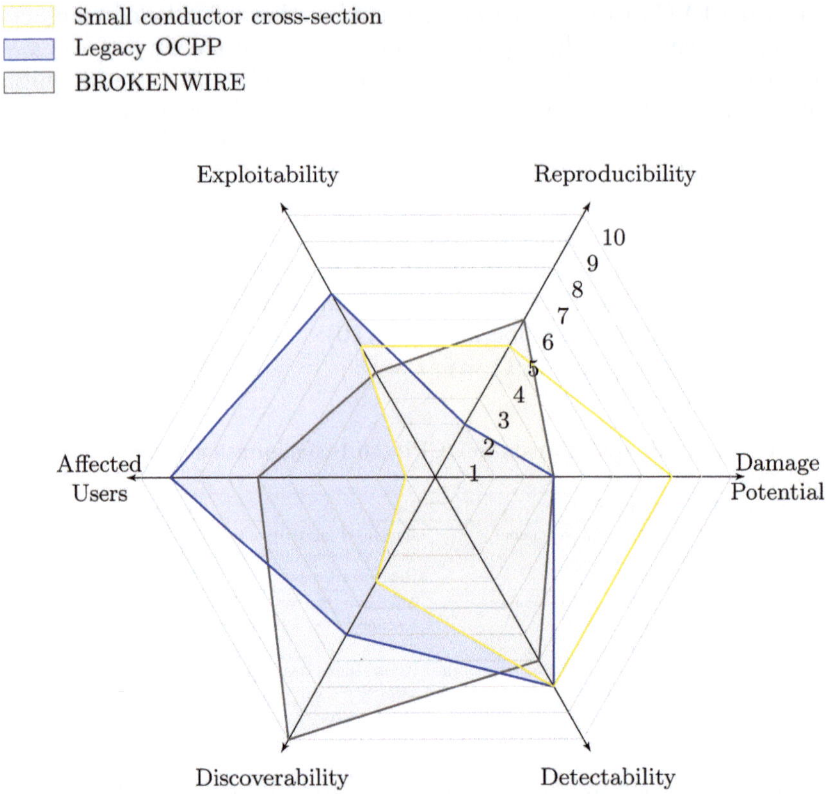

Fig. 4. Vulnerabilities with highest scoring and their impact across individual DREAD-D categories

5 Discussion

The goal of this work is to identify and evaluate existing vulnerabilities in the area of the EV charging infrastructure and to propose potential countermeasures. Table 2 summarizes all identified vulnerabilities, ranked by their overall DREAD-D scores. The scores are derived using a DREAD-based evaluation framework, which assesses vulnerabilities across six dimensions: Damage, Reproducibility, Exploitability, Affected Users, Discoverability, and Detectability. The vulnerability with the highest score is BROKENWIRE and ISO 15118 with TLS 1.2 has the lowest score.

Figure 4 illustrates the highest-scoring vulnerabilities in greater detail by visualizing their impact across individual DREAD-D categories. BROKENWIRE, although specific to a single type of charging connector, represents a significant threat due to its simplicity and the lack of fully effective countermeasures. This attack exploits weaknesses in communication protocols used by DC rapid chargers and can disrupt charging sessions remotely via electromagnetic interference.

Vulnerabilities in legacy OCPP implementations can disrupt the operation of entire charging parks, as this protocol is commonly used by CPOs to manage charging stations via the CSMS. This vulnerability can be exploited due to a lack of updates, but the countermeasure is correspondingly simple: always use the latest, most secure software version.

In terms of hardware-related weaknesses, modifications to conductor cross-sections present a subtle yet severe threat. Such changes are difficult for users to detect but could lead to catastrophic outcomes such as fires at charging stations or vehicles. Countermeasures to mitigate this hardware vulnerability include avoiding the use of external charging cables provided by third parties. At least for AC charging, users should only use their own charging cables that meet safety and compatibility standards. This reduces the risk of tampering or undetected modifications to the cable.

The findings underscore that as new technologies are integrated into EV charging infrastructure, robust security standards must be established. Specifically, standards must define a minimum level of cryptography to be used. This ensures that systems from different manufacturers communicate securely. Legacy software increases the risk of charging stations operating without proper encryption. To rule out further vulnerabilities, CPOs should regularly check their software for updates.

6 Conclusion

The advent of new technologies introduces new system vulnerabilities that can lead to security breaches and make these systems attractive targets for adversaries [18]. We examined that current standards exhibit vulnerabilities that are demonstrably exploitable by real-world attackers. These vulnerabilities present significant risks to the security and reliability of the EV infrastructure, highlighting the urgent need for robust security measures. EV charging attacks often exploit a chain of vulnerabilities or misconfigurations, yet adversaries consistently manage to cause damage, underscoring the importance of proactive security measures. A primary vulnerability of the EV charging infrastructure lies in its physical exposure. Attackers can exploit these vulnerabilities using modified cables or jammers to intercept or disrupt communication, thereby compromising the integrity of the charging process. We identify BROKENWIRE attacks and outdated OCPP versions as the vulnerabilities with the greatest potential impact. The consequences of such attacks can be significant, especially as more systemically important entities move to EVs, amplifying the impact of potential attacks. Attacks on the charging infrastructure threaten critical services such as ambulances, police, and fire departments that increasingly rely on EVs for transportation. Regular updates to standards are essential to address emerging threats and vulnerabilities in the EV charging infrastructure. Additionally, standards should prioritize security and avoid offering profiles with low security, as these are often adopted by manufacturers to reduce costs and efforts, further emphasizing the importance of stringent security measures.

In conclusion, our comprehensive analysis highlights the critical importance of addressing security aspects in the EV infrastructure to ensure its resilience against potential threats. By implementing proactive security measures, regularly updating standards, and fostering collaboration among stakeholders, we can mitigate risks and ensure the reliability and security of the EV infrastructure for the future.

References

1. Al-Jarrah, O.Y., Ramadan, O.A., Alsaify, B., Alkhushayni, S.: Comparative evaluation of machine learning-based controller area network intrusion detection systems. In: 2023 14th International Conference on Information and Communication Systems (ICICS), Irbid, Jordan (2023)
2. Alcaraz, C., Cumplido, J., Trivino, A.: OCPP in the spotlight: threats and countermeasures for electric vehicle charging infrastructures 4.0. Int. J. Inf. Secur. **22** (2023)
3. Alcaraz, C., Lopez, J., Wolthusen, S.: OCPP protocol: security threats and challenges. IEEE Trans. Smart Grid **8** (2017)
4. Bao, K., Valev, H., Wagner, M., Schmeck, H.: A threat analysis of the vehicle-to-grid charging protocol ISO 15118. Comput. Sci. Res. Dev. **33** (2018)
5. Berg, A., Svantesson, F.: Is your electric vehicle plotting against you?: An investigation of the ISO 15118 standard and current security implementations (2021). https://urn.kb.se/resolve?urn=urn:nbn:se:hh:diva-44918
6. Carroll, T., Redington, L., Moran-Schmoker, A., Murray, A.: Inventory of Public Key Cryptography in US Electric Vehicle Charging. Technical report (2023). https://www.osti.gov/servlets/purl/2204867/
7. Chalia, S., Seth, A.K., Singh, M.: Electric vehicle charging standards in india and safety consideration. In: 2021 IEEE 8th Uttar Pradesh Section International Conference on Electrical, Electronics and Computer Engineering (UPCON), Dehradun, India (2021)
8. D'Agostino, F.: Implementation of a PKI-based security communication and Value Added Service for EV charging using ISO 15118 standard. Laurea (2023). https://webthesis.biblio.polito.it/26753/
9. Deutsche Institut für Normung e. V.: DIN/TS 70121:2024-11 Elektromobilität - Digitale Kommunikation zwischen einer Gleichstrom-Ladestation und einem Elektrofahrzeug zur Regelung der Gleichstromladung im Verbund-Ladesystem (2024)
10. DKE, BDEW, ZVEH, ZVEI, VDE FNN, VDA: Technischer Leitfaden - Ladeinfrastruktur Elektromobilität (2023)
11. Engelhardt, M., Pfeiffer, F., Finkenzeller, K., Biebl, E.: Extending ISO/IEC 14443 Type A Eavesdropping Range using Higher Harmonics (2013)
12. Forschungsstelle für Energiewirtschaft e. V.: Normenlandschaft für die Elektromobilität (2023). https://www.ffe.de/veroeffentlichungen/normenlandschaft_fuer_die_elektromobilitaet/
13. Francis, L., Hancke, G., Mayes, K., Markantonakis, K.: Potential misuse of NFC enabled mobile phones with embedded security elements as contactless attack platforms. In: 2009 International Conference for Internet Technology and Secured Transactions, (ICITST) (2009). https://ieeexplore.ieee.org/document/5402513

14. Fries, S., Falk, R.: Electric Vehicle Charging Infrastructure – Security Considerations and Approaches (2012)
15. Fries, S., Falk, R.: Securely connecting electric vehicles to the smart grid. Int. J. Adv. Internet Technol. (2013)
16. Garofalaki, Z., Kosmanos, D., Moschoyiannis, S., Kallergis, D., Douligeris, C.: Electric vehicle charging: a survey on the security issues and challenges of the open charge point protocol (OCPP). IEEE Commun. Surv. Tutor. **24** (2022)
17. Gaton, B.: Tesla launches new EV charging battle, but the Plug War is already over (2022). https://thedriven.io/2022/12/21/tesla-launches-new-ev-charging-battle-but-the-plug-war-is-already-over/
18. Girdhar, M., Hong, J., You, Y., Song, T.J., Govindarasu, M.: Cyber-attack event analysis for EV charging stations. In: 2023 IEEE Power & Energy Society General Meeting (PESGM), Orlando, FL, USA (2023)
19. Habraken, R., Dolron, P., Poll, E., de Ruiter, J.: An RFID skimming gate using higher harmonics. In: Mangard, S., Schaumont, P. (eds.) RFIDSec 2015. LNCS, vol. 9440, pp. 122–137. Springer, Cham (2015). https://doi.org/10.1007/978-3-319-24837-0_8
20. Harnett, K., Harris, B., Chin, D., Watson, G.: DOE/DHS/DOT Volpe Technical Meeting on Electric Vehicle and Charging Station Cybersecurity Report (2018). https://rosap.ntl.bts.gov/view/dot/34991
21. Heidmaier, F., Neudorfer, H.: Steckersysteme für Elektrofahrzeuge. e & i Elektrotechnik und Informationstechnik **140** (2023)
22. Herberg, U., Mashima, D., Jetcheva, J.G., Mirzazad-Barijough, S.: OpenADR 2.0 deployment architectures: options and implications. In: 2014 IEEE International Conference on Smart Grid Communications (SmartGridComm), Venice, Italy (2014)
23. International Energy Agency: Global EV Outlook 2023: Catching up with Climate Ambitions. Global EV Outlook, OECD (2023). https://www.oecd-ilibrary.org/energy/global-ev-outlook-2023_cbe724e8-en
24. International Organization for Standardization: ISO 15118-2:2014 Road Vehicles – Vehicle-to-Grid Communication Interface – Part 2: Network and Application Protocol Requirements (2014)
25. Johnson, J., Berg, T., Anderson, B., Wright, B.: Review of electric vehicle charger cybersecurity vulnerabilities, potential impacts, and defenses. Energies **15** (2022)
26. Kern, D., Krauß, C., Zhdanova, M.: System Security Mechanisms for Electric Vehicles and Charge Points Supporting ISO 15118 (2022)
27. Köhler, S., Baker, R., Strohmeier, M., Martinovic, I.: Brokenwire : Wireless Disruption of CCS Electric Vehicle Charging (2022). http://arxiv.org/abs/2202.02104
28. Lohmiller, N., Kaniewski, S., Menth, M., Heer, T.: A survey of post-quantum cryptography migration in vehicles. IEEE Access (2025)
29. Metere, R., Pourmirza, Z., Walker, S., Neaimeh, M.: An Overview of Cyber Security and Privacy on the Electric Vehicle Charging Infrastructure (2022). http://arxiv.org/abs/2209.07842
30. Microsoft: STRIDE/DREAD, The DREAD approach to threat assessment (2023). https://docs.microsoft.com/en-us/windows-hardware/drivers/driversecurity/threat-modeling-for-drivers. Accessed 10 Feb 2025
31. Morosan, A.G., Pop, F.: OCPP security - neural network for detecting malicious traffic. In: Proceedings of the International Conference on Research in Adaptive and Convergent Systems, New York, NY, USA, RACS '17 (2017)

32. Nasr, T., Torabi, S., Bou-Harb, E., Fachkha, C., Assi, C.: Power jacking your station: in-depth security analysis of electric vehicle charging station management systems. Comput. Secur. **112** (2022)
33. Orcioni, S., Conti, M.: EV smart charging with advance reservation extension to the OCPP standard. Energies **13** (2020)
34. Pourmirza, Z., Srivastava, A.: Cybersecurity analysis for the communication protocol in smart grids. In: 2020 IEEE 8th International Conference on Smart Energy Grid Engineering (SEGE), Oshawa, ON, Canada (2020)
35. Pourmirza, Z., Walker, S.: Electric vehicle charging station: cyber security challenges and perspective. In: 2021 IEEE 9th International Conference on Smart Energy Grid Engineering (SEGE), Oshawa, ON, Canada (2021)
36. Rubio, J.E., Alcaraz, C., Lopez, J.: Addressing security in OCPP: protection against man-in-the-middle attacks. In: 2018 9th IFIP International Conference on New Technologies, Mobility and Security (NTMS), Paris (2018)
37. Sagstetter, F., et al.: Security challenges in automotive hardware/software architecture design. In: 2013 Design, Automation & Test in Europe Conference & Exhibition (DATE) (2013). https://doi.org/10.7873/DATE.2013.102
38. Sarieddine, K., et al.: Uncovering covert attacks on ev charging infrastructure: how OCPP backend vulnerabilities could compromise your system (2024)
39. Sarieddine, K., et al.: EV charging infrastructure discovery to contextualize its deployment security. IEEE Trans. Netw. Serv. Manag. **21** (2024)
40. Sayed, M.A., Atallah, R., Assi, C., Debbabi, M.: Electric vehicle attack impact on power grid operation. Int. J. Electr. Power Energy Syst. **137** (2022)
41. Skarga-Bandurova, I., Kotsiuba, I., Biloborodova, T.: Cyber security of electric vehicle charging infrastructure: open issues and recommendations. In: 2022 IEEE International Conference on Big Data (Big Data), Osaka, Japan (2022)
42. Tesla, Inc.: North American Charging Standard: Technical Specification (2022). https://tesla-cdn.thron.com/static/HXVNIC_North_American_Charging_Standard_Technical_Specification_TS-0023666_HFTPKZ.pdf
43. Upstream Security Ltd: Upstream's 2023 Global Automotive Cybersecurity Report. https://upstream.auto/reports/global-automotive-cybersecurity-report/
44. Van Aubel, P., Poll, E.: Security of EV-Charging Protocols (2022). http://arxiv.org/abs/2202.04631
45. Verband der Elektrotechnik Elektronik und Informationstechnik e.V.: DIN EN IEC 61851-1 VDE 0122-1:2019-12 Konduktive Ladesysteme für Elektrofahrzeuge (2017)
46. Zhou, C., et al.: ChargeX: exploring state switching attack on electric vehicle charging systems (2023). http://arxiv.org/abs/2305.08037

Data-Driven Approaches to Micromobility Demand Modeling

Ruben Röhner[1(✉)], Damir Ravlija[1], Ingo Trautwein[2], and Mirko Sonntag[1,2]

[1] Esslingen University of Applied Sciences, Flandernstraße 101, 73732 Esslingen am Neckar, Germany
ru.roehner@gmail.com

[2] Fraunhofer Institute for Industrial Engineering, Nobelstrasse 12, 70569 Stuttgart, Germany

Abstract. Shared micromobility services provide a flexible and sustainable alternative for urban and suburban mobility, especially for the first and last mile problems. It is crucial to understand the mobility patterns in the operating areas to provide the best experience for users of shared micromobility services. Effective demand modeling can provide data to test and evaluate fleet configurations in different but relevant mobility scenarios. This study utilizes statistical and deep learning techniques for demand modeling of a shared e-moped service operating in the urban and suburban areas of Stuttgart, Germany. It addresses the research gap of demand modeling in both urban and suburban areas by developing approaches based on models used in urban areas. Such models are usually presented in isolation for their use case, making them difficult to compare with each other. For this reason, in this work we also compare multiple model configurations based on different models and processing techniques. The results show that deep learning models, specifically LSTMs, provide the best results, outperforming the baseline and traditional models on most metrics. Using Voronoi partitioning and community clustering to aggregate trips and reduce spatial complexity led to better results for all evaluated models. Surprisingly, with the exception of Kullback-Leibler (KL) divergence, the inclusion of weather data resulted in worse performance for all other metrics.

Keywords: demand modeling · shared mobility · e-moped · micromobility · demand Generation · machine learning · deep learning

1 Introduction

The relevance of micromobility, including e-mopeds, has increased significantly in urban areas. This increase in popularity is due to the fact that they provide a flexible and efficient solution for short distances. Thereby, they address the first and last mile problems, i.e., the segments at the beginning and end of a journey that connect an origin or final destination of travelers to public transportation stations. Micromobility vehicles are often offered as a sharing service so that

L. Bechtel and T. Heer (Eds.): CCSSS 2025 PTT, pp. 37–52, 2026.
https://doi.org/10.1007/978-3-032-10569-1_3

users can rent them via smartphone. They benefit from continuous technological innovations that enhance their performance, durability, and sustainability. Shared micromobility services potentially reduce energy consumption, carbon emissions, and urban automobile traffic. This is achieved by shifting users from high-emission private vehicles to environmentally friendly shared micromobility. Consequently, these services play a key role in helping cities achieve their emissions reduction targets. This makes shared micromobility an interesting and sustainable alternative to private transportation by car [2].

This work focuses on the demand modeling for e-moped sharing services, particularly in urban and suburban areas. Unlike studies that aim to forecast future demand patterns using the information about the immediately preceding demand levels [8–10,12,13], we focus on demand modeling in order to generate synthetic demand patterns. In other words, the focus is on approximating the general distribution underlying the data in order to be able to generate data for traffic simulations. In doing so, demand modeling in this work also considers external factors, such as weather conditions, temperature, and the time of day.

This approach allows testing and evaluating different operational scenarios in simulation environments, which is unattainable with forecasting models that depend directly on historical data. This kind of demand model could be used to generate synthetic traffic in simulation tools like SUMO [15]. This work presents several methods for generating demand for the above-mentioned shared micromobility services. We compare approaches from traditional machine learning and deep learning. Finally, we also address the research gap of demand modeling in urban and suburban areas. Existing works focus on the modeling of urban areas. In the latter case, however, lower population density leads to a smaller number of e-moped rentals resulting in sparse trip data, which can negatively affect model performance. We address this challenge through spatial aggregation techniques and community clustering.

The rest of this paper is structured as follows: In Sect. 2, we provide a summary of the current state-of-the-art solutions for demand modeling in the area of shared micromobility. In Sect. 3, we first introduce the relevant preprocessing steps, including grid systems and community clustering. We then present the models implemented for demand modeling. In Sect. 4, the results to evaluate the models are presented. The results are discussed in Sect. 5, and Sect. 6 describes the findings of this research and provides insights into potential subject areas for future investigation.

2 Literature Review

This section provides an overview of the key literature on demand modeling in the shared micromobility sector. The literature review includes articles on all shared micromobility services due to the limited number of scientific articles addressing e-moped services. Most publications deal with demand forecasting for bike-sharing services. This section is split into three parts. The first part focuses on demand modeling using traditional machine learning approaches, the second part on deep learning techniques, and the final part summarizes the literature review results, highlights the research gaps, and provides an outlook on the study's contribution.

Traditional Machine Learning Approaches. In 2020, a study on demand modeling of e-scooter services was published [3]. The developed demand model is used in a simulator to test and improve different rebalancing strategies or similar operational differences aimed at enhancing the efficiency and user experience of such services. The public data used comes from the two American cities of Louisville and Minneapolis. The demand model is split into two parts, one modeling only the temporal component of the demand and the other modeling the spatial part. For temporal modeling, a Poisson regression is used with different parameters for every hour and type of day. The spatial modeling is based on kernel density estimation. Two years later, the same research group published an improved version of their demand model using a version of kernel density estimation with variable parameters based on the training data [17]. While the present work does not focus on exact coordinate generation, their approach could be implemented as an additional layer if precise locations are required for demand modeling.

Liu et al. [14] focused on modeling unfulfilled attempts to rent a bike, which is referred to in this study as "excess demand." A Two-Poisson regression and a Skellam regression were used to model the number of bikes rented and returned simultaneously for each bike docking station. The Skellam distribution is used to represent the difference between two Poisson distributions. Since this study simultaneously models the number of rentals and returns, this model can be used as an alternative to two distinct Poisson models.

Deep Learning Approaches. A literature review article on demand modeling of bike-sharing systems was published in 2022 by Jiang [7]. The results of the reviewed papers were divided into categories according to the input data type used for different deep learning models. Time series, graph, and grid data are the primary types of input used to model demand in bike-sharing systems. For time series data, Long Short Term Memory (LSTM) has been identified as the most used and performant model [7]. Conversely, when modeling graph data, Graph Convolutional Neural Network (GCN) is the preferred architecture [7]. For grid data as the input, the Convolutional Neural Network has been used the most [7]. A significant number of studies in this field focus on autoregressive models [7]. Autoregressive models are commonly used in time series forecasting. They would, however, not be usable in the simulator due to their direct reliance on the output of the previous historical values. Consequently, in this work, we have focused on models that generate demand based on temporal data in connection with external factors such as weather data.

Summary and Study Contribution. While substantial advancements have been made in the field of demand modeling of shared micromobility services, some research gaps remain. The majority of existing articles are based on large datasets containing millions of records from mostly densely populated urban centers [7]. This limits the usability of those models in less dense areas, like suburban areas. Almost all studies focus only on deep learning or traditional machine learning techniques while excluding a proper comparison of both methods [3,7,17]. Studies utilizing deep learning models mainly focus on autoregressive models, which depend directly on historical demand data. This makes them unsuitable for applications where historical data is only available for the training. To address these limitations, this work focuses on non-autoregressive demand modeling techniques using the data from the urban and suburban areas of Stuttgart, Germany.

The literature review identified that the vast majority of publications examined use a grid to aggregate the start and end points of the trips, which improves model performance [7]. Furthermore, community clustering is frequently utilized to group similar trips or grid cells into communities, which leads to an increase in model performance due to the similarity of trips inside a community [9,13,16]. Additionally, weather, points of interest (POI), or demographic data are often included as an extension of the trip data, mainly resulting in better-performing models [7]. Based on these insights, our models integrate grid systems, community clustering, and weather data to improve accuracy. POI and demographic data were not used to avoid making the models overly complex.

3 Methodology

In this section, we first present the key preprocessing steps used to prepare the trip data for training. Specifically, three distinct partitioning systems and a community clustering approach were used. After that, we present the traditional machine learning models and, finally, the deep learning models.

3.1 Data and Grid

Data utilized in this study were obtained from an e-moped sharing provider operating within the region of Stuttgart, Germany. The dataset was already preprocessed and enriched with weather information. It contains approximately 263,000 recorded trips, collected between October 2017 and October 2023. This makes it comparable with studies focused on docked bike systems [7] and larger than those focusing on e-scooter sharing systems [3]. Weather information was included using the Meteostat Python library, which collects data from national weather services such as DWD (Deutscher Wetterdienst) [1]. Furthermore, the months of November, December, January, and February were excluded due to the service provider's winter break. Each trip was described by start and end times, start and end locations, as well as temperature and precipitation information.

This free-floating sharing system allows customers to pick up and drop off e-mopeds at any location within the designated operating area. Consequently, the spatial distribution of e-mopeds presents certain modeling challenges. However, when modeling sharing services, spatial accuracy within a few hundred meters is sufficient, as customers of such sharing providers are willing to walk a short distance to the next vehicle [18]. For this reason, three distinct grid systems have been implemented to aggregate the trip data and thus reduce the spatial complexity. This study uses a 200×200 m square grid, a 1000×1000 m square grid, and a Voronoi partition. Specifically, the 1000×1000 m grid provides a coarse representation suitable for capturing broader urban mobility patterns, while the more granular 200×200 m grid better aligns with typical willingness to walk to an e-moped. This way, different levels of grid granularity as well as different ways of aggregating the trip data can be compared. While the 200×200 m square grid and the Voronoi partition are similar in size, their structures are different. The Voronoi cells are generated using road intersection data. Each cell is centered on a road intersection, thus partitioning the spatial area based on the underlying road network structure. Consequently, the origin and destination coordinates of the trip data were mapped to these grid systems, and the cell IDs were added to the dataset as a categorical feature.

3.2 Community Clustering

To further reduce the complexity of the more granular spatial aggregations, community clustering is used to cluster the 200×200 m grid and Voronoi cells, resulting in communities containing trip origins for similar trips. In this context, similar trips refer to trips with comparable temporal usage patterns, i.e., trips originating from cells that show similar hourly, daily, and seasonal demand patterns. The k-means algorithm has been used to generate communities of grid or Voronoi cells. The parameters used for this clustering are based on the temporal distribution of the trips, with their starting point inside the designated grid cell. The temporal distribution of trips is defined by the mean value and the standard deviation of the number of trips, aggregated by hour, day, weekday, and month. Prior to clustering, these features were normalized using z-transform to ensure that each dimension contributed equally to the clustering process and the initial number of clusters was determined by the rule of thumb $k \approx \sqrt{n/2}$, where n corresponds to the number of grid cells [11]. This number was continuously reduced, and the clusters were visually analyzed to identify a minimal and optimal number of communities. The visual analysis involved visually examining spatial coherence and cluster separation across potential community configurations. Finally, a total of 20 communities were selected. The community structure generated by this clustering is illustrated in Figs. 1 and 2, with colors representing clusters. Figure 1 displays the community clustering applied to the 200×200 m square grid and Fig. 2 the community clustering applied to the Voronoi partition. As can be observed in these figures, the different cell forms affect the clustering results. This is particularly noticeable in suburban areas, where the 200×200 m grid exhibits a greater diversity of clusters compared to the Voronoi partition.

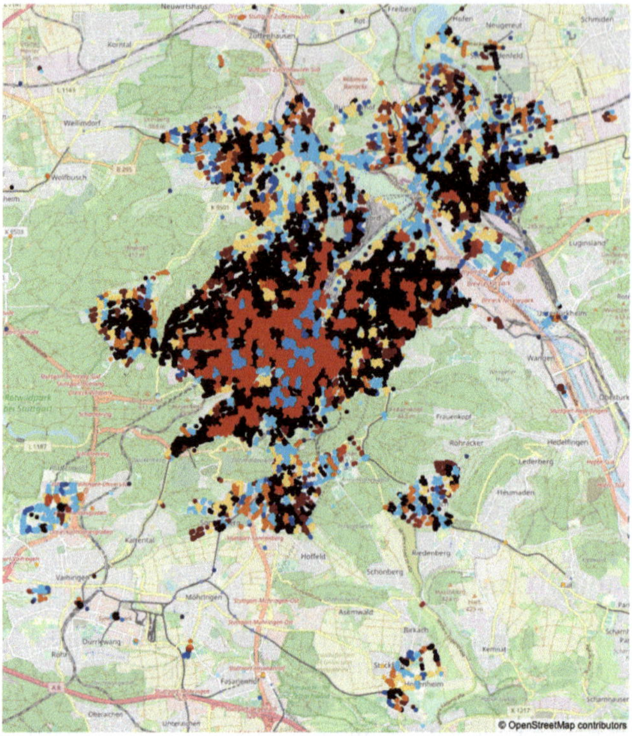

Fig. 1. Trip data clustered in communities: 200×200 m grid

3.3 Traditional Machine Learning Models

Based on the literature review on traditional machine learning models for demand modeling in the field of shared micromobility, we choose to implement a Poisson regression model, as described in [3] and [17]. We use the Negative Binomial regression model as an alternative for better comparison because it is widely used for modeling count data and is more robust when trained on sparse data [4]. The following section describes these two models and our implementation details.

Poisson Regression Model. The Poisson regression model is a widely used machine learning approach for modeling count data [4]. The Poisson regression assumes that the data to be modeled follows a Poisson distribution. In addition to that, the distribution's mean and variance are assumed to be equal. This assumption restricts the Poisson regression in the way that distributions with higher variance than their mean are not modeled well. This phenomenon is called overdispersion and is common in many real-world problems. The Poisson

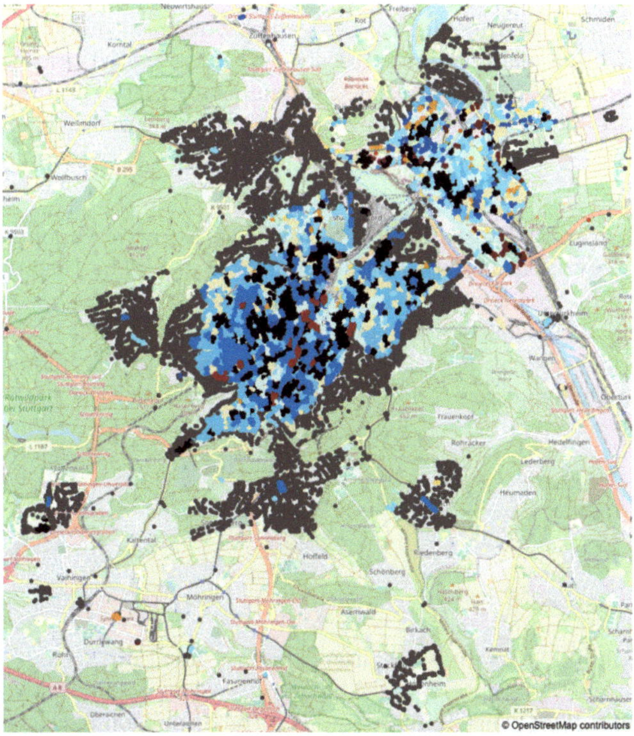

Fig. 2. Trip data clustered in communities: Voronoi partition

probability distribution is given by the following equation:

$$f(k;\lambda) = \frac{\lambda^k e^{-\lambda}}{k!} \tag{1}$$

The parameter λ represents the mean number of successes in the series. The parameter k represents the number of successes for which the probability mass function returns the corresponding probability [4]. During training, the model adapts the parameter λ to fit the observed data.

In this work, the Poisson regression model is trained based only on trip data. Three different model configurations were implemented. The first one is trained on trip data for each 1000×1000 m grid cell. The second one uses the 200×200 m grid system in combination with the discussed community clustering to train one model for each community. The last one is trained using the Voronoi partition, again utilizing the community clustering. The trip data is aggregated based on the configuration's spatial system, specifically the used grid system, and is then aggregated into three-hour bins. This results in a count data schema representing the number of trips that occur in the respective three-hour time bin within the designated grid cell. The input parameters for all three configurations are the three-hour time bin, the day of the week, and the month.

For the second and third configurations, which both use community clustering, an additional input parameter representing the designated grid cell is added. The output is a scalar representing the number of rentals for the designated cell. A separate model is trained for every cell or community, depending on the configuration.

Negative Binomial Regression Model. The Negative Binomial regression is another widely used model to model count data [4]. The Negative Binomial model is generally seen as more flexible and can handle overdispersion in contrast to the Poisson regression [4]. The mean and variance of their distributions are not assumed to be equal, as it is with the Poisson regression model (Sect. 3.3). The Negative Binomial regression is defined by the following probability mass function:

$$f(k;\mu,\alpha) = \frac{\Gamma\left(k+\frac{1}{\alpha}\right)}{\Gamma(k+1)\ \Gamma\left(\frac{1}{\alpha}\right)} \left(\frac{1}{1+\alpha\mu}\right)^{\frac{1}{\alpha}} \left(1-\frac{1}{1+\alpha\mu}\right)^{k} \tag{2}$$

$$\Gamma(k+1) = k! \qquad \Gamma\left(k+\frac{1}{\alpha}-1\right) = \left(k+\frac{1}{\alpha}\right)! \qquad \Gamma\left(\frac{1}{\alpha}\right) = \left(\frac{1}{\alpha}-1\right)! \tag{3}$$

The probability mass function uses the $\Gamma(\cdot)$ function, which is defined in Eq. 3. The parameter k represents the counts of events, μ represents the expected mean of the underlying distribution, and α is the dispersion parameter that controls the variance of the distribution. During training, the model optimizes both μ and α parameters to fit the observed data, allowing it to handle overdispersion that the Poisson model cannot take into account.

The Negative Binomial regression models used in this work were trained according to the previously discussed Poisson regression models. This means that three configurations for three different grid systems were implemented, utilizing the community clustering for the 200×200 m and Voronoi partition system. The input parameters, model training procedure, and output structure follow the same approach as described for the Poisson model configurations.

During the training process of the Poisson and Negative Binomial regression models, we encountered challenges related to convergence due to the sparseness of the trip data. For this reason, we aggregated the data in three-hour rather than one-hour bins. At this point, zero-inflated versions of the Poisson and Negative Binomial regression models have been tested to address this issue as well, but they didn't improve the performance. Further research on using zero-inflated models for demand generation under such sparse data conditions could lead to further improvement on this topic.

3.4 Deep Learning Models

In this section, the implemented deep learning models for this work are presented. We selected the LSTM model because of its popularity in demand modeling and its capability to capture both short-term and long-term dependencies in trip data. Another aspect is that LSTM models can be utilized as a non-autoregressive model, which is a requirement for this work (see Sect. 2). Firstly, the general architecture and relevant advantages of LSTMs are outlined. Then, the chosen network architecture for this work is described, and finally, the six different configurations trained are presented.

LSTM. Long Short Term Memory (LSTM) is a deep learning model developed by Hochreiter and Schmidhuber [5], which is a specialization of the Recurrent Neural Network (RNN), i.e., a neural network architecture with feedback connections. LSTMs are often used to model time series data. The LSTM was developed to solve the exploding/vanishing gradient problem. This problem describes the characteristic of RNN that the weights change too much or too little during backpropagation [5]. During backpropagation, weights are calculated as a function of the error between the expected value and the result. As a result, the model tends to overfit, i.e., training with new data no longer has an effect on the weights and thus on the entire model. This problem often occurs when modeling time series data if an attempt is made to capture long-term dependencies with these models.

The key feature of LSTM is the architecture of the individual cells, as shown in Fig. 3. An LSTM cell consists of three gates: the input gate, the output gate, and the forget gate. In addition to these three gates, LSTM cells have an internal memory $c(t)$. The three gates ensure that only the most important information is stored over a longer period of time, while new information $x(t)$ can still influence the model's internal memory. The input gate controls the amount of information that enters the internal memory from the input, so that only relevant data changes the internal memory. The forget gate determines which information is retained in the internal memory and which can be discarded. The output gate defines which information forms the new hidden state $h(t)$.

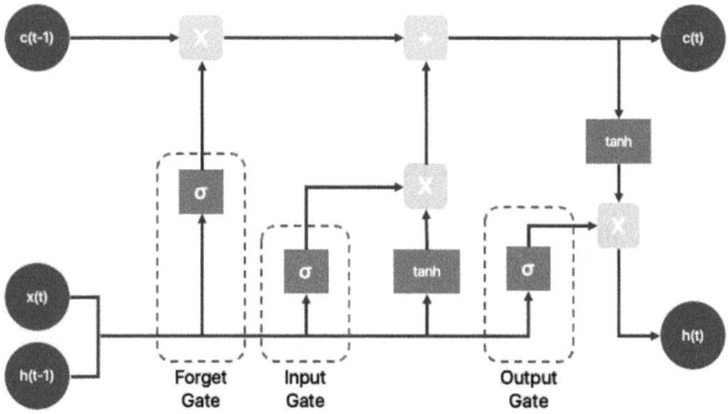

Fig. 3. LSTM cell

The LSTM model developed in this work consists of five LSTM layers, each containing 50 LSTM cells. A dropout layer with a dropout rate of 0.1 is added to the end of each LSTM layer to prevent the models from overfitting. The Adam optimizer with a learning rate of 0.01 and the Mean Squared Error (MSE) as the error function was used for model training. The final layer of the model is a dense layer, which reduces the number of output features to a scalar representing the demand, i.e., the number of rentals within the grid or Voronoi cell.

The trip dataset was divided into three distinct sets for the purposes of training, testing, and validation. Before splitting, the data were shuffled to ensure a representative distribution unaffected by concept drift in all three subsets. A 75:15:10 split of the data was selected for training, testing, and validation, respectively. The training process was conducted over 20 epochs, with a batch size of 32. To ensure the ability to replicate the training at a later point in time, a seed was utilized for the partitioning of the data into training, test, and validation sets, as well as for the dropout layers of the model. The training parameters and model architecture were derived from Liu et al. [12] but were adapted to the requirements of this work.

The LSTM-based demand model was trained using six distinct configurations, progressively increasing spatial complexity and incorporating environmental factors. Initially, the model was trained exclusively on trip data, aggregated into 1000×1000 m grid cells. For each grid cell, an individual LSTM model was trained using input features such as month, day of the week, and hour to model the demand within the corresponding cell. To enhance performance, the model was extended by integrating weather data, specifically temperature and precipitation, as additional input features while retaining the grid structure.

Subsequently, the spatial reduction approach was shifted to a community-clustering method, where grid cells were grouped into communities based on temporal trip distributions (see Sect. 3.2). A single LSTM model was then trained for each community, reducing the total number of models to 20. For cell-level modeling, the cell ID was added as a categorical feature to the input space. This reduction in the number of models allows the use of a finer grid resolution of 200×200 m. The model was further improved by incorporating weather data into this community-based configuration, leveraging both trip and environmental information.

As an alternative to square grid cells, Voronoi cells were introduced to better capture spatial heterogeneity, and these were similarly grouped into 20 communities, each with its own LSTM model. Finally, the Voronoi-based configuration was enhanced by adding weather data, therefore combining trip and environmental features to refine accuracy. Through these configurations, the same LSTM architecture was iteratively adapted to improve its ability to model demand across varying spatial and temporal conditions.

Table 1 presents all model configurations developed and evaluated in Sect. 3.3 and Sect. 3.4, highlighting the grid system, use of community clustering, and use of weather data.

Table 1. Overview of models, grid systems, use of community clustering, and use of weather data

Model	Grid System	Community Clustering	Weather Data
Poisson	1000×1000 m	✗	✗
Negative-Binomial	1000×1000 m	✗	✗
Poisson	200×200 m	✓	✗
Negative-Binomial	200×200 m	✓	✗
Poisson	Voronoi	✓	✗
Negative-Binomial	Voronoi	✓	✗
LSTM	1000×1000 m	✗	✗
LSTM	1000×1000 m	✗	✓
LSTM	200×200 m	✓	✗
LSTM	200×200 m	✓	✓
LSTM	Voronoi	✓	✗
LSTM	Voronoi	✓	✓

4 Results

In this section, the results from evaluating the models discussed in Sect. 3 are presented. In Table 2, the results for the Poisson and Negative Binomial models are presented, and in Table 3, the results from evaluating the LSTM models are displayed. All models were assessed using the mean absolute error (MAE), MSE, coefficient of determination (R^2), and the Kullback-Leibler (KL) divergence metrics. These metrics were aggregated across all cells for improved comparison among the different spatial aggregation methods. They were chosen because of their different interpretability. The MAE and the MSE describe the point accuracy of the demand models. The R^2 metric describes how well the demand models capture the variance of the whole trip distribution. In contrast to these metrics, the KL divergence assesses the similarity between the modeled and the actual distribution.

All model configurations were also compared to the baseline models, which compute the mean demand in the training dataset for each cell, depending on the used partitioning method. If such a model were applied to the test dataset, its R^2 value would be 0. In the following sections, we only include the best-performing baseline, i.e., the one applied to the Voronoi diagram. While the baseline calculated this way achieves a better MSE value and comparable results to the statistical models on other metrics, it performs significantly worse than the LSTM model with the same Voronoi partitioning. For all other partitioning systems, the corresponding baseline performs worse than the associated models.

4.1 Performance of Traditional Machine Learning Models

Table 2. Results for traditional machine learning models from Sect. 3.3

Model	MAE	MSE	R^2	KL Divergence
(0)	0.015344	**0.004206**	–0.014951	0.000118
(1)	0.121575	0.158624	–0.439623	**0.000066**
(2)	0.125233	0.160941	-0.471506	**0.000066**
(3)	0.004777	0.004947	–0.001137	0.000084
(4)	0.004785	0.004953	**–0.000204**	0.000084
(5)	**0.004403**	0.004780	–0.056200	0.000092
(6)	0.004637	0.004966	–0.089563	0.000091

(0) Baseline (Voronoi partition): mean of training data
(1) Poisson model using the large square grid
(2) Negative-Binomial model using the large square grid
(3) Poisson model using the small square grid
(4) Negative-Binomial model using the small square grid
(5) Poisson model using the Voronoi partition
(6) Negative-Binomial model using the Voronoi partition

The results from evaluating the traditional machine learning models are presented in Table 2. The Poisson model based on the Voronoi partition (model 5) demonstrated the best results regarding the MAE and MSE. However, when comparing the models using the R^2 metric, the Negative Binomial model utilizing the small grid system (model 4) performed the best. Based on the results considering the KL divergence, the Poisson and Negative Binomial models using the large square grid system (models 1 and 2) outperformed all other models.

Overall, the Poisson models consistently outperformed the Negative Binomial models regarding MAE and MSE across different grid systems. The R^2 metric showed similar results, except for the models based on Voronoi partitions, where the Negative Binomial model outperformed the Poisson model. The KL divergence shows mostly similar results for the Poisson and the Negative Binomial models, except for the Voronoi diagram-based models, where the Negative Binomial model shows slightly better results than the equivalent Poisson model.

When comparing the models based on the utilized grid system, the MAE and MSE prefer the Voronoi partition with a slight advantage over the small square grid system and a much worse performance using the large square grid system. Comparing the grid systems based on the R^2 metric, the small square grid system leads to a minor advantage over the Voronoi partition. The large square grid shows the worst performance for the R^2 metric as well. In contrast to the MAE,

MSE, and R^2 metrics, KL divergence shows the best results for the large grid system, poorer performance for the small grid system, and the poorest performance for the Voronoi partition. This suggests that while the Voronoi partition and small grid-based models capture point-level accuracy better, the large grid-based models represent the overall trip distribution better.

4.2 Performance of Deep Learning Model Configurations

Table 3. Results for deep learning models from Sect. 3.4

Model	MAE	MSE	R^2	KL Divergence
(0)	0.015344	0.004206	−0.014951	0.000118
(1)	0.059605	0.028057	−10.580745	0.000072
(2)	0.064695	0.033568	−24.384932	0.000071
(3)	0.002973	0.000951	−0.043849	0.000071
(4)	0.005058	0.001042	−0.168338	0.000070
(5)	**0.002496**	**0.000722**	**−0.000699**	0.000027
(6)	0.004218	0.000790	**−0.000699**	**0.000018**

(0) Baseline (Voronoi partition): mean of training data
(1) LSTM model using the large square grid
(2) LSTM model using the large square grid including weather data
(3) LSTM model using the small square grid
(4) LSTM model using the small square grid including weather data
(5) LSTM model using the Voronoi partition
(6) LSTM model using the Voronoi partition including weather data

The results for deep learning models, specifically the LSTM models, are presented in Table 3. The LSTM model utilizing the Voronoi partition system without including weather data (model 5) performed the best on the MAE and MSE metrics. In contrast, the LSTM model that includes weather data (model 6) showed the best results in terms of KL divergence. When comparing the models based on their R^2 score, both of these models displayed the best results.

The results show that the incorporation of weather data, independent of the grid system, led to poorer performance with respect to the MAE, MSE, and R^2 metrics. The difference in those metrics is higher for the large square system and much less for the small square and Voronoi partition systems. In contrast, the KL divergences indicated an opposing effect, leading to slightly better results when weather data were included as additional features. The differences in KL divergence are only marginal except for the Voronoi partition-based models, with a slightly larger improvement when incorporating weather data.

When comparing the results with respect to the different grid systems, the Voronoi partition, in combination with the community clustering, outperformed all others. The small square grid system (200×200 m) shows slightly worse performance, and the large square grid system (1000×1000 m) has the poorest results. The differences between the Voronoi and small square grid are only minor, but a rather big difference compared to the large square grid system.

4.3 Comparison

The results from the LSTM models compared to those from the Poisson and Negative Binomial models show that the LSTM models outperform statistical models. Notably, the values for the R^2 metric were all negative for all assessed models. This indicates that all models have difficulties modeling the variance of the underlying trip distribution. For both categories of models, the findings clearly indicate that the Voronoi partition system outperforms the other two. The small grid system experiences only a minor performance drop, while the large grid system displays more distinct performance differences. As described, the KL divergences show the opposite effect for traditional machine learning models when compared only with respect to the used grid systems.

5 Discussion

The results from evaluating both traditional machine learning and deep learning models show that the latter perform better. In most scenarios, Poisson models performed better than Negative Binomial models. Statistical and deep learning approaches faced challenges in modeling variance in the demand data, as indicated by the consistently negative R^2 values. This is an expected phenomenon when attempting to model sparse and highly variable data, such as mobility demand data from urban and suburban areas.

The results from Sect. 4 indicate that the grid systems, in conjunction with community clustering, significantly impact model performance. For the LSTM-based models, those using higher granular spatial aggregation displayed better outcomes regarding all evaluated metrics. In contrast, traditional machine learning models preferred a coarser spatial aggregation according to the KL divergence. These findings suggest that for deep learning models, presumably due to their higher complexity, finer grid systems, such as the described Voronoi partition, lead to superior models. For traditional machine learning models, the choice of spatial partitioning system depends on the application. Less granular partitioning proves more suitable for synthetic demand generation as demonstrated by higher KL divergence values. Conversely, finer partitioning is more advantageous for capturing point-level accuracy, as shown by improved MAE and MSE values. Choosing the right granularity and technique to aggregate mobility demand data spatially is a trade-off. Benefits of spatial aggregation are noise reduction and less complex demand models, but biases and local loss of detail can arise [6].

As seen in Sect. 4.2, incorporating weather data results in poorer performance in terms of the MAE, MSE, and R^2 metrics, along with a slight increase in the KL divergence. This suggests that models that include weather data struggle more with modeling the exact number of trips but show a slight benefit in capturing the overall distribution of trips. In the context of demand generation, this can be viewed as an improvement. However, further feature engineering of the incorporated weather data could lead to more significant improvements in model accuracy.

6 Conclusions

This work investigated approaches for the generation of synthetic demand patterns for shared micromobility services in urban and suburban environments where data sparsity presents modeling challenges. We examined deep and statistical machine learning methods for demand modeling in e-moped sharing. Three distinct models with different configurations, resulting in a total of 12 models, were developed, trained, and evaluated. The corresponding model definitions and evaluation procedure can be found in a GitHub repository[1].

The results show that deep learning models, specifically LSTM models, outperform traditional machine learning models, such as Poisson and Negative Binomial regression. Finer-granular grid systems, like the Voronoi-based partitioning system presented in combination with community clustering, performed best. Only the traditional machine learning models showed lower performance in modeling the whole trip distribution when using finer grid systems. To further improve the presented demand models, different techniques can be used, such as data augmentation to enlarge the available volume of training data and hyperparameter tuning in combination with cross-validation to make better use of the available training data. Additionally, further data aggregation and hybrid or hierarchical models in combination with regularization could be used to simplify the problem, prevent overfitting, and improve modeling of the whole trip distribution. As shown earlier, spatial data aggregation techniques, such as the presented grid systems and community clustering, had the most impact on modeling performances, and additional features, like weather conditions, didn't improve model accuracy. Therefore, aggregation methods and feature engineering are promising areas of research in this domain.

References

1. Meteostat developers: Data sources. https://dev.meteostat.net/sources.html. Accessed 28 Feb 2025
2. Abduljabbar, R.L., Liyanage, S., Dia, H.: The role of micro-mobility in shaping sustainable cities: a systematic literature review. Transp. Res. Part D: Transp. Environ. **92**, 102734 (2021). https://doi.org/10.1016/j.trd.2021.102734

[1] https://github.com/keim-hs-esslingen/mm-demand-modeling.

3. Ciociola, A., Cocca, M., Giordano, D., Vassio, L., Mellia, M.: E-scooter sharing: leveraging open data for system design. In: 2020 IEEE/ACM 24th International Symposium on Distributed Simulation and Real Time Applications (DS-RT), pp. 1–8 (2020). https://doi.org/10.1109/DS-RT50469.2020.9213514
4. Hilbe, J.M.: Negative Binomial Regression, 2nd edn. Cambridge University Press, Cambridge (2011)
5. Hochreiter, S., Schmidhuber, J.: Long short-term memory. Neural Comput. **9**(8), 1735–1780 (1997). https://doi.org/10.1162/neco.1997.9.8.1735
6. Hornberger, Z.T., Cox, B.A., Hill, R.R.: Effects of aggregation methodology on uncertain spatiotemporal data. arXiv preprint arXiv:1910.05125 (2019). https://doi.org/10.48550/arXiv.1910.05125
7. Jiang, W.: Bike sharing usage prediction with deep learning: a survey. Neural Comput. Appl. **34**(18), 15369–15385 (2022). https://doi.org/10.1007/s00521-022-07380-5
8. Jin, G., Cui, Y., Zeng, L., Tang, H., Feng, Y., Huang, J.: Urban ride-hailing demand prediction with multiple spatio-temporal information fusion network. Transp. Res. Part C: Emerg. Technol. **117**, 102665 (2020). https://doi.org/10.1016/j.trc.2020.102665
9. Kim, S., Choo, S., Lee, G., Kim, S.: Predicting demand for shared e-scooter using community structure and deep learning method. Sustainability **14**(5), 2564 (2022). https://doi.org/10.3390/su14052564
10. Kim, T.S., Lee, W.K., Sohn, S.Y.: Graph convolutional network approach applied to predict hourly bike-sharing demands considering spatial, temporal, and global effects. PLoS ONE **14**(9), e0220782 (2019). https://doi.org/10.1371/journal.pone.0220782
11. Kodinariya, T.M., Makwana, P.R., et al.: Review on determining number of cluster in k-means clustering. Int. J. **1**(6), 90–95 (2013). https://www.researchgate.net/publication/313554124_Review_on_Determining_of_Cluster_in_K-means_Clustering
12. Li, X.: Deep learning for short-term bike sharing demand forecast: spatial temporal usage characterization and feature fusion strategies. Phd thesis, Hong Kong Polytechnic University (2022). https://theses.lib.polyu.edu.hk/handle/200/12196
13. Lin, L., He, Z., Peeta, S.: Predicting station-level hourly demand in a large-scale bike-sharing network: a graph convolutional neural network approach. Transp. Res. Part C: Emerg. Technol. **97**, 258–276 (2018). https://doi.org/10.1016/j.trc.2018.10.011
14. Liu, X., Pelechrinis, K.: Excess demand prediction for bike sharing systems. PLoS ONE **16**(6), e0252894 (2021). https://doi.org/10.1371/journal.pone.0252894
15. Lopez, P.A., et al.: Microscopic traffic simulation using SUMO. In: 2018 21st International Conference on Intelligent Transportation Systems (ITSC), pp. 2575–2582 (2018). https://doi.org/10.1109/ITSC.2018.8569938
16. Pan, Y., Zheng, R.C., Zhang, J., Yao, X.: Predicting bike sharing demand using recurrent neural networks. Procedia Comput. Sci. **147**, 562–566 (2019). https://doi.org/10.1016/j.procs.2019.01.217
17. Pinna, M., Vassio, L., Giordano, D., Mellia, M.: Demand model generation from traces: adaptive kde data-driven optimization. In: 2022 6th International Conference on Smart Grid and Smart Cities, pp. 48–54 (2022). https://doi.org/10.1109/ICSGSC56353.2022.9963018
18. Reck, D.J., Martin, H., Axhausen, K.W.: Mode choice, substitution patterns and environmental impacts of shared and personal micro-mobility. Transp. Res. Part D: Transp. Environ. **102**, 103–134 (2022). https://doi.org/10.1016/j.trd.2021.103134

How to Tame GeNESIS: A Tutorial for Utilizing GeNESIS to Simulate Realistic Industrial Evaluation Scenarios

Samuel Müller(✉), Lukas Popperl, Lukas Bechtel, and Tobias Heer

University of Applied Sciences Esslingen, Esslingen am Neckar, Germany
{samuel.mueller,lukas.popperl,lukas.bechtel,tobias.heer}@hs-esslingen.de

Abstract. The growing interconnectivity of industrial networks enables new applications but poses security and performance challenges. To solve these challenges for industrial networks, researchers develop new algorithms and mechanisms. The evaluation of these solutions requires traffic simulation, which in turn requires realistic topologies and traffic traces. However, in most cases, topologies and traffic traces of industrial networks are confidential due to security concerns of factory operators. In previous work, we addressed the lack of disclosable industrial topologies and traffic traces with GeNESIS. GeNESIS generates realistic industrial network topologies and traffic traces. In this paper, we extend GeNESIS with output capabilities for common simulation tools, i.e., OMNeT++ and ns-3, and provide a step-by-step tutorial based on three realistic case studies.

Keywords: Industrial Networks · Evaluation · GeNESIS · OMNeT++ · ns-3 · Tutorial

1 Introduction

Industrial networks face increased connectivity between all end devices in a factory. Rather than operating in isolated machine networks, devices will exchange data across the entire factory network. This connectivity enables new use cases and business models, such as predictive maintenance and personalized manufacturing. Additionally, these industrial networks must maintain a high level of security, robustness, and performance. To meet these requirements, researchers continuously develop new mechanisms and algorithms. A key challenge remains the comparability with previous work. This challenge arises from a) the limited number of publicly available industrial network topology datasets, as companies conceal them to prevent attackers from gaining knowledge about their network, and b) the high costs of realistic network deployments. To address the lack of realistic industrial network topologies, in previous work, we published GeNESIS [3] (the **Ge**nerator for **N**etwork **E**valuation **S**cenarios of **I**ndustrial **S**ystems). GeNESIS is a tool able to generate realistic a) industrial network topologies, b) packet traces, and c) security configurations.

L. Bechtel and T. Heer (Eds.): CCSSS 2025 PTT, pp. 53–73, 2026.
https://doi.org/10.1007/978-3-032-10569-1_4

Researchers typically evaluate network configurations and optimizations for increased security, robustness, and performance with simulation tools, such as OMNeT++ [12] and ns-3 [10]. These tools require topologies, configurations of the network, and packet traces as input. GeNESIS generates all three required inputs, without being able to simulate the traffic itself. While the specific characteristics of the generated topologies, packet traces, and network configurations are randomized, the final outputs remain deterministic, allowing users to reliably reproduce identical results. However, the output of GeNESIS is not tailored for OMNeT++ and ns-3, requiring time-intensive and manual adjustments. Additionally, the flexibility of the GeNESIS generation process requires complex configurations, which reduces usability. In this paper, we address these shortcomings by making the following contributions: 1) We provide a comprehensive tutorial on how to generate network topologies with GeNESIS featuring three different case studies, 2) we equip GeNESIS with output capabilities for ready-to-import files for OMNeT++ and ns-3, and 3) we demonstrate the import capability of the GeNESIS output into OMNeT++ and ns-3.

The remainder of the paper is structured as follows: In Sect. 2, we compare GeNESIS with four other topology generators, focusing on the export capabilities to various simulation tools. Section 3 explores the fundamental concepts and structures of industrial network topologies utilized by GeNESIS to generate realistic topologies. In Sect. 4, we highlight the main features of GeNESIS. Section 5 demonstrates the GeNESIS workflow through three different case studies. Finally, we discuss future work and conclude the paper in Sect. 6.

2 Related Work

Realistic network topologies are the foundation for the simulation and evaluation of new algorithms and mechanisms. Exemplary research areas relying on realistic topologies include: routing optimization, network quality of service optimization, e.g., TSN and DetNet, or network security, e.g., firewalls and intrusion detection systems. Realistic topologies enable the application of experimental results to real-world scenarios. As a result, multiple network topology generators have emerged with varying features and use cases. Table 1 provides an overview of these network topology generators, highlighting available features and their focus, i.e., industrial networks (OT) or Internet networks (IT). The RFC 8345 [5] defines a YANG data model for network topologies and is widely used by network engineers in industrial networks. The data model contains information about the network nodes and can be augmented with additional data, e.g., firewall rules.

BRITE generates realistic Internet network topologies. There exist modules that facilitate the import into ns-3 and OMNeT++. Unfortunately, the topologies are not applicable to industrial networks and the output is not reproducible, i.e., each run results in a different output. As of today, BRITE is no longer maintained.

Table 1. An overview of existing topology generators and their features; Supported ●, not supported ○, no longer maintained †.

Topology Generators	ns-3	OMNeT++	RFC 8345	Reproducible	Traffic	Focus	Release
BRITE† [9]	●	●	○	○	○	IT	2000
RealNet [4]	○	○	○	○	○	IT	2008
FNSS [11]	●	●	○	●	●	IT	2013
GENIND [2]	○	○	○	○	○	OT	2023
GeNESIS [3]	●	●	●	●	●	OT	2024

RealNet generates realistic Internet network topologies with focus on routing applications such as BGP. RealNet does not offer export support for ns-3 or OMNeT++.

FNSS streamlines the simulation setup process, i.e., it generates new topologies or converts existing ones into the input formats required by network simulators. However, it focuses on IT networks and does not adhere to the typical characteristics of industrial networks, including industrial traffic profiles.

GENIND provides realistic industrial network topologies similar to GeNESIS. However, it is limited to three hierarchical layers and does not support export to ns-3 or OMNeT++.

None of the available network topology generators offer reproducible industrial networks with export capabilities to the discrete event simulators ns-3 and OMNeT+. Furthermore, all of them do not support output in RFC-8345 compliant format. The resulting network topologies are incomplete without integration into network simulation environments, except for BRITE and FNSS, which focus on IT networks and are not applicable to industrial networks. GeNESIS solves these shortcomings by providing export capabilities for RFC 8345, ns-3, and OMNeT++. Additionally, GeNESIS creates a shortened configuration representation for each generation, namely a GeNESIS tag. A GeNESIS tag can be used to reproduce all outputs of the referenced run and is short enough to be included as a footnote in publications. Also, GeNESIS is the only generator that offers realistic industrial traffic patterns and firewall rules. We explain all features of GeNESIS in Sect. 4.

3 Background Industrial Networks

Industrial networks follow hierarchical structures, to provide efficient data transport and security. The Purdue model [13] is the standard reference architecture for segmenting industrial networks into different layers. This segmentation is required by industrial security standards such as IEC 62443-3-2 [6]. A standardized naming convention for the different layer types has yet to be established. However, common definitions are:

Enterprise Layer Hosts IT infrastructure, servers, and business applications.

Supervisory Layer Facilitates communication between enterprise systems and industrial control systems.

Control Layer Manages real-time automation and supervisory control.

Field Layer Comprises field devices, sensors, and actuators, directly interacting with industrial processes.

Notably, an industrial network does not have to contain exactly four different layers matching these definitions. The presented definitions describe common layer roles. For example, a network can contain less layers, where some layers take on multiple roles, e.g., Supervisory and Control Layer, at the same time.

Within each layer, network configurations can adopt ring, line, star, or mesh structures, depending on the required levels of reliability and communication efficiency. Ring and mesh structures (cf. *Layer* $n+2$ in Fig. 1) offer high reliability through redundant paths, but increase complexity and infrastructure costs. Line and star topologies are simple to implement but lack failover mechanisms, making them less resilient to network failures.

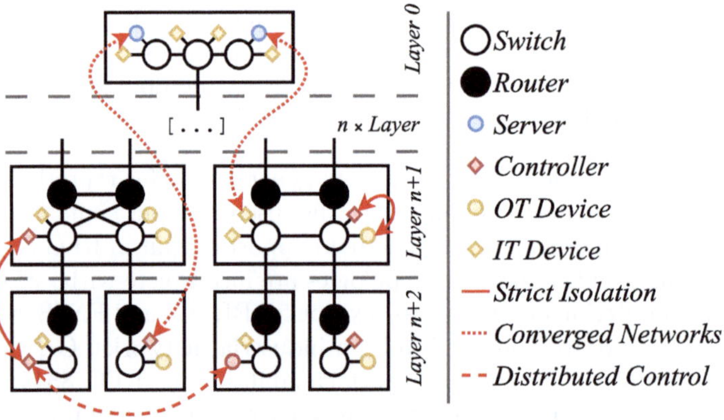

Fig. 1. Hierarchical network structure with varying subnet structures and different traffic profiles.

Beyond the physical topology, the traffic profiles within industrial networks further define the efficiency and the reliability. The traffic profiles inside industrial networks are (cf. Fig. 1): a) strict isolation, b) converged networks, or c) distributed control. Strict isolation is the simplest communication profile, limiting all communication to its corresponding subnet or restricting it to controller-to-controller communication in adjacent subnets. Converged networks allow communication from controllers and end devices to the enterprise layer, enabling predictive maintenance and centralized management. The distributed control communication envisioned in future industrial networks allows traffic between controllers and end devices across multiple zones, providing high redundancy and failover. Distributed control enables new use cases, e.g., smart factories or modular production.

The following section provides a comprehensive tutorial on the configurability, generation, and output capabilities of GeNESIS, enabling users to generate hierarchical industrial network topologies.

4 GeNESIS

GeNESIS is an actively maintained open-source Python project, published under the MIT license and available on GitHub[1]. Figure 2 presents an overview of the core features provided by GeNESIS and highlights our contributions introduced in version 1.2. As depicted, the typical workflow of GeNESIS consists of three steps: 1) the provision of a GeNESIS configuration for one or more evaluation scenarios, i.e., a network topology, packet traces, and security configurations, 2) the generation of the configured evaluation scenarios, and 3) the output of the generated evaluation scenarios in a variety of supported formats. We outline each of these steps in the following sections.

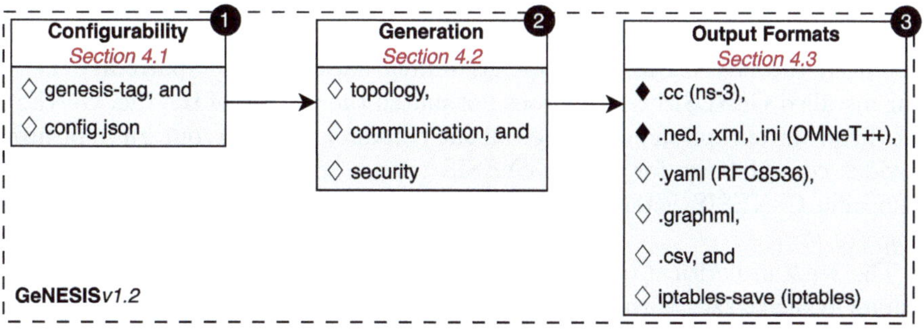

Fig. 2. The GeNESIS workflow visualizing new (♦ v1.2) and old (◇ v1.1) features.

4.1 Configurability

GeNESIS is configurable by one of two options: 1) by providing a GeNESIS-tag, and 2) via a JSON configuration file. We outline each of these options in the following sections.

GeNESIS-Tag. GeNESIS outputs a GeNESIS tag with each generation. It serves as a compressed representation of the configuration file used in the corresponding run, including all necessary information for reproducibility. In a later run, a user can configure GeNESIS by providing such a tag, which results in GeNESIS generating exactly the same outputs again. Hence, the tag is useful to exchange information about evaluation data without providing the actual data, e.g., by providing it as a footnote[2].

[1] https://github.com/hs-esslingen-it-security/hses-GeNESIS/tree/v1.2.

[2] genesis:v1.2#378·578·416::1·2·-1::1·0·0::1::2·4·2·1:2·-1·0·2:0·0·1·0::1·2·2·1:0·-1·-1·2:0·0·1·0#.

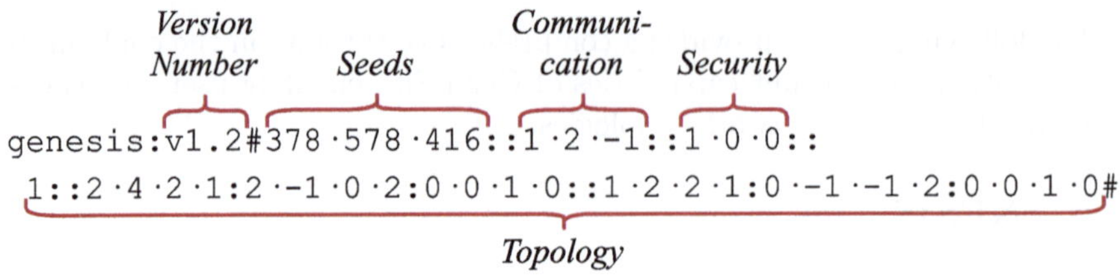

Fig. 3. A GeNESIS-tag with labeled segments.

Figure 3 displays a GeNESIS-tag and labels the different segments of the tag. The fist two segments contain unique values important for the reproducibility of GeNESIS outputs using a genesis-tag. Hence, we highlight the *version number* segment and the *seeds* segment in the following paragraphs. The last three segments directly map to values from a configuration file, i.e., they each translate to a same-named configuration-file segment. Hence, we further discuss the contents of the last tree segments in the next section.

The *version number* specifies the GeNESIS installation used to execute the referenced run. GeNESIS does not guarantee backwards compatibility, i.e., if your installed GeNESIS version does not match the version of the tag, GeNESIS will throw an exception to ensure output consistency. Note, our git repository provides commit tags for each GeNESIS release to ease the checkout process of specific GeNESIS versions, e.g., checkout GeNESISv1.0 with: *git checkout --tags/v1.0*.

The *seeds* are critical to the consistency of GeNESIS outputs when executed with a GeNESIS-tag, as the generation process of GeNESIS is not deterministic, i.e., it is partially based on random choices. However, GeNESIS uses a random number generator, capable to select the same sequence of random choices when provided with a number, i.e., a seed. Thus, GeNESIS requires seed information for repeatable outputs in later runs.

Configuration File. The usual procedure to configure GeNESIS is by providing a configuration file in JSON format. We updated the configuration file for better usability since the last GeNESIS version. The new version of the configuration file consists of three segments, each mapped to a specific generation step: 1) topology, 2) communication, and 3) security. Table 2 shows all parameters a user can configure for each segment, containing a) the name of the parameter, b) the default value of the parameter, and c) a short description of the parameters impact. Note, the configuration separates the main configurations of the topology segment into layer definitions. These layer definitions define the layout and contents of the different layers generated by GeNESIS.

Additionally, Table 2 highlights some parameters as *range parameters*. The values of range parameters can be set to a single integer or a list of three integers. For example, GeNESIS interprets the list [1, 3, 1] as a range with start value 1, inclusive final value 3 and a step size of 1. For each value inside the range parameter, GeNESIS performs the corresponding generation step separately. For example, with a *switch_count* value of [1, 3, 1] in the first layer definition, GeNESIS generates three different topologies with varying numbers of switches in the top layer: one, two, and three switches. If a user configures multiple range parameters in a configuration file, GeNESIS processes each range parameter individually, assuming the start values for all other range parameters. For example, with a configuration of a *switch_count* of [1, 2, 1] and a *max_hosts_per_switch* of [1, 2, 1] in the first layer, GeNESIS generates three network topologies: 1) a topology with one host connected to one switch in the enterprise layer, 2) a topology with two hosts connected to one switch in the enterprise layer, and 3) a topology with two switches each connected to one host in the enterprise layer.

Figure 4 visualizes the impacts of various parameters on the generation process of GeNESIS. Whereas Fig. 4a focuses on inter-subnet topology-related parameters, Fig. 4b focuses on intra-subnet topology-related parameters, and Fig. 4c focuses on traffic-related parameters. Note, the scope of this paper is a tutorial on the generation of network topologies and traffic for simulation. Therefore, this paper does not elaborate on the capabilities of GeNESIS to generate security features for generated networks. Hence, we do not illustrate the impacts of the configuration on the generated rulesets. The left side of each of these figures shows an extract of an exemplary configuration file containing various configuration parameters. The right side highlights the impacts of these parameters on the generated evaluation scenarios. For example, Fig. 4b shows, that the *switch_count* parameter value directly translates to the number of switches generated in a subnet.

4.2 Generation

The generation of evaluation scenarios by GeNESIS is an iterative process with multiple consecutive steps: 1) the generation of the network topology, 2) the generation of the network traffic, and 3) the generation of the security configurations for routers in the network. We explain each of these steps in the following sections.

Topology. GeNESIS generates the hierarchical tree-like network topology of industrial networks by sequentially creating and connecting subnets, branch by branch, until the network topology is complete. Figure 5 depicts an example subnet generation, consisting of the following steps: 1) The generation of switches. 2) The generation of routers, which GeNESIS only performs for subnets not inside the enterprise layer. Additionally, the number of routers varies depending on the structure of the subnet. If the subnet is redundant, i.e., it is of mesh or ring structure, GeNESIS generates two routers, else, GeNESIS generates one router. 3) The connection of all previously generated devices of the subnet based on the configured structure. 4) The generation of a fixed number of end-devices, configured with positive integer values. 5) The generation of other end-devices,

Table 2. Overview of configuration file parameters; Range parameter *.

Parameter	Default Value	Description
Topology		*Contains the necessary configurations for the topology generation.*
iterations	1	Number of topology generation repetitions.
layer_definitions	∅	List of layer definitions (see below); At least one layer definition is required for topology generation. An empty list will cause an exception.
Layer Definition		*Describes the layout and contents of one or more layers.*
*switch_count**	1	Number of switches in subnets within layers defined by this layer definition. In case of a negative value, the number of switches equals 2 × *subnet_descendats*.
*max_hosts_per_switch**	0	Number of hosts connected to each switch in subnets within layers defined by this layer definition.
structure	$\{line : 1\}$	Distribution of structures for subnets within layers defined by this layer definition. E.g., switches in layers with *structure* $\{line : 1, ring : 1\}$ have a 50:50 chance to either have a ring or line structure.
host_types	∅	Distribution of host types in subnets within layers defined by this layer definition. Positive numbers indicate a fixed number of hosts to generate in each subnet; Negative numbers indicate an indefinite number of hosts to generate, until each switch is connected to *max_hosts_per_switch* switches.
*repetitions**	1	Number of layers generated based on this layer definition.
*subnet_descendants**	1	Number of subnets in the next lower layer connected to subnets of layers defined by this layer definition.
Communication		*Contains the necessary configurations for the traffic generation.*
traffic_profile	*strict_isolation*	The traffic profile to use.
*upper_connection_bound**	−1	Maximal number of allowed communication pairs; Unlimited, if value is negative.
iterations	1	Number of communication generation repetitions; Only considered if *upper_connection_bound* is greater than zero.
Security		*Contains the necessary configurations for the security generation.*
*anomaly_count**	0	Minimal number of rule intersections in generated rulesets.
*stateful_percentage**	0	Percentage of stateful rules in generated rulesets; Clamped between 0 and 100.
iterations	1	Number of security generation repetitions; Only considered if either *anomaly_count* or *stateful_percentage* is greater than zero.

configured with negative integer values, until all switches connect to the configured number of hosts per switch.

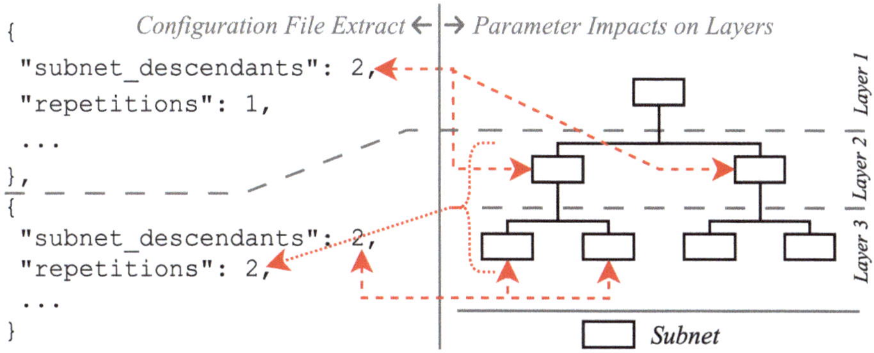

(a) Parameter impact on layer generation.

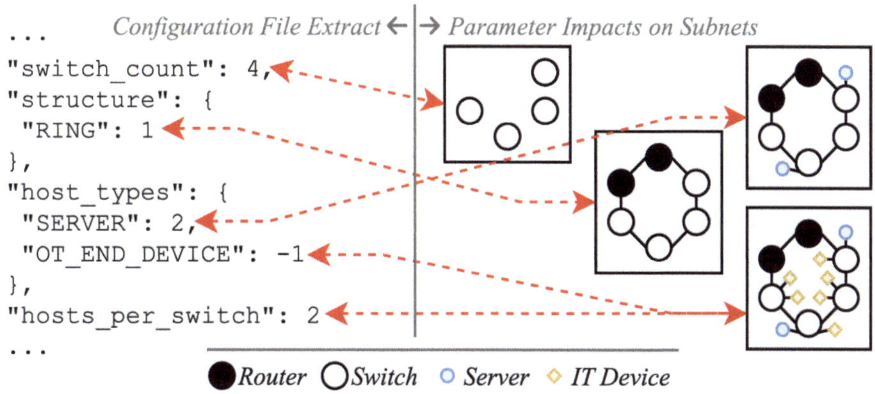

(b) Parameter impacts on subnet generation.

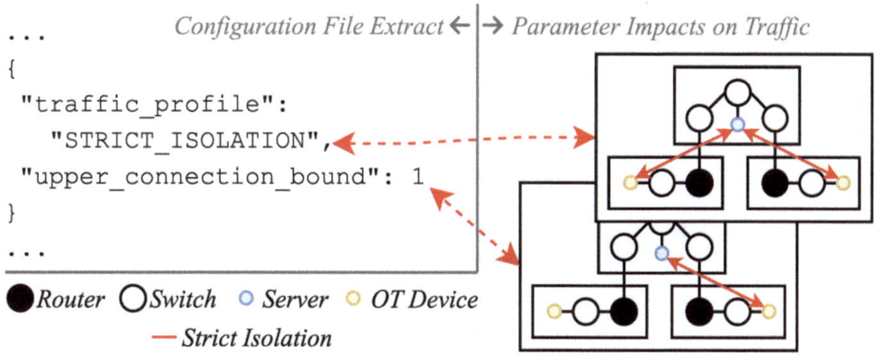

(c) Parameter impact on traffic generation.

Fig. 4. Configuration parameter impact on generation process.

Traffic. The generation of traffic, i.e., packets, is dependent on the previously generated network topology and the configured traffic profile. First, GeNESIS

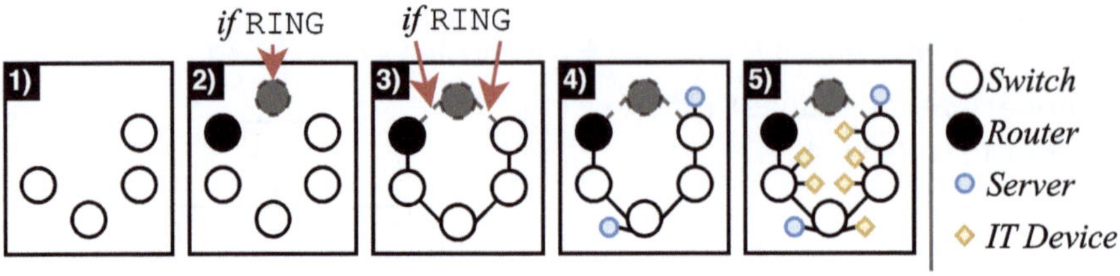

Fig. 5. Order of the subnet generation with line and ring structures.

determines all host-pair combinations that are able to communicate. Hereby, whether two devices can communicate with each other depends on two factors: 1) the accordance of the host-pair to the configured traffic profile and 2) the mutual support of a service over which the communication partners can communicate with each other. Table 3 shows all services GeNESIS potentially assigns to devices based on their type. Hereby, the support of a service is divided into requesting and/or sending data via the service. For example, a server can request data from all other device types via HTTP(S), but no other device type can request data from a server via HTTP(S). Note, in this paper, a server is defined as a hardware device containing virtual infrastructure such as virtualized controllers. Second, GeNESIS selects a random subset of valid host pairs if the user specifies an upper communication bound. Finally, GeNESIS sets the remaining host-pairs as communication partners and generates packets for each host pair based on the services both communication partners support.

Table 3. Services of generated routers (R), switches (Sw), servers (Sv), controllers (C), and IT/OT devices (IT/OT); Request data (→), Not Supported (–).

Service	End Devices						Protocol(s)	Port(s)
	R	Sw	Sv	C	IT	OT		
HTTP/HTTPS	→	→	←	→	↔	→	TCP	80/443
SSH	→	→	↔	↔	↔	–	TCP	22
OPC UA	→	→	↔	↔	–	→	TCP	4840
NETCONF	→	→	↔	←	–	–	TCP	830
IP Camera	–	–	↔	–	↔	–	RTSP, TCP	554
Modbus/TCP	–	–	←	↔	–	↔	TCP	502
Ethernet/IP	–	–	←	↔	–	↔	TCP, UDP	44818/TCP, 2222/UDP
EtherCAT	–	–	←	↔	–	↔	UDP	34980
ProfiNet	–	–	←	↔	–	↔	UDP	3496[2-4], 53247

Security. The generation of the security configurations of the routers within the network depends on the configurations and previously generated traffic. First, GeNESIS adds an empty ruleset with the default action DROP to all routers. Then, GeNESIS adds ACCEPT rules to the rulesets by utilizing the previously generated traffic. Specifically, GeNESIS defines the source and destination information of the packets as the definite set of allowed inter-subnet connections inside the network and adds corresponding ACCEPT rules to the rulesets of each router between the source and destination addresses of every packet. As the default rule of each router is set to DROP, this ensures that only the previously generated packets are allowed. All other traffic is dropped at subnet borders. Concisely, GeNESIS creates a whitelisting ruleset in all routers, allowing only the previously generated traffic. A user can for example utilize these realistic firewall rulesets to test and evaluate novel optimization algorithms to improve network performance.

4.3 Output Formats

GeNESIS supports a variety of different output formats. Figure 6 displays all output file formats supported by GeNESIS v1.2 to store its generated data. The figure arranges these files in the folder structure GeNESIS creates for each generation iteration, highlighting default output-files and optional output-files, which require specific command line options to be created.

```
/
└─ hses_genesis
   └─ output
      └─ <configuration-name>
         └─ <generation-run-timestamp>
            ├─ <generation-run-iteration-id>×
            │  ├─ graphs
            │  │  ├─ ● graph.graphml
            │  │  ├─ ○ graph.jpg ........................ −img
            │  │  ├─ ○ graph.png ........................ −img
            │  │  └─ ○ ietf-topology.yang.json .......... −yang
            │  ├─ ns3
            │  │  └─ ○ genesis.cc ....................... −ns3
            │  ├─ omnetpp
            │  │  ├─ ○ graph.ned ........................ −omnet
            │  │  ├─ ○ interfaces.xml ................... −omnet
            │  │  └─ ○ omnetpp.ini ...................... −omnet
            │  ├─ packets
            │  │  └─ ● packets.csv
            │  ├─ rulesets
            │  │  └─ ○ <router-id>-iptables-save× ....... −ipt
            │  ├─ ● .genesistag
            │  └─ ● config.json
            ├─ ● .genesistag
            └─ ● config.json
```

Fig. 6. The GeNESIS output folder structure with default output (●) and special output (○), which requires specific command line options (... −*flag*); Multiple file/folder instances possible (×).

The default outputs are 1) the *graph.graphml*-file, which contains all topology and security information, 2) the *packets.csv*-file, which contains packet related information, 3) *config.json* files, containing the output-correlated GeNESIS configuration, and 4) *.genesistag* files, containing the GeNESIS-tag for the reproducibility of the generated outputs. GeNESIS outputs the *config.json* and *.genesistag* files for both a) the overall generation process, containing all configuration information provided by the user, and b) each generation iteration caused by, e.g., multiple iterations of the topology generation step.

The optional output-files and their corresponding command line options include 1) images, i.e., *graph.jpg* and *graph.png* with −*img*, to visualize the topology graph of the generated network, 2) a *.json*-file containing a yang model of RFC 8345 with −*yang*, 3) firewall ruleset files in *iptables-save*-format for each router with −*ipt*, and 4) an *omnetpp* and *ns-3* folder with −*omnet* and −*ns*3 respectively, containing files relevant for the simulation of the generated traffic with OMNEeT++ and ns-3.

The *omnetpp* and *ns3* folders are a new feature in GeNESISv1.2 and a major contribution of this paper. The *omnetpp* folder contains three files: a) the *graph.ned* file, which describes the topology, i.e., what devices exist and how they are connected, b) the *interfaces.xml* file, which contains the IP address and IP network information for all devices, and c) the *omnetpp.ini* file, which contains the services of each device and the packet descriptions for the simulation. In contrast to *OMNeT++*, *ns-3* describes all simulation components, i.e., the network topology and traffic, in a single file. GeNESIS outputs this file, i.e., *genesis.cc*, in the folder *ns3*.

The next section guides readers through three case studies, enabling them to generate outputs with GeNESIS that can be imported into simulators.

5 GeNESIS Workflow Application

In this section, we apply the GeNESIS workflow to three different case studies. Table 4 highlights these case studies, focusing on their network topology and traffic profiles.

Table 4. Quick reference for all case studies.

Section	Scenario	Subnet Structure	Traffic Profile	Layer Count
Section 5.1	EPIC [1]	Ring, Star	Converged Network	3
Section 5.2	SWaT [8]	Ring, Star, Line	Strict Isolation	4
Section 5.3	Next-Generation Network [7]	Mesh, Ring	Distributed Control	2

We elaborate on each of the case studies in their corresponding sections, providing detailed descriptions on how to setup a corresponding GeNESIS configuration file. Additionally, we provide the configuration files of the case studies in the resource folder of the GeNESIS project on GitHub. Note, the related work describing our use-case scenarios did not specify firewall-specific security configurations. Also, OMNeT++ and ns-3 currently do not support the simulation of security features. Hence, we skip the configuration of the security mechanisms in all case studies and use the default values of GeNESIS for all security-specific parameters during generation (cf. Sect. 4.1).

5.1 Case Study 1 EPIC

In this section, we create a configuration to generate the Electric Power and Intelligent Control (EPIC) testbed [1] with GeNESIS. EPIC is an advanced research and development platform designed to evaluate and enhance the cybersecurity of energy and power systems. The testbed provides realistic and scalable environments for network security research. Readers interested in the generation results can use this GeNESIS-tag[3] to recreate our results.

[3] genesis:v1.2#556·178·835::1·1·-1::1·0·0::1::1·5·1·1:2·0·0·0:0·1·0·0::6·13·1·1:0·-1·0·2:1·0·0·0::1·2·2·1:0·-1·-1·2:0·1·0·0#.

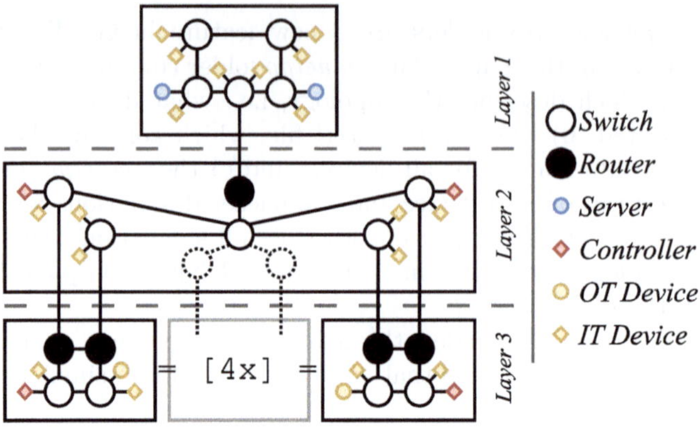

Fig. 7. EPIC testbed network topology including eight subnets with a mix of ring and star subnet structures.

Topology. Figure 7 highlights the topology of the EPIC testbed. To generate this topology with GeNESIS, we complete the following steps: 1) we add the *topology* segment to the configuration file, and 2) we add *layer_definitions* to the topology segment, configured as visualized in Table 5.

Communication. To add a communication logic matching the descriptions of EPIC to the network topology, we complete the following steps: 1) we add the *communication* segment to the configuration, and 2) we set the value of the *traffic_profile* parameter to *converged_network*, as the communication patterns of EPIC match the converged network traffic profile.

5.2 Case Study 2 SWaT

In this section, we create a configuration to generate the SWaT testbed [8] with GeNESIS. SWaT is a modern industrial control system for security and research training. The testbed focuses on the security of industrial networks by segmenting the network into four layers. Readers interested in the generation results can use this GeNESIS-tag[4].

Topology. Figure 8 provides an overview of the network topology of the SWaT testbed. To generate this topology with GeNESIS, we complete the following steps: 1) we add the *topology* segment to the configuration, 2) we add *layer_definitions* to the topology segment. Table 6 highlights necessary configuration parameters to generate the outlined topology.

[4] genesis:v1.2#60·723·928::1·0·-1::1·0·0::1::1·3·2·1:2·-1·0·0:0·0·1·0::
6·13·1·1:0·-1·-1·2:1·0·0·0::1·2·2·2:0·-1·-1·2:0·1·0·0#.

Table 5. Quick reference for the EPIC testbed layer definitions; Server (s), controller (c), IT device (it), OT device (ot).

Parameter	Value	Reasoning
Layer 1		
switch_count	5	In layer 1, subnets contain five switches.
max_hosts_per_switch	2	In layer 1, two end devices connect to each switch.
device_type	$\{s : 2,$	In layer 1, subnets contain two servers.
	$it : -1\}$	In layer 1, subnets contain IT devices.
structure	$\{ring : 1\}$	In layer 1, subnets have a ring structure.
Layer 2		
switch_count	13	In layer 2, subnets contain 13 switches.
max_hosts_per_switch	2	In layer 2, two end devices connect to each switch.
device_type	$\{c : 2$	In layer 2, subnets contain two controllers.
	$it : -1\}$	In layer 2, subnets contain IT devices.
structure	$\{star : 1\}$	In layer 2, subnets have a star structure.
subnet_descendants	6	In layer 2, one subnet connects to six subnets in layer 3.
Layer 3		
switch_count	2	In layer 3, subnets contain two switches.
max_hosts_per_switch	2	In layer 3, two end devices connect to each switch.
device_type	$\{c : 2,$	In layer 3, subnets contain two controllers.
	$it : -1,$	In layer 3, subnets contain IT devices.
	$ot : -1\}$	In layer 3, subnets contain OT devices.
structure	$\{ring : 1\}$	In layer 3, subnets have a ring structure.

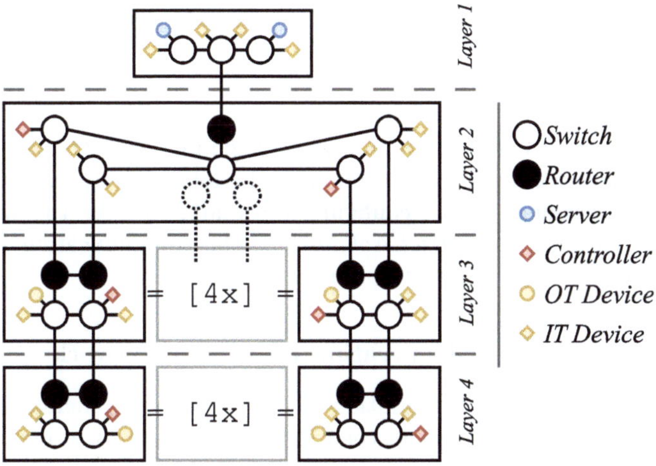

Fig. 8. SWaT testbed network topology including 14 subnets with a mix of line, star and ring structures.

Table 6. Quick reference for the SWaT testbed layer definitions; Server (s), controller (c), IT device (it), OT device (ot).

Parameter	Value	Reasoning
Layer 1		
switch_count	3	In layer 1, subnets contain three switches in layer 1.
max_hosts_per_switch	2	In layer 1, two end devices connect to each switch.
device_type	$\{s: 2,$	In layer 1, subnets contain two servers.
	$it: -1\}$	In layer 1, subnets contain IT devices.
structure	$\{line: 1\}$	In layer 1, subnets have a line structure.
Layer 2		
switch_count	13	In layer 2, subnets contain 13 switches.
max_hosts_per_switch	2	In layer 2, two end devices connect to each switch.
structure	$\{star: 1\}$	In layer 2, subnets have a star structure.
	$\{c: 2,$	In layer 2, subnets contain two controllers.
device_type	$it: -1,$	In layer 2, subnets contain IT devices.
	$ot: -1\}$	In layer 2, subnets contain OT devices.
subnet_descendants	6	In layer 2, one subnet connects to six subnets in layer 3.
Layer 3		
switch_count	2	layer 3, subnets contain two switches.
max_hosts_per_switch	2	layer 3, two end devices connect to each switch.
structure	$\{ring: 1\}$	layer 3, subnets have a ring structure.
	$\{c: 2,$	layer 3, subnets contain two controllers.
device_type	$it: -1,$	layer 3, subnets contain IT devices.
	$ot: -1\}$	layer 3, subnets contain OT devices.
repetitions	2	Layer 3 and layer 4 are identical. Hence, the layer 3 definition is used twice to generate both layer 3 and layer 4.

Communication. To add a communication logic matching the descriptions of SWaT to the network topology, we complete the following steps: 1) we add the *communication* segment to the configuration, and 2) we set the value of the *traffic_profile* parameter to *strict_isolation*, as the communication patterns of SWaT are mappable to the strict isolation traffic profile.

5.3 Case Study 3 Next-Generation Industrial Network

In this section, we create a configuration to generate a next-generation industrial testbed [7] with GeNESIS. This testbed reflects the increasing digitalization of operational processes in industrial networks. Due to the migration of control processes to central, virtual controllers, the network topologies become flatter, i.e., include fewer layers, in comparison to current network topologies. However, in return, subnets become bigger and more complex to handle. For example, mesh structures require special protocols and increase the number of intra-subnet paths, which complicates the calculation of necessary bandwidth and resources. Readers interested in the results of the generation can use this GeNESIS-tag[5] to recreate our results.

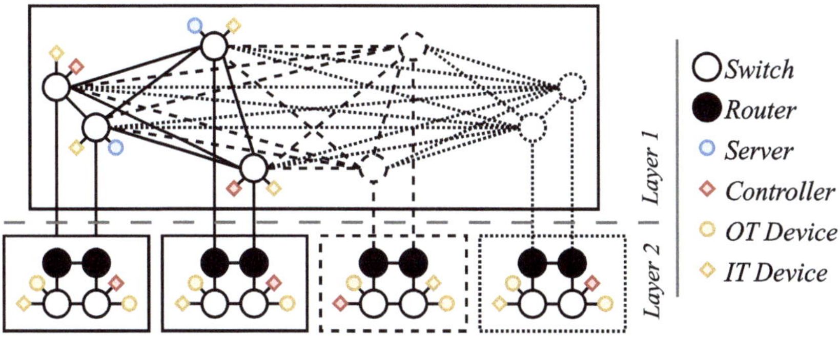

Fig. 9. Next generation network topology with a dynamic number of layer 1 switches and layer 2 subnets.

Topology. Figure 9 displays the topology of the next generation network. Note, the authors did not specify the structures of included subnets. Hence, we give the top layer a mesh structure and the lower subnets a ring structure, as such structures are the standard for subnets in industrial networks for redundancy reasons. To generate this topology with GeNESIS, we complete the following steps: 1) we add the *topology* segment to the configuration, and 2) we add *layer definitions* to the topology segment, configured as visualized in Table 7.

Communication. To add a communication logic matching the descriptions of the next-generation industrial network to the network topology, we complete the following steps: 1) we add the *communication* segment to the configuration, and 2) we set the *traffic_profile* to *distributed_control*, as the described communication of the next-generation network is mappable to the distributed control traffic profile.

5.4 Simulation Integration

This section describes how to import the evaluation scenarios generated with GeNESIS into OMNeT++ and ns-3. For visual clarity, we explain the process based on the *example* scenario of GeNESIS, located in the resource folder of the GitHub project. The output data can be generated using this GeNESIS-tag[6].

[5] genesis:v1.2#838·638·358::1·2·-1::1·0·0::1::2.4.1·-1·2·1:2·-1·0·2:0·0·0·1::1·2·2·1:0·-1·-2·2:0·1·0·0#.

[6] genesis:v1.2#192·678·926::1·2·-1::1·0·0::1::2·4·2·1:2·-1·0·2:0·0·1·0::1·2·2·1:0·-1·-1·2:0·0·1·0#.

Table 7. Quick reference for the next generation network layer definitions; Controller (c), IT device (it), OT device (ot).

Parameter	Value	Reasoning
Layer 1		
switch_count	-1	In layer 1, subnets have a variable switch count depending on the *subnet_descendants* value of layer 1.
max_hosts_per_switch	2	In layer 1, two end devices connect to each switch.
	$\{c: 2,$	In layer 1, subnets contain two controllers.
device_type	$s: 2,$	In layer 1, subnets contain two servers.
	$it: -1\}$	In layer 1, subnets contain IT devices.
structure	$\{mesh: 1\}$	In layer 1, subnets have a mesh structure.
subnet_descendants	$[2, 4, 1]$	This is a range value. In three separate topologies, subnets in layer 1 connect to two, three and four different subnets in layer 2.
Layer 2		
switch_count	2	In layer 2, subnets contain two switches.
max_hosts_per_switch	2	In layer 2, two end devices connect to each switch.
	$\{c: 2,$	In layer 2, subnets contain two controllers.
device_type	$it: -1,$	In layer 2, subnets contain IT devices.
	$ot: -1\}$	In layer 2, subnets contain OT devices.
structure	$\{ring: 1\}$	In layer 2, subnets have a ring structure.

OMNeT++. When loading the *graph.ned* output file of GeNESIS into an OMNeT++ project, OMNeT++ creates a visualization of the network. Figure 10 displays this visualization. The topology in OMNeT++ is identical to the topology generated and visualized in Fig. 11. The similarity between these two topologies indicates a successful import into OMNeT++. Adding the *interfaces.xml* file and the *omnetpp.ini* file to the same OMNeT++ project as the *graph.ned* file completes the simulation setup. Note, the generated *graph.ned* file contains a default package path. To successfully start the simulation, one must adapt this path to match the actual path of the OMNeT++ project. When the path is adjusted, OMNeT++ is able to simulate the generated traffic.

NS-3. A ns-3 simulation consists of a descriptive *.cc* file. Hereby, the *.cc* file describes the network topology as well as the traffic patterns that ns-3 simulates. GeNESIS generates such an ns-3 compatible file, i.e., *genesis.cc*, with the *-ns3* flag (cf. Sect. 4.3). The generated file must be placed inside the *scratch* folder of the ns-3 installation. Afterward, the simulation can be executed with the *./ns3 run genesis.cc* command.

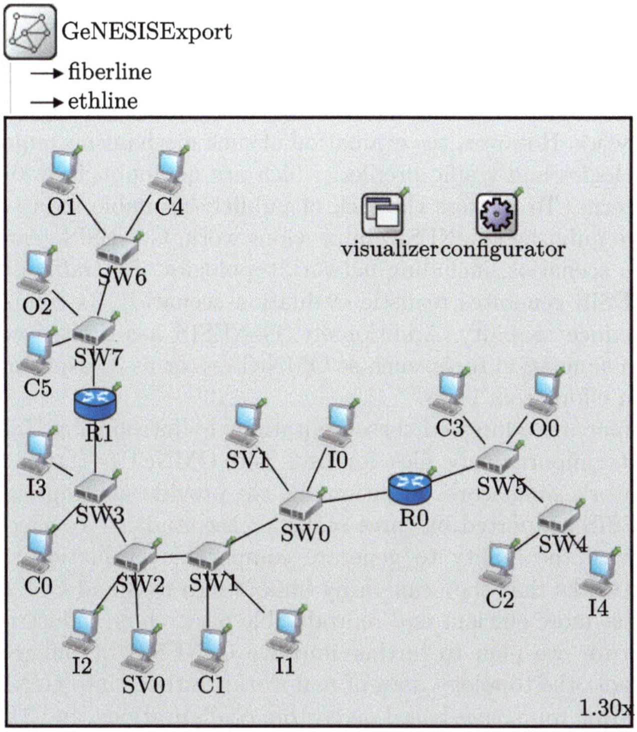

Fig. 10. Network topology in OMNeT++ with routers (Rn), switches (SWn), servers (SVn), controllers (Cn), IT devices (In), and OT devices (On).

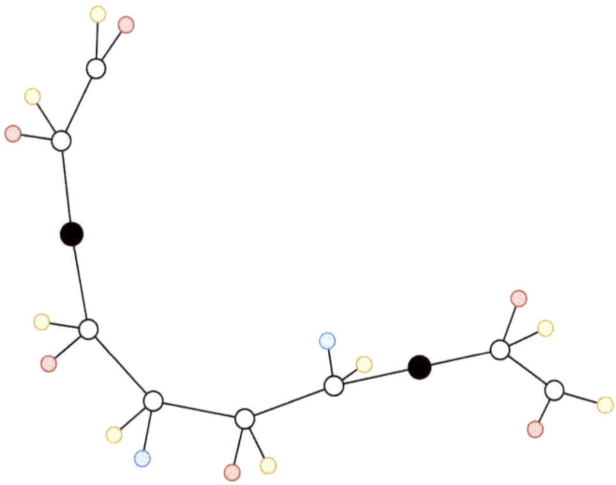

Fig. 11. Generated topology with routers ●, switches ○, servers , controllers , and IT/OT devices .

6 Conclusion and Future Work

The increasing connectivity of next-generation industrial networks requires new mechanisms and algorithms to guarantee the security, performance, and reliability of the network. However, the evaluation of such mechanisms requires realistic network topologies and traffic profiles, which are not publicly available due to security concerns. To address the lack of publicly available industrial network topologies, we published GeNESIS in previous work. GeNESIS generates realistic evaluation scenarios, including network topologies and traffic profiles. Even though GeNESIS generates realistic evaluation scenarios, its complicated configurations reduce usability. Additionally, GeNESIS has limited compatibility with common simulation tools, such as OMNeT++ or ns-3, requiring additional compensation effort from users.

In this paper, we addressed these limitations by introducing GeNESIS v1.2, which outputs import-ready files for ns-3 and OMNeT++, two of the most common network simulators. Additionally, we provide a comprehensive tutorial on GeNESIS supported by three realistic case studies. We effectively equip researchers with the ability to generate comparable evaluation scenarios for industrial networks that they can easily import into ns-3 and OMNeT++. Our work facilitates more efficient and reproducible research on industrial networks.

In the future, we plan to further improve GeNESIS by integrating 1) the ability to import the topology data of real-world testbeds into GeNESIS, 2) the scaling of existing topologies based on custom configurations, and 3) the integration of the generated security configurations into ns-3 and OMNeT++, as soon as realistic firewall models become available. Additionally, we plan to improve the realism of generated traffic, which is currently based on traffic-profile permissions and random values. Thus, we plan to integrate common traffic behaviors into the traffic generation of GeNESIS.

Acknowledgement. This work has been funded by the Deutsche Forschungsgemeinschaft (DFG, German Research Foundation) – Project-ID 528745080 - FIP 68. Additionally, this research was supported by the project "FHP: Qualifizierung und Entwicklung des professoralen Personals der Hochschule Esslingen für zukunftsweisende Themen" (FKZ: 03FHP115) as part of the Federal States Program "FH-Personal", funded by the BMBF and MWK Baden-Württemberg. The authors alone are responsible for the content of the paper.

References

1. Adepu, S., Kandasamy, N.K., Mathur, A.: EPIC: an electric power testbed for research and training in cyber physical systems security. In: Computer Security: ESORICS International Workshops, CyberICPS and SECPRE. Barcelona, Spain (2018)
2. Alrumaih, T.N., Alenazi, M.J.: GENIND: an industrial network topology generator. Alexandria Eng. J. **79** (2023)

3. Bechtel, L., Muller, S., Menth, M., Heer, T.: GeNESIS: generator for network evaluation scenarios of industrial systems. In: IEEE International Conference on Emerging Technologies and Factory Automation (ETFA) (2024)
4. Cheng, L., Hutchinson, N.C., Ito, M.R.: RealNet: a topology generator based on real internet topology. In: International Conference on Advanced Information Networking and Applications (2008)
5. Clemm, A., Medved, J., Varga, R., Bahadur, N., Ananthakrishnan, H., Liu, X.: A YANG data model for network Topologies. RFC 8345 (2018)
6. International Electrotechnical Commission (IEC): IEC 62443-3-2. Security for industrial automation and control systems – Part 3-2: Security risk assessment for system design (2020)
7. Lautenschlaeger, W., Frick, F., Christodoulopoulos, K., Henke, T.: A scalable factory backbone for multiple independent time-sensitive networks. J. Syst. Architect. **119**, 102277 (2021)
8. Mathur, A.P., Tippenhauer, N.O.: SWaT: a water treatment testbed for research and training on ICS security. In: International Workshop on Cyber-physical Systems for Smart Water Networks (CySWater). Vienna, Austria (2016)
9. Medina, A., Matta, I., Byers, J.: BRITE: a flexible generator of internet topologies. Tech. rep., USA (2000)
10. Riley, G.F., Henderson, T.R.: The ns-3 Network Simulator. Berlin, Heidelberg (2010)
11. Saino, L., Cocora, C., Pavlou, G.: A toolchain for simplifying network simulation setup. In: Proceedings of the 6th International ICST Conference on Simulation Tools and Techniques. SIMUTOOLS 2013, Brussels, Belgium (2013)
12. Varga, A.: The OMNET++ discrete event simulation system. In: Proceedings of the ESM'2001 9 (2001)
13. Williams, T.: The purdue enterprise reference architecture. Proc. Triennal World Congress Int. Fed. Autom. control (IFAC) **26**(2), 559–564 (1993)

I Still Know Who You Scanned Last Summer: An Update on the Landscape of Internet Scanners

Markus Schramm(✉), Nils Lohmiller, Sabrina Kaniewski, and Tobias Heer

Esslingen University of Applied Sciences, Esslingen, Germany
{markus.schramm,nils.lohmiller,sabrina.kaniewski,
tobias.heer}@hs-esslingen.de

Abstract. The proliferation of Internet-connected services and devices has led to more vulnerabilities on the Internet. These vulnerabilities are often discovered through Internet-wide scans conducted by various groups of users with different intentions, both benign and malicious. This work investigates these scanning activities by operating six globally distributed honeypots over a 20-month period. We examine scanning organizations, which scanning tools they use, and their behavioral patterns, e.g., the number of scans and covered ports. We observe that the introduction of new services on the honeypots, namely SSH, Telnet, HTTP, and HTTPS, correlates with a general increase in scanning activity. We identify temporally focused scanning patterns that indicate strategic approaches by different scanning entities. In this analysis, we found that the scanning tools were not being updated frequently, possibly due to the need to adapt the interaction between tools or due to the risk of new bugs. This study provides valuable insights on the evolving landscape of Internet-wide scanning and its implications for cybersecurity.

Keywords: Honeypot · Port Scan · Internet Scanning · Scanning Tools

1 Introduction

The Internet scanning landscape is constantly evolving, driven by the rapid growth of connected devices. As more and more devices are connected to the

We thank *IPinfo* who support our research by IP lookups free of charge.

This research was supported by the project "FHP: Qualifizierung und Entwicklung des professoralen Personals der Hochschule Esslingen für zukunftsweisende Themen" (FKZ: 03FHP115) as part of the Federal States Program "FH-Personal", funded by the BMBF and MWK Baden-Württemberg. The authors alone are responsible for the content of the paper.

L. Bechtel and T. Heer (Eds.): CCSSS 2025 PTT, pp. 74–91, 2026.
https://doi.org/10.1007/978-3-032-10569-1_5

Internet, the number of potentially vulnerable systems has increased. Different groups of users, both benign users, e.g., researchers, and malicious actors use scanning techniques to identify these vulnerable systems or prepare for attacks. The increasing use of scanning creates significant challenges for cybersecurity, including the difficulty of distinguishing between legitimate and malicious scans.

In previous work [8], we deployed six honeypots to investigate scanners, their scanning tools used, and their specific scanning behavior. We particularly focused on scans targeting Internet of Things (IoT) services, such as AMQP (port 5672), CoAP (port 5683), MQTT (port 1883), and OPC UA (port 4840). In this paper, we analyze how the Internet scanning landscape has developed during an extended period from June 1, 2023 to January 31, 2025. The scanning landscape relates to the organizations conducting scans and the tools they use, such as ZMap and Masscan. In addition to the existing IoT services AMQP, CoAP, MQTT, and OPC UA, we installed HTTP, HTTPS, SSH, and Telnet services on the honeypots to include even more services in the analysis. We investigate whether the introduction of the new services results in an increase in the number of scans on other ports. We also investigate differences in scanning activity across these services and identify new scanners such as the *Technical University of Denmark (DTU)* and *TU Dresden*. We further focus on shifts in scanning tool use and scanning frequency, highlighting the temporary but substantial fluctuations in the occurrence of scanning activities and adaptive nature of Internet-wide scanning. These findings contribute to a more nuanced understanding of the intentions behind scanning activities, offering an updated view of the evolving Internet scanning landscape. To simplify the data analysis process for other researchers and service operators, we provide the code for the data analysis pipeline and evaluation on GitHub[1].

The remainder of this paper is structured as follows. In Sect. 2, we present related work on the analysis of Internet scanning. In Sect. 3, we present the honeypot and analysis infrastructure. We describe the updated process we established for identifying scanners and scanning tools in Sect. 4. In Sect. 5, we present identified organizations and their scanning behavior. We conclude this work in Sect. 6.

2 Related Work

Numerous studies focus on Internet and port scanning, characterizing, e.g., the patterns of scanning tools used and most frequently targeted ports. In a previous work [8], we analyzed scanning traffic received over eight months on six IoT honeypots running the common IoT services AMQP, CoAP, MQTT and OPC UA, located on different continents. We identified scanners that scan these honeypots, categorized their scanning behavior, e.g., the port range they scan and the time between scans, and analyzed their scanning tools used. In this section, we briefly discuss recent research efforts published since this previous

[1] https://github.com/hs-esslingen-it-security/hses-honeypot.

study, focusing on long-term observation studies that monitor and analyze Internet scanning activity over extended periods. These studies provide insights into the evolution of scanning tools, such as ZMap and Masscan, and their impact on scanning behavior, enabling then-and-now comparisons of scanning patterns.

Durumeric et al. [4] provide a comprehensive analysis of ZMap's adoption over ten years since its release. ZMap is a widely used Internet scanning tool, evident by the share observed in the analyzed data from a network telescope (i.e., unsolicited Internet traffic sent to unassigned IP address space). The study highlights the distribution of ZMap traffic in overall scans and across different ports. The study also offers insights into industry adoption, revealing that organizations such as *Palo Alto Networks* and *Rapid7* predominantly use ZMap for attack surface management. Additionally, other non-profit organizations and companies, including *BinaryEdge*, *Censys*, and *Shadowserver*, leverage ZMap to gather data on IP addresses, threat actors, and Internet services. Notably, we also identified these organizations and their use of ZMap in previous work [8].

Similarly, Griffioen et al. [6] asses Internet-wide TCP scanning over a ten-year period, also using data from a network telescope. Their analysis covers measurement periods from 2015 to 2024, examining up to two months of data from the first half of each year, excluding Samba and Telnet traffic. They discuss the evolution and development of scanning actors, their tooling, and targets. The study reveals high volatility in Internet-wide scanning, with targeted ports and major campaigns shifting rapidly, sometimes within weeks or months. Scanning activities are also increasingly influenced by short-term trends, e.g., because of newly reported vulnerabilities, which we also observed on the honeypots. The authors further identify an increase in the number of collaborative scans and scans targeting a broad number of ports, including full-range scans. Additionally, the study highlights geographical shifts in scanning activity and changes in tool adoption, with a notable increase in the adoption of common scanning tools.

Munteanu et al. [9] analyze traffic collected over a 15-month period from November 2021 to March 2023, using a globally distributed honeyfarm comprising 221 honeypots deployed across 55 countries. Their study uses Cowrie honeypots to monitor SSH and Telnet activity, revealing substantial differences in session volumes and threat types observed across the honeypots. The authors categorize session characteristics into five types: no credential, failed login, no command execution, command execution, and command execution with file download. Furthermore, they classify the interactions into scanning, scouting, and intrusion behavior, providing detailed insights into the geographic distribution of IPs, interaction times, and client interactions, i.e., common commands and file hashes, of the different behaviors.

In comparison with these studies, we provide updated insights into scanning organizations and their behaviors, specifically examining the impact of newly deployed services on the honeypots alongside existing IoT services.

3 Honeypot and Analysis Infrastructure

We employ a honeypot infrastructure as detailed in previous work [8]. This infrastructure consists of six Amazon Web Services (AWS) EC2 instances running Ubuntu 24.04. The instances run in six different AWS regions: Cape Town, London, Mumbai, Northern California, São Paulo, and Tokyo (cf. Fig. 1). Distributing the honeypots across multiple regions allows us to collect information about differences in scanning behavior related to scanned destinations.

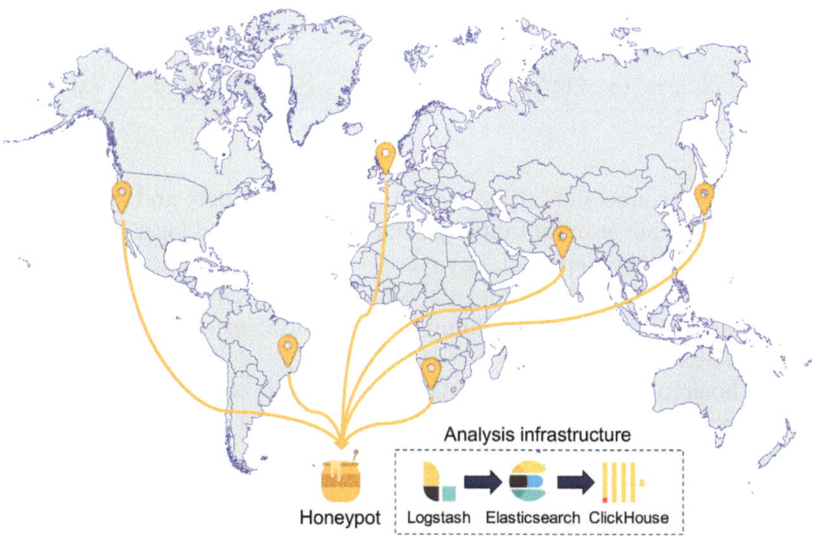

Fig. 1. Geographical distribution of the six honeypots and the analysis infrastructure.

Each honeypot is configured to run services for the IoT protocols AMQP, CoAP, MQTT, and OPC UA, simulating small building automation systems. Moreover, we expanded the infrastructure since the last report to include HTTP and HTTPS services using Nginx[2], as well as SSH and Telnet services using Cowrie[3]. Cowrie simulates a Debian system and logs SSH login attempts and commands executed by attackers over Telnet. Similarly, Nginx logs interactions with HTTP and HTTPS, such as requested paths. One exception to this service deployment is the Northern California honeypot. Instead of Cowrie, this honeypot hosts an XZ honeypot designed to investigate the exploitation of the XZ vulnerability in SSH, known as CVE-2024-3094 [10]. Table 1 provides an overview of all running services. We highlighted the newly deployed services and added the date when they were deployed. The HTTP honeypot is running since April 2024, the HTTPS, SSH, and Telnet honeypots since May 2024.

[2] https://nginx.org.
[3] https://github.com/cowrie/cowrie.

Table 1. Services running on each honeypot. Services added since the last report are highlighted.

Service	Software	Protocol	Port	Deployment
AMQP	RabbitMQ (v3.11.16)	TCP	5672	Jun. 2023
CoAP	aiocoap Python package (v0.4.3)	UDP	5683	Jun. 2023
MQTT	HiveMQ (hivemq-ce-2021.3)	TCP	1883	Jun. 2023
OPC UA	opcua-asyncio Python package (v0.9.95)	TCP	4840	Jun. 2023
HTTP	Nginx (v1.26.1)	TCP	80	Apr. 2024
HTTPS	Nginx (v1.26.1)	TCP	443	May 2024
SSH	Cowrie (v2.5.0)	TCP	22	May 2024
Telnet	Cowrie (v2.5.0)	TCP	23	May 2024

We log every connection attempt to any TCP/UDP port and following packets on each honeypot using iptables log rules. All generated logs, including those from iptables and the deployed services, are parsed using Logstash and stored in an Elasticsearch database. For analysis, we load the data into a ClickHouse database, a high-performance column-oriented database system. This analysis pipeline is visualized in Fig. 1.

As the honeypots are hosted on AWS, there is a potential bias in the results, since we only observe scanners scanning this part of the Internet. Thus, we cannot distinguish scanners that solely scan the AWS address space from those that scan the entire or a large part of the IPv4 address space. However, we hypothesize that the scanners that scan the honeypots on AWS also scan other parts of the Internet [8].

4 Identification of Scanners and Scanning Tools

In this paper, we continue the analysis of the scanning behavior of scanning organizations identified in previous work [8], along with newly identified scanning organizations. Additionally, we identify the specific scanning tools used by these scanners and investigate any changes in their utilization shares compared to previous analyses. In this section, we provide a recap of the methods used to identify scanning organizations and scanning tools.

4.1 Identification of Scanners

We identify scanners by leveraging IP information obtained from the *IPinfo.io* API[4], including details such as Autonomous System (AS) name, hostname, and company name. This process involves querying the API for each IP address observed in the iptables logs and then analyzing the returned information for

[4] https://ipinfo.io.

specific keywords. For example, we search for keywords such as '*scan*', '*measurement*', and '*security*' to identify general scanning organizations. Additionally, we search for keywords such as '*university*', '*institute*', and '*research*' to identify academic institutions. The overall workflow to identify scanners is displayed in Fig. 2. This workflow enables us to effectively identify scanning organizations such as Censys (hostname $*$.*censys-scanner.com*) or research organizations such as *Georgia Institute of Technology*. Newly identified organizations in this work include universities, such as *TU Berlin*, *TU Dresden*, and the University of Michigan, as well as non-research-focused organizations, such as *Cybcube*, *Modat*, and *Qualys*. In addition, we identify individuals conducting scans, such as *Bill Demirkapi* and *Yevgen*.

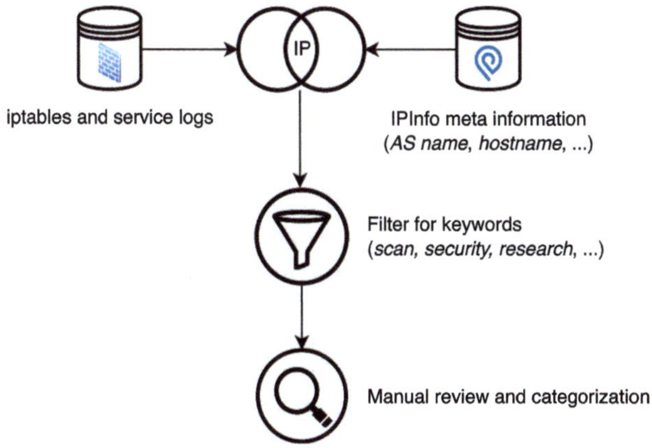

Fig. 2. Workflow to identify scanners.

4.2 Identification of Scanning Tools

We focus on identifying commonly used scanning tools, including ZMap, Masscan, Unicorn, and Nmap. Additionally, we aim to detect packets originating from the Mirai botnet and its variants.

Table 2. Fingerprints of common Internet scanning tools and Mirai botnet variants.

Tool	Fingerprint	Source
ZMap (< v4.1.0)	IP-ID = 54321	[5]
Masscan	IP-ID = destIP $\oplus$ destPort $\oplus$ SeqNum	[5]
Nmap	Different combinations of values in TCP fields	[7]
Unicorn	$SeqNum_1 \oplus SeqNum_2 = destIP_1 \oplus destIP_2 \oplus srcPort_1 \oplus srcPort_2 \oplus ((destPort_1 \oplus destPort_2) \ll 16)$	[5]
Mirai variants	destIP $\oplus$ SeqNum = 0	[13]

Common Scanning Tools. To identify specific scanning tools, we employ fingerprinting techniques, which involve extracting distinctive information encoded in packet header fields. Specifically, we use the fingerprints presented by Ghiëtte et al. [5] and Tanaka et al. [13], which are based on unique encodings in TCP/IP header fields. Table 2 provides an overview of the fingerprints for common scanning tools, including ZMap, Masscan, Nmap, and Unicorn. Since the last analysis [8], ZMap received an update that invalidates its previously known fingerprint. In earlier versions, ZMap set the IP-ID value to 54321. However, this behavior was removed in version v4.1.0 released in May 2024 [4]. Consequently, from version v4.1.0 onward, ZMap can no longer be detected using its IP-ID fingerprint. To assess the impact of this change, we investigate whether the update influences the results, specifically by examining if a decrease in ZMap's share is noticeable following the release of version v4.1.0.

Mirai Botnet. In this work, we also take a deeper look at the Mirai botnet and its variants. Mirai is a botnet that consists of infected hosts on the Internet. Infected hosts scan the Internet for new victims and try to attack them using a set of vulnerabilities. Initially, infected hosts tried to connect to victims using Telnet on ports 23 and 2323 by brute-forcing the credentials. Some threat actors adapt the publicly available Mirai code and, e.g., extend it so that it exploits additional vulnerabilities. This results in new Mirai-like botnets. Previously, we limited the identification of Mirai and its variants to the ports 23 and 2323. We removed this constraint for the analysis in this paper, as the fingerprint of Mirai-like bots is precise enough so that the number of false positives does not increase significantly when observing all ports (cf. Table 2). As a result, we can investigate which other ports are a target of Mirai-like botnets.

5 Evaluation

In this section, we present how the scanning behavior of the identified organizations and the use of scanning tools changed. The evaluation period ranges from Jun. 1, 2023 to Jan. 31, 2025. In this period, the honeypots received 154917569 TCP and UDP packets from 4102918 unique IP addresses. We compare the scanning behavior during this extended period with the previous evaluation period that ranged from Jun. 1, 2023 to Jan. 31, 2024.

After we deployed the new SSH, Telnet, HTTP, and HTTP services on the honeypots, the number of received packets increased. The main reason for the increasing number of packets is the interaction of scanners with the services. For example, a scanner that performs an HTTP request contributes around 5 packets to the total number of received packets on the honeypot: TCP SYN, TCP ACK, HTTP request, TCP FIN, and TCP ACK. This leads to the problem that a scanner that interacts extensively with one or more services is overrepresented in the evaluation. Therefore, we introduce the metric *distinct scan* that we use as a replacement for the number of TCP and UDP packets. We define a distinct scan as a) a scanner that checks whether a port is open (i.e., a port scan) or

b) the interaction of a scanner with a service. This means that each port scan and interaction counts only as one scan in the evaluation. During the evaluation period, the honeypots received 100736613 distinct scans.

5.1 Organizations Conducting Scans

In previous work, we identified 47 different scanning routines from 43 distinct organizations [8]. If an organization runs multiple scanners with different goals or if they are operated by different departments, we call each of these different scanners a scanning routine. We distinguish scanning routines using information about IP addresses as described in Sect. 4.1. Using this technique, we identified 67 scanning routines from 62 distinct organizations. During the evaluation period from June 1, 2023 to January 31, 2025, 18.8% of all scans originated from the identified organizations. In previous work [8], we showed the number of received TCP and UDP packets that the identified organizations sent to each honeypot using a heatmap. Building on this previously established methodology, Fig. 3 shows the number of distinct scans that each identified organization performed per honeypot. The number of distinct scans is indicated by the color in each cell. The darker the hue, the more distinct scans we have recorded. Newly identified organizations are highlighted in bold. We use the categorization introduced in previous work [8] to categorize the identified organizations into three categories (cf. Fig. 3): i) universities or organizations that conduct scans for research *(Research, R)*, ii) companies or organizations that scan the Internet as part of their security services *(Commercial, C)*, and iii) organizations with other intentions or whose intent is not clear *(Other, O)*. For easier identification of the categories in the heatmap, we colored the labels of research organizations blue, commercial organizations purple, and other organizations green.

The results are comparable to the previous work: most organizations scan all honeypots equally and the number of distinct scans strongly differs between the organizations. However, some organizations, e.g., *Georgia Tech*, have significantly altered their scanning patterns by scanning the Mumbai honeypot almost exclusively. Maybe they scan only parts of the Internet, possibly switching the subnets or geographical areas from time to time. Some organizations have almost stopped scanning, e.g., *RWTH Aachen* only sent 40 packets after the evaluation period of the previous work. This can be due to a change in scanning behavior or they are only interested in specific events or targets. Conversely, other organizations, e.g., *research.knoq.nl* and *University of Colorado*, maintained consistent behavior, suggesting that these organizations aim to get a consistent view of the services running on the Internet over time. Newly identified organizations include *Modat* and *Qualys*, both of which show that scanners also focus on scanning only certain geographical areas. *Modat* only scans the Cape Town and São Paulo honeypots and *Qualys* exclusively scans the Tokyo honeypot. Among the newly identified scanners are *Bill Demirkapi* and *Yevgen*, two individuals who claim to scan the Internet for research purposes. Both are responsible for fewer scans than the other organizations, but they show that individuals can perform Internet scanning too, regardless of their motivation. These findings highlight the

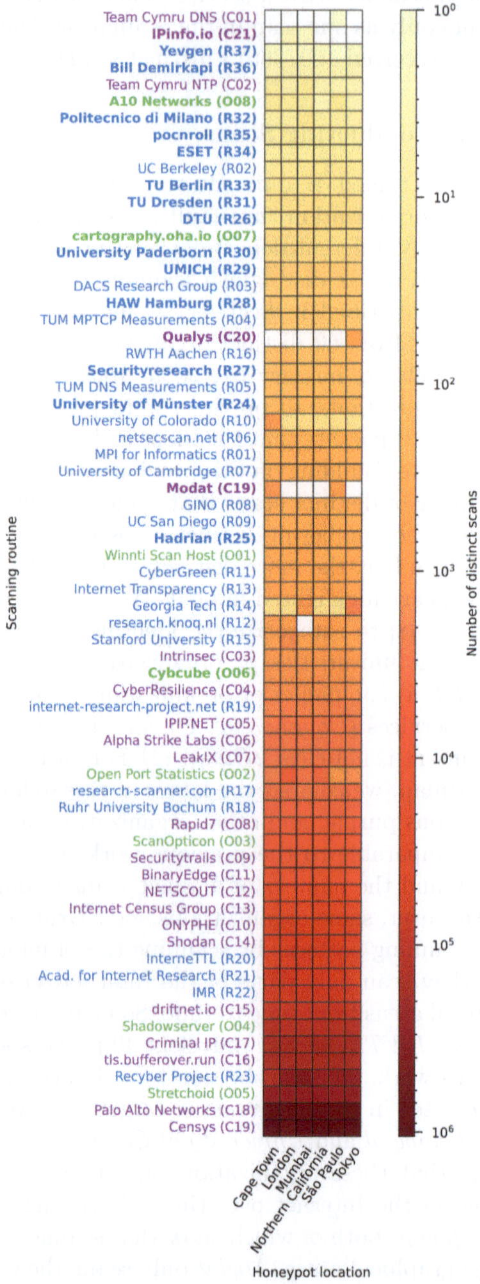

Fig. 3. Number of distinct scans from all 67 identified scanning routines across the six honeypots. Newly identified scanning routines are highlighted in bold. The organization's label colors indicate the three different organization categories.

dynamic nature of scanning practices across different organizations and emphasize the importance of continuous monitoring to understand evolving trends in the scanning landscape.

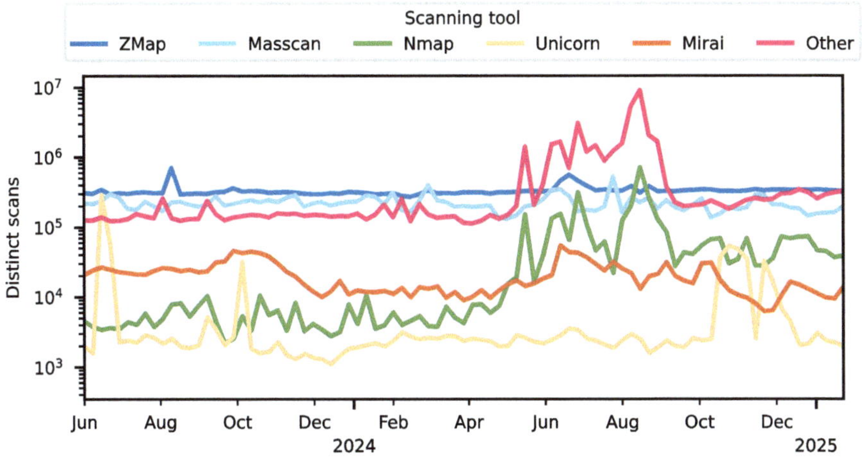

Fig. 4. Number of distinct scans per scanning tool.

5.2 Use of Scanning Tools

ZMap, Masscan, Unicorn, and Nmap are common tools used by scanners to automate the scanning of a large number of IP addresses and ports. In this section, we analyze how the share of these scanning tools changes over time. Particularly, we analyze the change caused by the deployment of the additional services on the honeypots. In addition, we provide a deeper look at the scanning behavior of Mirai-like botnets. To identify the scanning tools, we use the fingerprints introduced in Sect. 4.2.

Figure 4 shows the number of distinct scans on the honeypots for each scanning tool in intervals of 7 days. First, we look at the change in the number of distinct scans conducted using ZMap. As mentioned in Sect. 4, ZMap removed the IP-ID fingerprint from the packets it sends. This means that we cannot identify packets sent by ZMap with version v4.1.0 released in May 2024 and onward using IP-ID fingerprints. If scanners update their ZMap versions, the number of distinct scans sent using ZMap should decrease, while the number of distinct scans from other scanning tools should increase. However, as shown in Fig. 4, the number of distinct scans using ZMap remains almost constant throughout the observation period. This stability in scanning activity suggests that scanner operators update their scanning tools only infrequently. The lack of willingness to upgrade may be due to the need to disrupt running scanning pipelines during upgrades, which may require significant changes to data processing workflows.

Another reason may be that scanner operators do not want to risk breaking the scanning pipeline due to bugs in the new scanning tool version. This observation highlights the trade-off between maintaining operational continuity and adopting the latest scanning tool versions, which may impact the overall efficiency and effectiveness of large-scale Internet scanning operations.

The number of distinct scans using other scanning tools increases after the deployment of the HTTP, HTTPS, SSH, and Telnet services on the honeypots in April and May 2024. This shows that the number of scans using tools that can possibly interact with the services increases. In contrast, the number of distinct scans using ZMap, Masscan, and Unicorn does not change. There is a spike in the number of distinct scans using other scanning tools and Nmap in the period between May and September 2024. This increased scanning activity consists mainly of the increased scanning activity on port 443, which we discuss in Sect. 5.3.

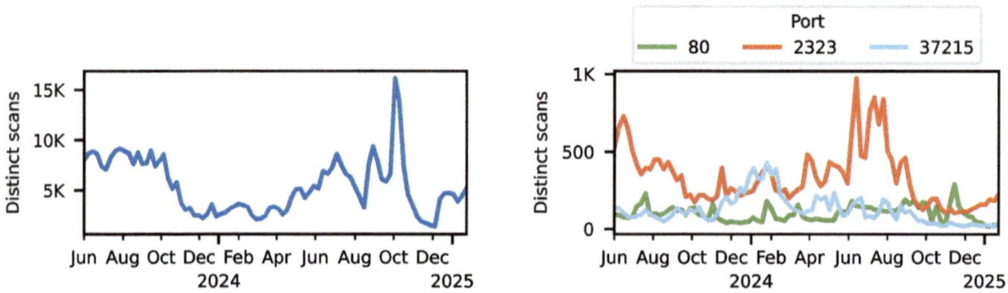

(a) Mirai variants on port 23. (b) Mirai variants on other ports.

Fig. 5. Number of distinct scans on different ports from unique IPs from hosts infected by Mirai variants.

In the following, we take a deeper look at the behavior of Mirai-like botnets. Figure 4 shows the overall change of distinct scans originating from Mirai-infected hosts across all ports. Figure 5 shows the ports most often scanned by Mirai-like botnets and includes each IP only once within the interval of 7 days. This prevents a single host from disrupting the number of distinct scans by sending many packets, as we aim to get an overview of the number of all hosts in botnets on the Internet. The number of distinct scans differs between the ports, as different Mirai-like botnets exploit different vulnerabilities. This also leads to spikes at different points in time. In general, the ports 23 and 2323 show the most scanning activity while there is less activity on the other ports. The reason for this is that every Mirai variant targets Telnet. Which other vulnerabilities a Mirai variant exploits depends on the variant. Decreasing activity of Mirai variants can be observed on all ports from July 2024 onward. This reduction can be possibly attributed in part to the successful intervention by the FBI during the beginning of the previous year [3]. The FBI operation involved taking control of and subsequently shutting down the primary servers that hosted the command

and control infrastructure for a Mirai-like botnet [11]. This action significantly disrupted the operational capabilities of this botnet, leading to a decrease in its scanning and infection attempts.

Even after the FBI intervention, there were increasing numbers of distinct scans by other Mirai-like botnets. In November 2024, there was a botnet that started to exploit a vulnerability registered as CVE-2024-12856 [14]. This vulnerability affects the HTTP service of Four-Faith industrial routers, and, therefore, led to an increased number of distinct scans on port 80. In May and June, two botnets exploited different vulnerabilities on HTTP services that possibly led to another increase on port 80 [1,12]. There are even more spikes during the observation period that can eventually be attributed to a botnet. However, sometimes the differentiation between botnets is not clear if their time of activity overlaps.

5.3 Scanning Behavior

In this section, we analyze how the scanning behavior changed over time and compares to previous findings. First, we present the scanning behavior on well-known ports, followed by a deeper look at the scanning behavior on the most scanned ports, and finally, the organizations' individual scanning behaviors.

To give an overall view of the ports scanned on the honeypots, we present a heatmap in Fig. 6. The heatmap shows the ports 0 to 1023 on the y-axis and the observation period in an interval of 7 days on the x-axis. The color of a cell indicates the number of distinct scans on the corresponding port across all honeypots within 7 days. We chose the first 1024 ports, as these are the well-known ports assigned by IANA [2]. These ports are used by many common services, which means that they experience increased scanning activity. The heatmap shows that scanners scan a wide range of ports with a focus on ports used by common services, e.g., the ports 22 (SSH), 53 (DNS), 80 (HTTP), 389 (LDAP), and 443 (HTTPS). The most scanned ports host the HTTPS, SSH, Telnet, and HTTP services running on the honeypots. Before the deployment of these services in April and May 2024, port 22 was not among the top 4 most scanned ports. This indicates that scanners detect the new services and interact with them or perform more port scans. The heatmap also reveals time frames with an increased scanning activity across a large number of ports through vertical bars that are lighter than the surrounding cells on the left and right. For example, there is such a vertical bar around mid-June 2024.

The deployment of the SSH, Telnet, HTTP, and HTTPS services in April and May 2024 resulted in a significantly altered scanning behavior. Figure 7 shows the scanning activity on the most scanned ports 22, 23, 80, and 443, which are also the ports on which the new services are running. The deployment of these services has led to an increased scanning activity targeting the associated ports. We detected temporary but substantial fluctuations in the number of distinct scans, indicating that scanners, potentially operated by threat actors, gained interest in these newly available services. An example for such a fluctuation is the increase in distinct scans targeting port 443 in August 2024. We believe that this increase is related to the increased interest following the disclosure of

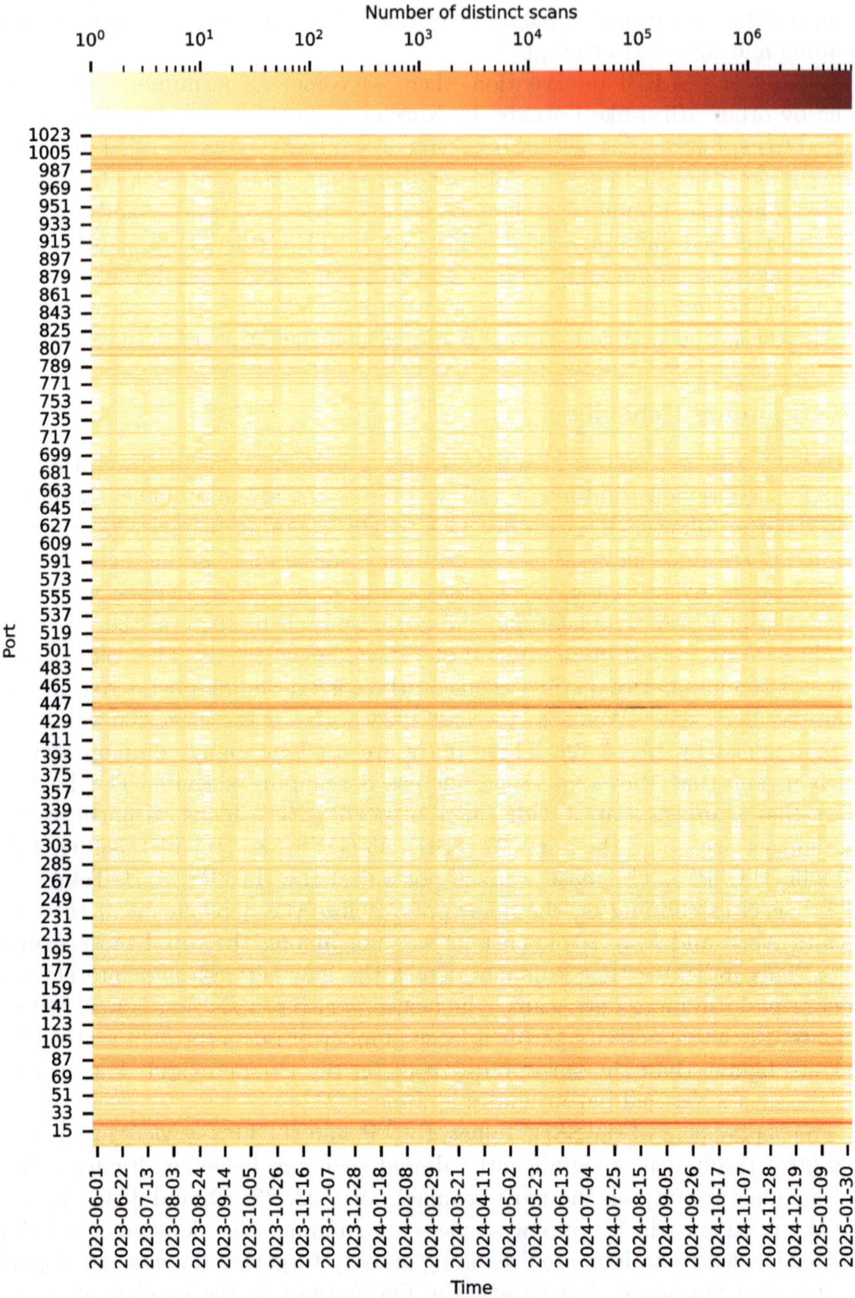

Fig. 6. Number of distinct scans on the ports 0 to 1023 on all honeypots in an interval of 7 days.

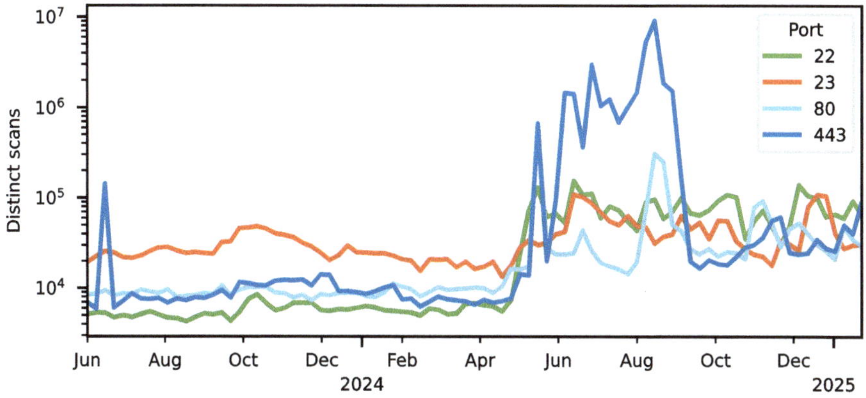

Fig. 7. Number of distinct scans on the most scanned ports.

a vulnerability. Unfortunately, we have not been able to identify a unique CVE that explicitly involves HTTPS and port 443. CVEs are standardized, unique identifiers for publicly known vulnerabilities in software and hardware products. There are at least four CVEs that could explain the increased interest (CVE-2024-30080, CVE-2024-30103, CVE-2024-55591, CVE-2024-39573). These CVEs affect various systems such as Microsoft Message Queuing or FortiOS and FortiProxy. They allow remote code execution or exploit the Node.js websocket module. While the initial spike in traffic subsided after a short period, the sustained elevated activity on this port remains notably higher than the activity observed before the deployment of the new services.

As the research focus of the honeypots prior to the introduction of the new services was on IoT services, we list in Table 3 the organizations that sent packets to at least one of the IoT services on the honeypots, i.e. AMQP, CoAP, MQTT or OPC UA. This allows to compare the behavior of organizations that scan IoT services with previous work [8]. The second column of the table shows the number of scanned TCP and UDP ports. The third column shows the number of distinct scans on all ports as well as the share of distinct scans of the IoT services. Days scanned is the percentage of days with at least one scan. The average scan interval denotes the number of days between two distinct scans on the same port. We calculate the scan interval separately for each honeypot location so that the scan interval is independent of the location. We highlight the increase of the average scan interval compared to previous work in red and a decrease in blue. For an increase or decrease to be highlighted, the change of the average scan interval must be larger than one day. In the last two columns, we list histograms to show which ports the organizations scan and at which times they scan. For better readability, we included red lines on the x-axis and y-axis of the histograms. The port histograms contain red lines to mark the end of the well-known ports (1024) and the beginning of the ephemeral ports (49152) on the x-axis. On the y-axis, the red lines mark the number of 50 distinct scans in the port histograms and 50 distinct scans in the time histograms. The time histograms show the distinct scans on the London honeypot only. For the organization *Modat*, we did not include a time histogram in the table because they did not scan the London honeypot. We highlighted distinct scans of the IoT ports in the time histogram in pink. However, as there are only few distinct scans on the IoT ports, the pink areas near the x-axis are difficult to see. They are best to see for organizations that have a higher share of distinct scans on the IoT ports, e.g., *Ruhr University Bochum* and *driftnet.io*.

For some of the organizations identified, we observe that the scanning activity has increased since the deployment of the new services. For example, *Palo Alto Networks* and *driftnet.io* show an increased scanning activity. Further analysis reveals that *Palo Alto Networks* increased the number of distinct scans in general, while *driftnet.io* only increased the number of distinct scans for the new services. However, the increase of distinct scans visible in the time histogram of *driftnet.io* results from an increase of distinct scans before the deployment of the new services. In contrast to this, we also observe that the scan activities of some organizations, such as *Acad. for Internet Research*, were limited in time and suddenly stopped. Many organizations show a different average scan interval compared to the findings in the previous work. Of the 21 organizations for which we presented the average scan interval in previous work, 8 show a similar average scan interval, while 12 have an increased and only 1 organization a reduced average scan interval on all ports. For some organizations, the average scan interval for all ports has increased, while the average scan interval for IoT ports remains almost the same. For example, the average scan interval of *Censys* increased by around 85 days, while the average scan interval of the IoT ports did almost not change. This supports the findings of Griffoen et al. [6] that scanners are increasingly scanning for specific events or specific ports. Other organizations increased their average scan interval on all ports, including IoT ports, e.g., *BinaryEdge* and *Recyber Project*. Only *ONYPHE* reduced their average scan interval from about 15 to about 7 days. Some of the newly identified organizations also scan IoT services, e,g., *A10 Networks*, the *Technical University of Denmark (DTU)*, and *Modat*.

Table 3. Scanning behavior characteristics of organizations that probe at least one of the IoT ports (AMQP, CoAP, MQTT, and OPC UA). We define the percentage of days with at least one distinct scan as days scanned. Distinct scans per port shows the distinct scans across all ports using a histogram with 611 bins; the red lines on the x-axis mark the end of well-known (1024) and the beginning of ephemeral ports (49152); the red line on the y-axis at 50 distinct scans allows a comparison between organizations. Distinct scans over time shows the distinct scans of IoT and non-IoT ports across the observation period on the London honeypot using a histogram with one bin per day; the red line on the y-axis at 50 distinct scans allows a comparison between organizations.

Organization	#Ports		#Dis. Scans		Days Scanned		Avg. Scan Interval (days)		Dis. Scans per Port	Dis. Scans over Time
	TCP	UDP	All	IoT	All	IoT	All	IoT		
A10 Networks	24	9	56	7.1 %	0.7 %	0.1 %	88.0 d	-		
Acad. for Internet Research	1473	1	328246	0.5 %	11.2 %	8.8 %	10.1 d	10.5 d		
Alpha Strike Labs	181	63	15924	1.2 %	96.0 %	2.6 %	61.5 d	90.7 d		
BinaryEdge	831	25	66197	3.1 %	92.4 %	6.4 %	47.1 d	31.7 d		
cartography.oha.io	29	0	202	3.0 %	4.8 %	0.2 %	115.9 d	-		
Censys	65535	45638	5919437	2.1 %	99.8 %	99.8 %	142.9 d	1.1 d		
Criminal IP	15800	715	972973	0.2 %	99.6 %	28.5 %	16.3 d	21.0 d		
driftnet.io	15639	23	444312	3.0 %	99.8 %	36.5 %	71.2 d	8.1 d		
DTU	8	4	180	56.1 %	2.7 %	1.4 %	18.3 d	16.5 d		
IMR	65534	0	387207	0.2 %	1.6 %	0.5 %	17.2 d	5.0 d		
Internet Census Group	367	44	122480	2.2 %	99.8 %	22.3 %	17.7 d	15.0 d		
InterneTTL	371	113	259216	0.3 %	19.1 %	18.3 %	5.7 d	5.5 d		
Modat	619	1	1718	1.1 %	1.1 %	0.6 %	6.5 d	1.7 d		
NETSCOUT	95	83	100286	2.6 %	98.1 %	48.9 %	8.8 d	2.0 d		
ONYPHE	2149	26	174510	1.0 %	97.7 %	17.9 %	7.7 d	12.2 d		
Palo Alto Networks	40117	106	4739806	0.5 %	99.8 %	97.2 %	4.9 d	1.1 d		
Rapid7	166	22	35140	0.7 %	52.0 %	5.9 %	22.9 d	32.6 d		
Recyber Project	65535	3	1545187	0.0 %	99.8 %	3.3 %	100.7 d	98.4 d		
Ruhr University Bochum	25	7	26247	43.3 %	76.4 %	75.7 %	56.5 d	1.0 d		
RWTH Aachen	20	3	668	54.6 %	9.9 %	2.1 %	55.2 d	69.4 d		
Shadowserver	291	45	721103	3.4 %	99.8 %	99.4 %	1.2 d	1.1 d		
Shodan	3792	88	237043	1.1 %	99.8 %	33.3 %	68.1 d	10.2 d		
Stanford University	761	2	4458	0.4 %	10.7 %	0.3 %	18.2 d	74.3 d		
Stretchoid	827	68	1593963	1.2 %	99.8 %	96.6 %	4.8 d	1.2 d		
tls.bufferover.run	1220	0	979399	0.3 %	99.8 %	34.5 %	5.3 d	3.6 d		

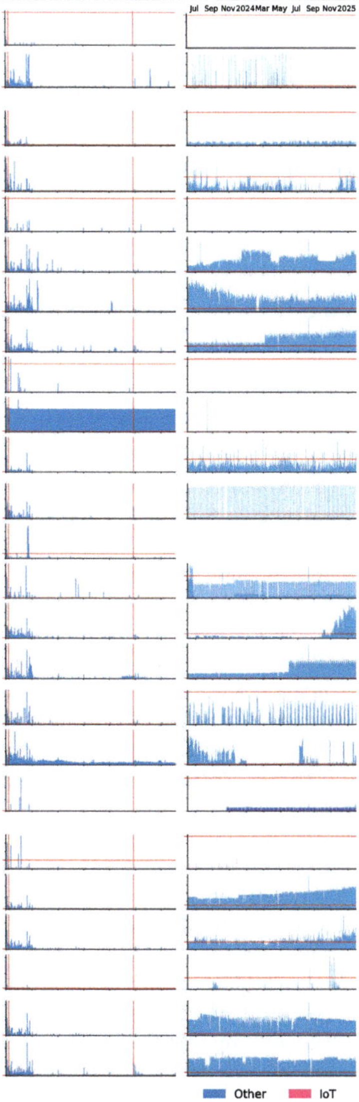

6 Conclusion

We analyzed the behavior of Internet scanners over a time period of 20 months and compared it to the behavior of scanners on the same honeypots in previous work [8]. In addition, we deployed four new services, HTTP, HTTPS, SSH, and Telnet, on the honeypots and analyzed how the scanners changed their scanning behavior. The deployment of new services led to a substantial increase in scanning activities, highlighting the responsiveness of scanners and threat actors to changes on the Internet. Interestingly, despite potential identification risks through the fingerprint, we observed a consistent use of older ZMap versions, suggesting a reluctance among scanners to update their tools. This behavior may be influenced by concerns about disrupting established scanning pipelines or the need for extensive modifications to data processing workflows. While there are fluctuations in the number of distinct scans by hosts that are infected by Mirai-like botnets, we noted a decline in Mirai-like botnet activity, which can be attributed to the ongoing efforts of the FBI to dismantle the infrastructure of Mirai-like botnets. Furthermore, the analysis revealed that individual scanning organizations exhibited highly distinctive and temporally focused scanning patterns, indicating specialized strategies or targeted interests in specific vulnerabilities or services. These findings underscore the dynamic nature of the scanning landscape and emphasize the importance of continuous monitoring and adaptation in network defense strategies.

References

1. Ahmed, D.: Mirai-like botnet targets Zyxel NAS devices in Europe for DDoS attacks. https://hackread.com/mirai-botnet-zyxel-nas-devices-europe-ddos-attacks/. Accessed 6 Mar 2025
2. Cotton, M., Eggert, L., Touch, J., Westerlund, M., Cheshire, S.: RFC 6335: Internet Assigned Numbers Authority (IANA) procedures for the management of the service name and transport protocol port number registry (2011)
3. Court, U.S.D.: In the matter of charge and seizure of infected devices and command-and-control servers in the united states that are part of a Mirai botnet, https://www.justice.gov/d9/2024-09/redacted_24-mj-1484_signed_search_and_seizure_warrant_for_disclosure.pdf. Accessed 9 Mar 2025
4. Durumeric, Z., Adrian, D., Stephens, P., Wustrow, E., Halderman, J.A.: Ten years of ZMap. In: Proceedings of the 2024 ACM on Internet Measurement Conference (2024)
5. Ghiëtte, V., Blenn, N., Doerr, C.: Remote identification of port scan toolchains. In: IFIP International Conference on New Technologies, Mobility and Security (NTMS) (2016)
6. Griffioen, H., Koursiounis, G., Smaragdakis, G., Doerr, C.: Have you SYN me? Characterizing ten years of Internet scanning. In: Proceedings of the 2024 ACM on Internet Measurement Conference (2024)
7. Liao, S., et al.: A comprehensive detection approach of Nmap: principles, rules and experiments. In: International Conference on Cyber-Enabled Distributed Computing and Knowledge Discovery (CyberC) (2020)

8. Mayer, J., et al.: I know who you scanned last summer: mapping the landscape of Internet-wide scanners. In: IFIP Networking Conference (2024)
9. Munteanu, C., Saidi, S.J., Gasser, O., Smaragdakis, G., Feldmann, A.: Fifteen months in the life of a honeyfarm. In: Proceedings of the ACM on Internet Measurement Conference (2023)
10. Red Hat, Inc.: CVE-2024-3094 detail. https://nvd.nist.gov/vuln/detail/cve-2024-3094. Accessed 27 Feb 2025
11. Ries, U.: FBI schaltet riesiges Botnet aus Heim-Routern, Webcams und NAS-Geräten ab. https://www.heise.de/news/Heim-Router-Webcams-NAS-Geraete-Riesiges-IoT-Botnet-vom-FBI-abgeschaltet-9939939.html. Accessed 6 Mar 2025
12. SOCRadar: Attackers Attackers exploit Ivanti Connect Secure zero-day vulnerabilities to deploy webshells (CVE-2023-46805, CVE-2024-21887). https://socradar.io/attackers-exploit-ivanti-connect-secure-zero-day-vulnerabilities-to-deploy-webshells-cve-2023-46805-cve-2024-21887/. Accessed 6 Mar 2025
13. Tanaka, A., Han, C., Takahashi, T.: Detecting coordinated Internet-wide scanning by TCP/IP header fingerprint. IEEE Access **11**, 23227–23244 (2023)
14. Toulas, B.: New Mirai botnet targets industrial routers with zero-day exploits, https://www.bleepingcomputer.com/news/security/new-mirai-botnet-targets-industrial-routers-with-zero-day-exploits/. Accessed 6 Mar 2025

A Performance Comparison of the Homomorphic Encryption Schemes CKKS and TFHE

Clemens Krüger(✉), Bhavinkumar Moriya, and Dominik Schoop

University of Applied Sciences Esslingen, Esslingen am Neckar, Germany
clemens.krueger@hs-esslingen.de

Abstract. Homomorphic encryption (HE) is a promising technique for privacy-preserving data analysis. Several HE schemes have been developed, with the Cheon-Kim-Kim-Song (CKKS) and Fast Fully Homomorphic Encryption over the Torus (TFHE) schemes being two of the most advanced. However, due to their differences, it is hard to compare their performance and suitability for a given application. We therefore conducted an empirical study of the performance of the two schemes in a comparable scenario. We benchmarked the commonly used operations addition, multiplication, division, square root, evaluation of a polynomial and a comparison function, each on a common pair of datasets with 2^{16} 32-bit integers. Since the CKKS scheme is an approximate scheme, we set a requirement of at least 32 bits of precision to match that of the input data. Our results show that CKKS outperforms TFHE in most operations. TFHE's only advantage is its fast bootstrapping. Even though TFHE performs bootstrapping after every operation, while CKKS typically performs bootstrapping only after a certain number of multiplications, CKKS's bootstrapping still presents a bottleneck. This can be seen specifically with the comparison operation, where TFHE is much faster than CKKS in many settings, as it requires several bootstrapping operations in CKKS due to its multiplicative depth. Generally speaking, CKKS should be preferred in applications which can be parallelized. CKKS's advantages decreases in applications with a large depth that require many bootstrapping operations.

Keywords: Homomorphic Encryption · Performance · CKKS · TFHE

1 Introduction

Homomorphic encryption (HE) enables computations on encrypted data, making it possible to perform data analysis in a privacy-preserving way. In 2009, Craig Gentry proposed the first fully homomorphic encryption scheme, which was able to perform a theoretically unlimited number of additions and multiplications [13]. Over the years, many more schemes have been proposed which improved the capabilities and performance of HE. The newest and most promising of these schemes are the CKKS and TFHE schemes [20]. The two schemes

L. Bechtel and T. Heer (Eds.): CCSSS 2025 PTT, pp. 92–108, 2026.
https://doi.org/10.1007/978-3-032-10569-1_6

work in very different ways. CKKS uses real numbers as inputs, whereas TFHE uses bits or small integers. Also, CKKS uses a batching technique which allows for parallelized operations on multiple values, whereas TFHE encrypts individual values. These differences make it very hard to determine which scheme is most appropriate for a given application. In this paper, we perform a study to compare the performance of the two schemes for several operations executed on a common dataset. It is structured as follows: In Sect. 3 we provide background information about homomorphic encryption and the two schemes we utilized for this study. In Sect. 4 we show our experimental setup including choice of hardware, software and measurements. Section 5 lists all operations on which we performed benchmarks. In Sect. 6 we show and discuss the results of our measurements. Finally, we conclude the paper in Sect. 7.

2 Related Work

Several publications have performed various comparisons between the different FHE schemes as well as between their implementations. Jiang et al. [18] performed an empirical study of several schemes, including Brakerski-Gentry-Vaikuntanathan (BGV), Brakerski/Fan-Vercauteren (BFV), CKKS and TFHE. In addition, they tested different implementations of these schemes, such as Microsoft SEAL, IBM HElib and PALISADE. However, in their benchmarks they specifically differentiate between arithmetic operations (such as addition and multiplication) and logic operations (such as AND/OR gates). Furthermore, they do not consider bootstrapping in their measurements. Such approach makes it challenging to develop selection criteria for CKKS and TFHE.

Zhu et al. [30] compared the performance and accuracy of the CKKS scheme in the three libraries OpenFHE, HElib and Microsoft SEAL with the example of a convolutional neural network. They do not consider any other schemes for their evaluation.

Rahman et al. [25] performed benchmarks on the three schemes BGV, BFV and CKKS in multiple libraries in the context of their performance on IoT devices. None of these works specifically benchmark the performance of the two schemes CKKS and TFHE in comparable circumstances, i.e. on the same datasets and using the same operations. This makes it hard to make an informed choice as to which scheme should be chosen for an application.

Gouert et al. [15] performed a series of benchmarks on multiple schemes including CKKS and TFHE. They implemented their benchmarks in several libraries. Their tests include arithmetic calculations as well as bit-wise and relational ones. However, at the time of their study in 2023, TFHE only supported bit-wise operations and not yet operations on small integers (see Sect. 3.2 for more detail). Additionally, they do not utilize bootstrapping for the CKKS scheme, which limits their benchmarks to calculations with low multiplicative depth and changes the requirements for parameter choice.

3 Background

In this section, we introduce the two FHE schemes CKKS and TFHE, which we have chosen for this study. We give an overview of the two schemes' characteristics, ciphertext structures as well as the problems on which their security is based.

3.1 CKKS

The Cheon-Kim-Kim-Song (CKKS) [6] scheme is a fully homomorphic encryption scheme designed for approximate arithmetic on real numbers. CKKS is based on the Ring Learning With Errors problem (RLWE) [26], which is a variant of the Learning With Errors problem (LWE). In LWE, secret data is represented as a set of linear equations with small errors added to them. Its security is based on the idea that it is hard to distinguish the secrets from the errors. The problem can be reduced to certain lattice problems, which are considered quantum safe. CKKS uses an encoding scheme that maps real numbers to integer coefficients of polynomials. The numbers are multiplied by a scaling factor Δ, which dictates the precision of the numbers after the decimal point. This encoding method uses a batching technique, where multiple real numbers are encoded into one CKKS plaintext. These plaintext batches can then be encrypted, and homomorphic calculations are performed element-wise on each value (Single Instruction, Multiple Data (SIMD) approach). CKKS itself is a leveled scheme, meaning that the maximum number of consecutive multiplications (called the multiplicative depth d) needs to be defined during setup.

Ciphertexts in CKKS are represented as elements of the polynomial ring $\mathbb{Z}_q[X]/(X^N + 1)$, where N is the degree of the polynomials, also called the ring dimension, and q is referred to as the ciphertext modulus. This modulus is constructed as the product of multiple large prime numbers (modulus chain), specifically $q = q_0 \cdot q_1 \cdot ... \cdot q_d$. The prime q_0 is the first modulus in this chain, and it is used during decryption. The primes q_i $(1 \geq i \leq d)$ are very close in size to the scaling factor Δ. There is one of these for each level corresponding to the multiplicative depth.

The scheme offers a bootstrapping operation [5], which is able to reset the level, allowing for a theoretically unlimited number of operations. During bootstrapping the scheme's decryption mechanism is evaluated homomorphically. Consequently, it is possible to reset the multiplicative depth without needing to decrypt the ciphertext. The added error terms introduce a certain amount of noise to the ciphertexts. This noise increases with every subsequent operation, especially through multiplications.

To handle the noise growth during multiplication, CKKS has a special rescaling operation. After each multiplication, the ciphertext is divided by the scaling factor and one modulus q_i is dropped, effectively reducing the left-over multiplicative depth. When all levels are exhausted, only the modulus q_0 is left, which can then be used for decryption. While the scaling factor Δ controls the maximum precision after the decimal point, the difference between q_0 and Δ specifies the maximal number of bits before the decimal point.

3.2 TFHE

The Torus Fully Homomorphic Encryption (TFHE) scheme [8] is based on the RLWE problem as well as a variant called Torus LWE (TLWE). The scheme is based on the FHEW [11] scheme, which it improved by providing a very fast bootstrapping operation. TFHE's bootstrapping is also referred to as functional bootstrapping or programmable bootstrapping (PBS), because it allows to evaluate a function during bootstrapping without additional performance costs. This is achieved through lookup tables, which can be evaluated as a byproduct of the bootstrapping. TFHE's bootstrapping procedure is so optimized, that it is executed by default after every operation.

TFHE is a hybrid scheme which combines techniques from traditional LWE constructions as well as Gentry-Sahai-Waters (GSW) [14]. Its fundamental arithmetic and encoding occur on the torus ($\mathbb{T} = \mathbb{R}/\mathbb{Z}$), giving it its name.

A homomorphic arithmetic is performed on a TLWE (Torus Learning With Errors) ciphertext. A TLWE ciphertext is constructed using a generalization of the LWE problem, following the footprint of [3] (that defined the General LWE problem) and [14].

Originally, TFHE ciphertexts represented individual bits, and the operations were simply binary gates such as AND. Recently, however, the scheme was expanded to support multi-bit ciphertexts up to 8 bits, which are often referred to as small integers. From these small integers, one can then construct encryptions of larger integers (e.g. 32 bits), by splitting them into multiple ciphertexts. This can be done in two ways:

- Radix representation: A given integer is represented in a base $B \in \mathbb{N}$ (at most 4 bits integer). If a given integer $m \in \mathbb{N}$ is represented as $m = m_0 + m_1 \cdot B + m_2 \cdot B^2 + \cdots + m_k \cdot B^k$, then each m_i is encrypted independently.
- Chinese Reminder Theorem (CRT) representation: The given integer $n \in \mathbb{N}$ is represented as a product of many small coprime integers of size at most 4 bits.

The CRT representation can potentially be faster than the radix-based one, however it does not support all operations on ciphertexts. To perform operations on larger integers on the basis of multiple small integers, a carry is often needed. Therefore, the space of a small integer is divided into a message space and a carry space.

Now, we briefly discuss the building blocks of the TFHE scheme. Let s be a secret key (which is basically a binary vector or a polynomial with binary coefficients). The phase is a function ϕ_s from $\mathbb{T}^n \times \mathbb{T}$ to $\mathbb{T}$ defined as $\phi_s(\mathbf{a}, b) = b - s \cdot \mathbf{a}$. In TLWE, the phase is the main building block.

The TLWE works well for linear operations. However, non-linear operations are not supported by TLWE. To tackle this problem, various schemes have been proposed over the years. Among all of them, the most common solutions are the BGV scheme [3] and the GSW scheme [14]. TFHE builds on top of the GSW scheme to solve the issue of non linear operations. GSW is fully homomorphic and its security is based on the security of the LWE problem. A generalized scale invariant version of GSW is called TGSW (in the same line as TLWE). The scheme relies on a gadget decomposition function. The canonical gadget decomposition is used to introduce an external product between TGSW and TLWE ciphertext, which is homomorphic to a product of two plaintexts. To ease the circuit construction, the scheme introduces the `CMux` gate, which evaluates one of the two tasks based on the validity of the encrypted message. The most important tool of the TFHE is a fast bootstrapping. The scheme introduces gate bootstrapping (it is performed after every gate), which is the fastest in the lineage of [11,13]. They have also introduced circuit bootstrapping, which has been recently improved by [28].

The scheme uses deterministic weighted finite automata (det-WFA) to evaluate specific arithmetic functions largely used in applications, such as addition (and multi-addition), multiplication, squaring, comparison and max, etc. For further details on det-WFA one may refer to [4,10].

4 Experimental Setup

We compare the performance of the two schemes CKKS and TFHE for several operations. To make the results comparable, we perform our measurements in the same environment. In the following, we describe the setup of our study, including utilized hardware, software libraries and dataset, as well as which parameter sets we use and which measurements we take.

4.1 Hardware

We performed our measurements on a system with 2 Intel Xeon Gold 5315Y (3.2GHz) and 512GB RAM running Ubuntu 22.04.4. We did not utilize any multi threading other than what our chosen libraries (see Sect. 4.3) perform out of the box.

4.2 Dataset

All operations are evaluated using a common dataset to ensure a meaningful comparison across the two schemes. The dataset consist of two randomly generated sequences A and B of 65,536 (2^{16}) unsigned 32-bit integers each. Sequence A is employed for the measurement of unary operations such as square root, while the elements of A and B serve as the operands for binary operations such as addition.

The input representation varies depending on the encryption scheme. In CKKS, numbers are scaled down to the range [0,1], with the smallest distinguishable step being $2.3283064e-10$. In contrast, TFHE operates on small integers, which can be combined to represent bigger integers (see Sect. 5 for more detail).

4.3 Software Libraries

There are many different software libraries that implement common FHE schemes, including CKKS and TFHE. Some are specific to certain schemes, others implement multiple schemes in one library. In this section, we list libraries that implement CKKS, TFHE or both and explain our choice of library for this study. It should be noted that many more FHE implementations exist, such as Apple's Swift HE library. However, we excluded them because they do not implement either CKKS or TFHE. We also excluded libraries such as Liberate. FHE [9], NuFHE [22] and REDcuFHE [12]. While they do implement CKKS and TFHE respectively, they run on GPUs, which is out of scope for this paper.

Table 1. Libraries that implement CKKS or TFHE

Library	CKKS	TFHE	Maintained
OpenFHE [1]	✓	✓	✓
PALISADE [23]	✓	✓	
HELib [16]	✓		✓
Microsoft SEAL [21]	✓		✓
TFHE-rs [29]		✓	✓
HEAAN [17]	✓		✓
TFHE [27]		✓	
Lattigo [19]	✓		✓

Table 1 lists the commonly used libraries for the two chosen schemes and indicates whether they are still actively maintained. The libraries OpenFHE and PALISADE are the only ones on the list that implement both schemes. PALISADE is the predecessor of OpenFHE. All its features were added to OpenFHE and it is no longer maintained. The TFHE library is also abandoned. They are the original implementations of CKKS and TFHE respectively, created by the schemes' authors.

For the CKKS scheme, the actively maintained options are therefore OpenFHE, HELib, Lattigo, HEAAN and Microsoft SEAL. To make our study relevant for realistic scenarios, we require specific features with regards to CKKS, namely bootstrapping support and encrypted polynomial approximation (e.g. through Chebyshev polynomials) to allow more than basic addition and multiplication. Both HELib and SEAL do not support either. Furthermore, SEAL does not appear to support necessary parameter sets, specifically a sufficiently high ring dimension. Both Lattigo and OpenFHE implement the necessary features. HEAAN was originally published by Seoul National University as a reference implementation for the original CKKS scheme. Since then however, it has been maintained by the company Cryptolab Inc, which consists of some of the original authors of the scheme. It supports bootstrapping as well as polynomial approximations. For this study, we chose the OpenFHE library (v1.2.3) for CKKS.

For the TFHE scheme, we are left with OpenFHE and TFHE-rs. In its original form, the TFHE scheme operated purely on binary values. Over time, the capability to calculate on multi-bit inputs was added. As described in Sect. 4.2, our benchmarks are executed on datasets containing 32-bit integers. To work with these inputs in TFHE, we need to have the ability to combine these small integers to construct bigger integers from them. The TFHE-rs library provides the option to perform the available operations on multiple integer sizes, where a bigger integer is transparently composed by multiple small integers. The OpenFHE library only has sporadic support for ciphertexts bigger than individual bits: Basic operations are implemented in the form of binary gates (AND, OR, etc.). Small integers are only supported for specific functions such as sign evaluation. There is no built-in support for larger integers such as 32 bits. Therefore, we choose the TFHE-rs library (v0.11) for the TFHE benchmarks in this study.

4.4 Parameter Choice

When it comes to the choice of cryptographic parameters for any given scheme, the overall goal is to achieve a certain security level while still maintaining the best possible performance. For this study, our goal is to maintain a minimum security level of 128 bits. In contrast to TFHE, where bootstrapping is typically automatically performed after every operation, CKKS requires more nuance. Its bootstrapping is a costly operation, which is why it is usually not executed after every operation, but rather in larger intervals. While some of our tested operations by themselves would not require bootstrapping due to their small depth, our goal is to show the performance of the operations as though they were part of a larger algorithm in order to make them more representative. We therefore select a parameter set for CKKS that allows bootstrapping while allowing the required precision of 32 bit for this evaluation. In addition, we need to ensure that our parameter set satisfies a minimum security level of 128 bits. Table 2 shows our chosen parameters set.

Table 2. CKKS Parameter Set

Parameter	Value
Security Level	128 bit
Ring Dimension	2^{16}
Multiplicative Depth	26
ScaleModSize	51
FirstModSize	53

The security of a CKKS parameter set is mainly driven by the relationship between the ring dimension and the ciphertext modulus ($\frac{N}{q}$). The ciphertext modulus is defined as $q_0 \cdot q_1 \cdot ... \cdot q_d$, where q_0 is the FirstModSize, q_1 to q_d are the ScaleModSize and d is the multiplicative depth. We therefore need to find the best trade-off between the scaling factors and the ring dimension. On the one hand, we need the scaling factors to facilitate our 32 bit precision requirement and the depth to be high enough to avoid bootstrapping too often, while on the other hand keeping the ring dimension low for performance. Our goal is to keep the ring dimension from exceeding 2^{16}, as performance typically degrades rapidly after this point. However, this requires us to set our parameters tightly, because limiting the ring dimension also requires us to limit the ciphertext modulus `Q` in order to keep 128 bits of security. The maximum possible size of the scaling factor (`ScaleModSize`) in this configuration was 51 bits, with a first modulus size (`FirstModSize`) of 54. We then set the multiplicative depth to 26, of which 12 will be consumed during bootstrapping. This leaves us with 14 multiplications between bootstrapping operations.

For TFHE, we utilize the parameter set `PARAM_MESSAGE_2_CARRY_2_KS_PBS`, which is provided by the TFHE-rs library. It defines that each small integer ciphertext consists of 2 bits of message space and 2 bits of carry space. `KS_PBS` specifies that the so-called key switching operation is performed before bootstrapping, which is the faster option.

This parameter set utilizes a tweaked uniform noise distribution and provides a minimum of 128 bits of security with a bootstrapping failure probability fixed at $\texttt{p}_{\texttt{error}} = 2^{-64}$.

4.5 Measurements

All measurements are performed for unary operators such as the square root on every element of dataset A and for binary operators such as addition on every element pair (a_i, b_i) from dataset A and B respectively. In the case of CKKS, the datasets are divided into batches and then encrypted, whereas TFHE encrypts every value separately.

Throughout the paper, we will consider the throughput, latency and precision of each operation. Since the CKKS scheme operates on batches of multiple values in each ciphertext, whereas TFHE ciphertexts contain individual values, we need to distinguish between the time it takes to calculate an operation on a (pair of) ciphertext(s), versus the amortized time for a single (pair of) value(s).

Latency is defined as the time it takes to complete an operation on a ciphertext, i.e. the latency until the result is returned after starting an operation.

Throughput is defined here as the amortized runtime for an operation on a single value from the previously defined dataset of 32-bit integers in the representation of the respective scheme. In the CKKS scheme, this is therefore determined by dividing the latency by the batch size. In TFHE, latency and throughput are the same, due to the lack of ciphertext batching.

The **Precision** gives for each operation the relative error of the homomorphically calculated and then decrypted results compared to the results calculated in plaintext. Specifically, the relative error for each result $r_i = Dec(Enc(a_i) \circ_{HE} Enc(b_i))$ with $a_i \in A, b_i \in B$ is calculated as $\frac{|(a_i \circ b_i) - r_i|}{max(A \circ B)}$, where $max(A \circ B)$ denotes the maximum possible result of the operation $\circ_{HE}$.

We will use this measurement to determine the parameter set for the encryption, specifically for the CKKS scheme, where a trade-off between precision and performance is possible depending on the parameters. The goal is to select the aforementioned parameters so that the relative error does not exceed 2^{-32}, i.e. the minimum relative error throughout all measurements must not go beneath the 32-bit precision we defined for the input datasets. It is important to note that we do not compare the precision among the benchmarked operations. We simply set a minimum precision to ensure a fair comparison between the schemes.

To test the influence of CKKS's batching technique, we perform our CKKS measurements with two different batch sizes, namely 8192 and 1. We chose the 8192 as a representative for a higher batch size, as it is a good compromise. We test this batch size in comparison with the lowest possible batch size of 1.

5 Operations

This section provides a list of the operations we chose to benchmark. For each scheme, we provide details on how the operations are implemented respectively. In the CKKS scheme, all operations are executed on multiple values at the same time, due to the batching technique of the ciphertexts. Therefore, every operation follows a SIMD approach. In TFHE, all operations are based on 32-bit integers, which are constructed from several small integer ciphertexts as described in Sect. 3.2.

5.1 Addition

CKKS: Addition is one of the natively supported operations in the CKKS scheme. The addition is performed on two ciphertexts, each of which contain a number of encrypted values. Therefore, the addition in CKKS can be seen as element-wise addition of two vectors.

TFHE: TFHE-rs uses element-wise addition of two vectors of small integers of the form $(a_1, a_2, \cdots, a_n, b)$ (where b is the number of small integers that form a single 32 bit integer) to perform the addition of the corresponding plaintexts. If the results become larger than the 32 bit limit, they overflow.

5.2 Multiplication

CKKS: The CKKS scheme handles multiplication in a similar way as addition: When two ciphertexts are multiplied, the result corresponds to an element-wise multiplication of two vectors of numbers. However, multiplication consumes levels, because a rescaling operation is applied to reduce the growth of the plaintext magnitude.

TFHE: In TFHE-rs, multiplication of two ciphertexts follows techniques introduced in GSW [14]. It uses a flattening method (called Gadget matrix) that modifies vectors without affecting dot products.

5.3 Division

CKKS: The division operation is not natively supported in the CKKS scheme. If the divisor is known as plaintext, then the inverse of the divisor can be calculated easily and then multiplied as a plaintext constant. If the divisor is encrypted, the calculation of the inverse $1/x$ is typically approximated using techniques such as Chebyshev polynomials. With the range of the dataset for this paper being $(0, 1)$, a problem presents itself: Since $1/x$ is undefined at $x = 0$, the approximation for x near 0 is not accurate. An alternative would be to keep the original scale of $(0, 2^{32}]$. However, this would lead to very large bounds for the approximation, which significantly decreases the accuracy of the result, even with a high polynomial degree. Additionally, this requires a large ciphertext magnitude. Since the maximum ciphertext magnitude is determined by the difference between the size of the first modulus and of the scaling factor, this either requires the reduction of the scaling factor (leading to lower precision after the decimal point) or the increase of the first modulus (possibly making it larger than typical word sizes such as 64-bit and therefore reducing performance). Ideally, one would choose an approximation interval that is both small and not close to 0 (i.e. ≥ 1), such as $(1, 2)$. In this case, the required degree for achieving high precision is quite low, as the interval is small and not close to 0. When developing an application using CKKS, one should make sure that any ciphertexts that are to be divided are scaled accordingly. In this paper, we assume an interval of $(1, 2)$.

TFHE: Division in TFHE is performed as integer division. The operation results in a separate quotient and remainder.

5.4 Square Root

CKKS: Just like the division operation, the square root is not natively supported in CKKS, and should therefore be approximated using the same techniques as the division operation. This approximation is much more straightforward however, as it is well defined in the range $(0, 1)$.

TFHE: The square root cannot be executed natively in TFHE either. It must be approximated. We do this by applying the Newton-Raphson method, which approximates the integer closest to the square root of an encrypted integer $N \in \mathbb{Z}$ using i iterations. The method can be seen in Algorithm 1.

5.5 Polynomial Evaluation

To test a more complex calculation that includes several additions and multiplications, we choose a random polynomial $f(x) = x^5 + 5x^4 + 4x^3 + x^2 + 2x$

Algorithm 1. Newton-Raphson square root approximation

Require: $N \in \mathbb{Z}, i \in \mathbb{N}$
Ensure: Approximated square root of N

```
x ← N/2
for i ← 1 to i do
    x ← 1/2 * (x + N/x)
end for
return x
```

which we evaluate in encrypted form. In FHE, it is important to keep the multiplicative depth as low as possible, which is why we evaluate our polynomial based on the Paterson-Stockmeyer method [24], making it possible to evaluate it with a depth of $\sqrt{n}$ instead of the polynomial degree n: We first divide f into two lower-degree polynomials $f_1(x) = x^3 + 5x^2 + 4x$ and $f_2(x) = x^2 + 2x$. We can then calculate $f(x) = x^2 * f_1(x) + f_2(x)$, resulting in a maximum depth of 3 non-scalar multiplications, instead of 5. As this calculation simply consists of a number of additions and multiplications, they can be implemented easily in both CKKS and TFHE.

5.6 Comparison Operation

CKKS: Performing comparisons in encrypted form is one of the most challenging operations in FHE, while at the same time being commonly used in many applications. The operation is not natively supported in CKKS. In addition, it is hard to approximate accurately as it is a step function and therefore not continuous. General approximation techniques such as Chebyshev polynomials are not suitable for this purpose. There has been some research into approximation techniques specific to this purpose. Cheon et al. [7] constructed two polynomials $g(x)$ and $f(x)$ with a certain degree n which, when combined, are able to approximate the general shape of a step function. They then propose to iteratively apply $g(x)$ d_g times, followed by $f(x)$ d_f times to approach a step function with the desired precision. Their proposed algorithm for comparison is shown in Algorithm 2.

The authors determined that the optimal combination of the parameters d_f, d_g and n is to select $n = 4$ and to set d_f and d_g as high as necessary until the required precision is achieved. For this paper, we follow this recommendation while setting the parameters high enough such that the relative error introduced by the approximation and the encryption combined does not exceed 2^{-32}.

TFHE: The comparison in TFHE is performed using a comparator circuit. Since TFHE supports logic operations, such a circuit can be evaluated in encrypted form without the need for approximation.

Algorithm 2. Comparison Function by Cheon et al.

Require: $a, b \in [0, 1], n, d_f, d_g \in \mathbb{N}$
Ensure: Approximated value of 1 if $a > b$, 0 if $a < b$ and 0.5 otherwise

```
x ← a − b
for i ← 1 to d_g do
    x ← g_n(x)
end for

for i ← 1 to d_f do
    x ← f_n(x)
end for
return (x + 1)/2
```

5.7 Bootstrapping

CKKS: The bootstrapping operation in CKKS resets the depth to allow for additional operations to be performed. However, bootstrapping also introduces noise to the ciphertext and therefore limits its precision. To reach our precision goal of 32 bits, we apply the iterative bootstrapping method developed by Bae et al. [2], which is implemented in the OpenFHE library.

TFHE: Since TFHE performs bootstrapping by default as part of each operation, we do not benchmark the bootstrapping operation by itself. In the case of functional bootstrapping, the calculation is performed as part of the bootstrapping itself through the use of look-up tables.

6 Results

In the following, we present and discuss the results of our study. We show measurements for the CKKS operations with two different batch sizes, as well as for the TFHE operations. Each result shows both the throughput (amortized runtime per individual input) and the latency (runtime of a whole operation). The precision of the individual measurements is not detailed here, as the primary objective was to guarantee a minimum precision threshold among all results.

6.1 Throughput

Figure 1 shows the throughput for an individual execution of each operation. As discussed above, for CKKS the throughput corresponds to the amortized runtime defined as the runtime of a batch divided by the batch size.

It is immediately clear that CKKS has a much better throughput when using higher batch sizes throughout all measured operations.

When using a higher batch size, it can be seen that for the basic operations of addition and multiplication, the CKKS scheme shows much better throughput compared to TFHE. Here, CKKS only requires fractions of a millisecond, while

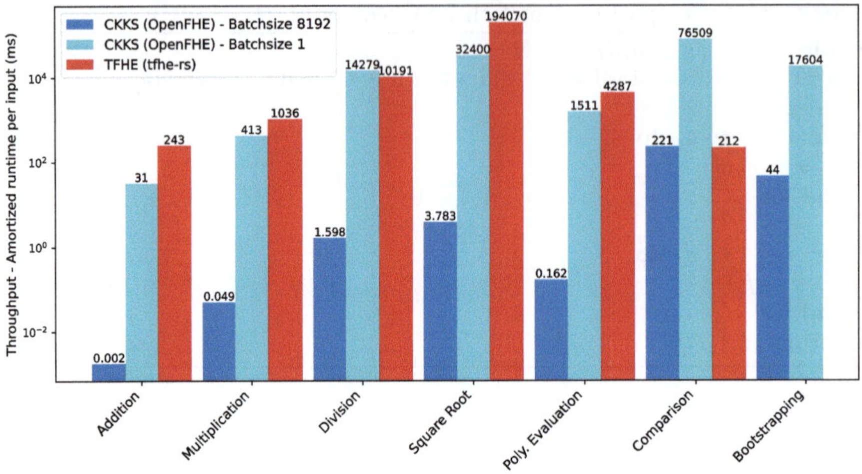

Fig. 1. Throughput of all benchmarked operations (milliseconds)

TFHE is on the order of hundreds of milliseconds to a second. The division and square root calculation in CKKS is considerably slower than the addition and multiplication, due to the fact that it needs to be approximated. To achieve our chosen precision requirements, the approximation is performed using Chebyshev polynomials with very high orders, which increases the complexity. However, CKKS still performs better than TFHE here. The division specifically appears to be a hard operation in TFHE, as a single execution takes about 10 s. The square root is the only operation in our list which cannot be calculated directly in TFHE, but must be approximated just like in CKKS. Here, we used the Newton-Raphson method. Due to its iterative nature and the fact that it uses costly divisions, the runtime is extremely high.

For the evaluation of our polynomial, we see the same trends as with addition and multiplication. We chose this benchmark to showcase how performance scales when several basic operations are used to calculate a more complex function. The polynomial evaluation consists of three ciphertext-ciphertext multiplications, three multiplications by constant and four additions. As we can see, the two schemes exhibit similar performance scaling compared to the individual additions and multiplications.

The comparison function on the other hand shows very different results. Here, the throughput is almost identical between the two schemes. This can be attributed to the fact that approximating the comparison function is difficult due to it being a discontinuous function. As it requires a large number of multiplications for accurate results, regular bootstrapping operations must be performed throughout the approximation, to avoid excessive depth. However, the bootstrapping operation in CKKS is much slower compared to TFHE, where bootstrapping is performed as part of every single operation with the use of the aforementioned functional bootstrapping, which is why we did not benchmark it separately. It should be noted that CKKS does not require bootstrapping to be performed after every operation. Due to its high cost, bootstrapping should be performed as little as possible. As can be seen in the graph, a single bootstrapping operation with batch size 8192 takes 44 ms per slot. Throughout the comparison function, we need to perform four bootstrapping operations. These operations make up a large part of the approximation.

6.2 Latency

Figure 2 shows the latency of each tested operation, i.e. the time it takes for one operation (batch) to finish. These results are identical to the throughput in the case of CKKS with batch size 1 as well as TFHE. The only difference is for CKKS with a higher batch size. One can see that for basic addition and multiplication, CKKS still outperforms TFHE, albeit with less margin. The same goes for the polynomial evaluation. The division function on the other hand is now slightly slower compared to TFHE. When looking at the latency, the comparison function is an extreme outlier. It is now vastly outperformed by the TFHE comparison function. It can be seen that the main driver for this effect is the performance of the bootstrapping operation. With higher batch size, this operation takes considerably longer compared to lower batch sizes. This is in contrast to the other operations in CKKS, where batch size appears to have almost no influence.

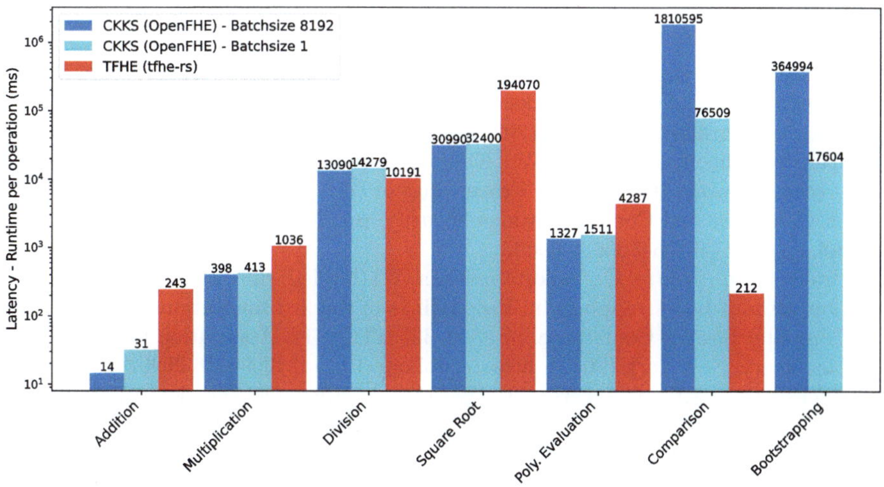

Fig. 2. Latency of all benchmarked operations (milliseconds)

7 Conclusion

Our evaluation of the schemes CKKS and TFHE show their respective strengths and trade-offs across different types of calculations. We tested the two schemes on multiple commonly used operations, each performed on a common dataset and with equal requirements for result precision. CKKS shows significant advantages when applications can leverage its batching capabilities. Lower batch sizes in CKKS do not appear to influence the latency in most calculations, except for the bootstrapping operation. The bootstrapping in CKKS seems to be the main bottleneck of performance, especially at higher batch sizes. The comparison operation is a prime example for an operation that is affected by this, as it requires multiple bootstrapping operations to avoid the depth to become excessive.

As CKKS is an approximate scheme, the precision of the results can be adjusted in order to achieve a certain trade-off between precision and runtime. In our study, we utilized a target precision of 32 bits. Increasing or decreasing the precision would have considerable impact on the runtime. The first reason for this, is that the approximated functions for division, square root and comparison would require higher degree polynomials or more iterations to achieve higher precisions and vice versa. Additionally, different precision targets would also affect the necessary parameters for CKKS, potentially requiring different ring dimensions, which would have an additional impact on performance.

References

1. Al Badawi, A., et al.: Openfhe: Open-source fully homomorphic encryption library. In: proceedings of the 10th workshop on encrypted computing & applied homomorphic cryptography, pp. 53–63 (2022). https://doi.org/10.1145/3560827.3563379
2. Bae, Y., Cheon, J.H., Cho, W., Kim, J., Kim, T.: META-BTS: bootstrapping precision beyond the limit. In: Proceedings of the 2022 ACM SIGSAC Conference on Computer and Communications Security, pp. 223–234. ACM (2022). https://doi.org/10.1145/3548606.3560696
3. Brakerski, Z., Gentry, C., Vaikuntanathan, V.: (leveled) fully homomorphic encryption without bootstrapping. In: Proceedings of the 3rd Innovations in Theoretical Computer Science Conference, pp. 309–325. ITCS '12. Association for Computing Machinery, New York (2012). https://doi.org/10.1145/2090236.2090262
4. Buchsbaum, A.L., Giancarlo, R., Westbrook, J.R.: On the determinization of weighted finite automata. SIAM J. Comput. **30**(5), 1502–1531 (2000). https://doi.org/10.1137/S0097539798346676
5. Cheon, J.H., Han, K., Kim, A., Kim, M., Song, Y.: Bootstrapping for approximate homomorphic encryption. In: Nielsen, J.B., Rijmen, V. (eds.) EUROCRYPT 2018. LNCS, vol. 10820, pp. 360–384. Springer, Cham (2018). https://doi.org/10.1007/978-3-319-78381-9_14
6. Cheon, J.H., Kim, A., Kim, M., Song, Y.: Homomorphic encryption for arithmetic of approximate numbers. In: Takagi, T., Peyrin, T. (eds.) ASIACRYPT 2017. LNCS, vol. 10624, pp. 409–437. Springer, Cham (2017). https://doi.org/10.1007/978-3-319-70694-8_15

7. Cheon, J.H., Kim, D., Kim, D.: Efficient homomorphic comparison methods with optimal complexity. In: Moriai, S., Wang, H. (eds.) ASIACRYPT 2020. LNCS, vol. 12492, pp. 221–256. Springer, Cham (2020). https://doi.org/10.1007/978-3-030-64834-3_8
8. Chillotti, I., Gama, N., Georgieva, M., Izabachène, M.: TFHE: fast fully homomorphic encryption over the torus. J. Cryptol. **33**(1), 34–91 (2020). https://doi.org/10.1007/s00145-019-09319-x
9. DESILO: Liberate.FHE: A New FHE Library for Bridging the Gap between Theory and Practice with a Focus on Performance and Accuracy (2023). https://github.com/Desilo/liberate-fhe
10. Droste, M., Gastin, P.: Weighted Automata and Weighted Logics, pp. 175–211. Springer, Heidelberg (2009). https://doi.org/10.1007/978-3-642-01492-5_5
11. Ducas, L., Micciancio, D.: FHEW: bootstrapping homomorphic encryption in less than a second. In: Oswald, E., Fischlin, M. (eds.) EUROCRYPT 2015. LNCS, vol. 9056, pp. 617–640. Springer, Heidelberg (2015). https://doi.org/10.1007/978-3-662-46800-5_24
12. Folkerts, L., Gouert, C., Tsoutsos, N.G.: REDsec: running encrypted discretized neural networks in seconds. In: Network and Distributed System Security Symposium (NDSS), pp. 1–17 (2023)
13. Gentry, C.: Fully homomorphic encryption using ideal lattices. In: Proceedings of the 41st Annual ACM Symposium on Theory of Computing, pp. 169–178. ACM (2009). https://doi.org/10.1145/1536414.1536440
14. Gentry, C., Sahai, A., Waters, B.: Homomorphic encryption from learning with errors: conceptually-simpler, asymptotically-faster, attribute-based. In: Canetti, R., Garay, J.A. (eds.) CRYPTO 2013. LNCS, vol. 8042, pp. 75–92. Springer, Heidelberg (2013). https://doi.org/10.1007/978-3-642-40041-4_5
15. Gouert, C., Mouris, D., Tsoutsos, N.: Sok: New insights into fully homomorphic encryption libraries via standardized benchmarks. Proceedings on Privacy Enhancing Technologies (2023). https://doi.org/10.56553/popets-2023-0075
16. Halevi, S., Shoup, V.: Design and implementation of HElib: a homomorphic encryption library. Cryptology ePrint Archive (2020)
17. HEaaN library. https://web.archive.org/web/20230627031842/https://github.com/snucrypto/HEAAN
18. Jiang, L., Ju, L.: FHEBench: Benchmarking fully homomorphic encryption schemes
19. Lattigo v6 (Aug 2024). https://github.com/tuneinsight/lattigo, ePFL-LDS, Tune Insight SA
20. Marcolla, C., Sucasas, V., Manzano, M., Bassoli, R., Fitzek, F.H., Aaraj, N.: Survey on fully homomorphic encryption, theory, and applications. Proc. IEEE **110**(10), 1572–1609 (2022). https://doi.org/10.1109/JPROC.2022.3205665, publisher: IEEE
21. Microsoft SEAL (release 4.1). https://github.com/Microsoft/SEAL
22. Nufhe, July 2019. https://github.com/nucypher/nufhe
23. PALISADE library. https://palisade-crypto.org/
24. Paterson, M.S., Stockmeyer, L.J.: On the number of nonscalar multiplications necessary to evaluate polynomials. SIAM J. Comput. **2**(1), 60–66 (1973). https://doi.org/10.1137/0202007
25. Rahman, T., Osmani, A.M.I.M., Rahman, M.S., Shibly, M.M.A., Islam, S.: Benchmarking fully homomorphic encryption libraries in IoT devices. In: Proceedings of the 11th International Conference on Networking, Systems, and Security, pp. 16–23. ACM (2024). https://doi.org/10.1145/3704522.3704546
26. Regev, O.: On lattices, learning with errors, random linear codes, and cryptography. J.ACM **56**(6), 34:1–34:40 (2009). https://doi.org/10.1145/1568318.1568324

27. TFHE library. https://github.com/tfhe/tfhe
28. Wang, R., et al.: Circuit bootstrapping: Faster and smaller. In: Joye, M., Leander, G. (eds.) Advances in Cryptology – EUROCRYPT 2024, pp. 342–372. Springer, Cham (2024). https://doi.org/10.1007/978-3-031-58723-8_12
29. Zama: TFHE-rs: A pure rust implementation of the TFHE scheme for boolean and integer arithmetics over encrypted data
30. Zhu, H., Suzuki, T., Yamana, H.: Performance comparison of homomorphic encrypted convolutional neural network inference among HElib, microsoft SEAL and OpenFHE. In: 2023 IEEE Asia-Pacific Conference on Computer Science and Data Engineering (CSDE), pp. 1–7. IEEE (2023). https://doi.org/10.1109/CSDE59766.2023.10487709

Tracking Micromobility-Battery-SOC-Levels with 3D-SUMO-Simulations Based on Real World Ride-Data

Emanuel Reichsöllner[1(✉)], Damir Ravlija[1], Andreas Freymann[2], and Mirko Sonntag[1]

[1] University of Applied Sciences, Esslingen, Germany
{emanuel.reichsoellner,damir.ravlija}@hs-esslingen.de,
andreas.freymann@iao.fraunhofer.de
[2] Fraunhofer IAO, Stuttgart, Germany
mirko.sonntag@hs-esslingen.de

Abstract. Micromobility vehicles such as e-bicycles, e-scooters, or e-mopeds are increasingly popular in urban areas. These vehicles are small, lightweight, and energy efficient and have great potential to be a perfect piece of the puzzle for sustainable mobility, especially for short trips in crowded cities. However, a crucial challenge is still the simulation of the vehicles' SOC levels, especially within hilly and steep terrains as this topography has a significant impact on the vehicle's battery. Knowing the SOC levels helps to plan battery swapping, charging, and reallocation operations of the vehicles. Thus, the focus of this paper is the determination of the SOC levels of a micromobility vehicle fleet based on a traffic simulation. We use an experimental feature of the microscopic traffic simulation environment SUMO to simulate micromobility trips in 3D. To appropriately model the influence of altitude differences on SOC levels, we also consider topological map information. The simulation is performed in the hilly terrain of Stuttgart, Germany and is validated with data from a local micromobility fleet provider. The presented improvements can further be utilized to assist in the development and optimization of micromobility fleet relocation strategies and charging point positioning algorithms.

Keywords: micromobility · shared mobility · traffic simulation · SUMO · elevation data · traction battery · SOC

1 Introduction

A decade ago, micromobility vehicles such as e-scooters, e-bikes or e-mopeds have become increasingly popular in many cities around the world. There are several reasons for the rise of micromobility vehicles, such as the potential to

L. Bechtel and T. Heer (Eds.): CCSSS 2025 PTT, pp. 109–124, 2026.
https://doi.org/10.1007/978-3-032-10569-1_7

reduce traffic in cities, offer cheaper travel costs, be more flexible in comparison to a car, or the enjoyment factor of driving a tiny vehicle. All of this was made possible by breakthroughs in battery research, which led to lightweight and cost-effective lithium ion batteries [1]. These batteries were first available in small consumer goods such as cellphones and cameras [1]. Later, lithium ion batteries with higher capacities were also used as traction batteries for micromobility vehicles and electric cars [2]. Besides the advantages of micromobility, there is still a challenge coming along with micromobility. Due to the fact that the "free-floating" model allows parking the vehicle wherever the user wants after a trip, the need to know and estimate the state of charge (SOC) of the vehicles increases. This information helps to establish a charging plan for the vehicles. In addition, an essential factor that influences the SOC level is hilly and steep terrain, which requires consideration of the altitude within the area where the vehicles move. Nowadays, when comparing micromobility vehicles with electric cars, it is noticeable that electric cars usually use a recuperation system that increases their range [3] and balances the negative effect of hilly and steep terrain on the range [4]. Conversely, micromobility vehicles are usually not equipped with recuperation systems due to their low recuperation potential and the high cost of power electronics that enable energy regeneration [5]. This leads to a significant loss of range for micromobility vehicles on uneven terrain. For micromobility providers, the determination of the SOC levels of their vehicles is an essential and necessary task [6]. Therefore, this paper presents an approach to simulate micromobility vehicles in hilly and steep terrain, track the state of charge (SOC) of the traction battery, and validate the results with real-world data. Traditionally, traffic simulation tools mainly focus on cars in 2D maps to model critical road sections and complex intersections with the aim of predicting traffic congestions [7] and finding solutions to increase traffic flow [8]. The use case presented in this work is a niche and therefore requires certain adjustments to standard *SUMO* traffic simulation models. These adjustments mainly comprise the shift from a 2D to a 3D map to improve the SOC tracking accuracy and the modeling of a battery-powered micromoblity vehicle.

The rest of this paper is structured as follows. Section 2 describes related work and highlights differences to this paper. In Sect. 3, the required preprocessing steps for the real-world ride-data are described. Section 4 describes the steps to create a 3D-*SUMO* model for battery powered micromobility vehicles, including *OpenStreetMap* data import, addition of topographical map information, and vehicle modeling. In Sect. 5, simulated data is compared to the real-world data. Finally, Sect. 6 summarizes this work and gives an outlook for future works.

2 Related Work

In this section, related work is presented that encompasses the microscopic traffic simulation environment *SUMO* in general, as well as further works, which consider electric vehicle simulations, bicycle simulations, and the inclusion of topographical map data.

2.1 Microscopic Traffic Simulation with *SUMO*

The traffic simulation environment *SUMO* [9] provides comprehensive features to perform accurate microscopic traffic simulations where each vehicle and its dynamics are modeled individually. To setup a traffic simulation model, a variety of data is needed. *SUMO* provides a large set of tools and scripts to collect and process the required data. With the *OSMWebWizard* [19] map data can easily be imported from *OpenStreetMap* [22] and random traffic of cars, buses, trams, motorcycles, bicycles, pedestrians and other types can be generated, so that a basic simulation model can be created within a few steps. Most traffic simulation tools like *SUMO* [9] initially focused mainly on accurate modeling of car traffic with 2D-maps. In reality, it is not sufficient to consider just cars, because the traffic modes are increasingly mixed and therefore many other vehicle types and pedestrians are also included in *SUMO*. Due to its comprehensive abilities and the open source approach, *SUMO* provides an ideal base for researchers and developers to add customized features for specific use cases.

2.2 Electric Vehicle Simulation with *SUMO*

In 2019 the paper *Evaluation of the Energy Consumption Model Performance for Electric Vehicles in SUMO* [13] and in 2021 the paper *Accurate physics-based modeling of electric vehicle energy consumption in the SUMO traffic microsimulator* [14], were published, both evaluating the potential and limitations of the *SUMO* EV energy consumption model [26]. Both works are focused on electric cars and not on micromobility vehicles.

2.3 Bicycle Simulation with *SUMO*

In 2023, the results of a workshop on the state of bicycle modeling in *SUMO* were published by A. Roosta et al. [10]. The goal of it was to identify required improvements to address the specific behavior of cyclists in *SUMO*. In this context, they identify the need for a bicycle vehicle type similar to the moped type we define below, and mention the challenges associated with the inclusion of elevation data into SUMO.

In the same year, Kaths and Roosta published a framework for simulating cyclists in *SUMO* [11], which provides a specific *CyclistModel*. This model represents the flexible behavior of cyclists and other non-lane-based road users, which quickly change between bicycle lanes and adjacent sidewalks [11]

2.4 *SUMO* Simulation using topographical (3D) maps

In 2018, Codeca and Härri published the *Monaco SUMO Traffic (MoST) Scenario* [12], which was the first freely available mobility scenario with elevation data based on proprietary topographic information. In 2024, Freymann et al. [15] published the toolset *SUMO3D4MicroMobility* [23] to simulate realistic micromobility trips in hilly and steep terrain. This toolset provides an easy-to-use workflow to add elevation data to the by default 2D SUMO network files. Compared to the MoST-Scenario [12], which uses proprietarly topographic map data, SUMO3D4MicroMobility [23] is based on the free *Open Topo Data* API [17].

This work also shows a proof of concept of how elevation changes and the energy consumption of an e-bicycle in hilly terrain could be tracked. However, this proof of concept lacks the comparison with real world energy consumption (SOC) values, where the current work is performed to close this gap. However in the current work the micromobility vehicle type is an e-moped instead of an e-bike.

3 Preprocessing of the Real World Ride-Data

For validation of the described approach, a dataset of 100.000 rides of a local micromobility provider in Stuttgart in the time period from beginning of 2020 until end of 2023 is used. The relevant ride-data comprise the start- and end-location (longitude and latitude), the trip-length and the loss of the battery SOC level in percent. In the following subsections the preprocessing steps for this real word ride-data are described.

3.1 Remove Short Trips up to 5 Km

The provided SOC-loss percentages of the real world ride-data, used to compare and validate the simulation results, are only given in integer values. There is no information, whether these integer values are assigned by rounding or truncating the real world SOC-loss percentages. Especially for shorter trips with small SOC-loss percentages the result-comparison is strongly affected by rounding or truncating the decimal places, which leads to intrinsic comparison errors. Typically micromobility rides are in a range of 2.6 km to 4.2 km [18], which contradicts the requirement for long rides with high SOC-loss percentages to avoid deviations by comparing to simulation-result due to rounding effects of the real world SOC integer values. After performing this step, from the total 100000 rides, 19552 rides with a trip-length greater than 5 km remained.

3.2 Reducing the Geographical Area

In Fig. 1 the area of Stuttgart with the initial real world ride-dataset with all 100.000 start positions is shown. To keep the simulation model small and efficient, the considered map area is reduced to the area marked with a yellow box, where the majority of the rides take place.

From the remaining 19552 rides with a trip-length greater than 5 km, only those rides within the yellow box should further be considered. Therefore the start- and end-position, as well as the whole path in between must be located with the yellow box. To perform this step, for each ride it was checked, whether *SUMO* finds a valid route within the yellow box shown in Fig. 1. After performing this step from the 19552 rides of the previous step, 4619 rides remained.

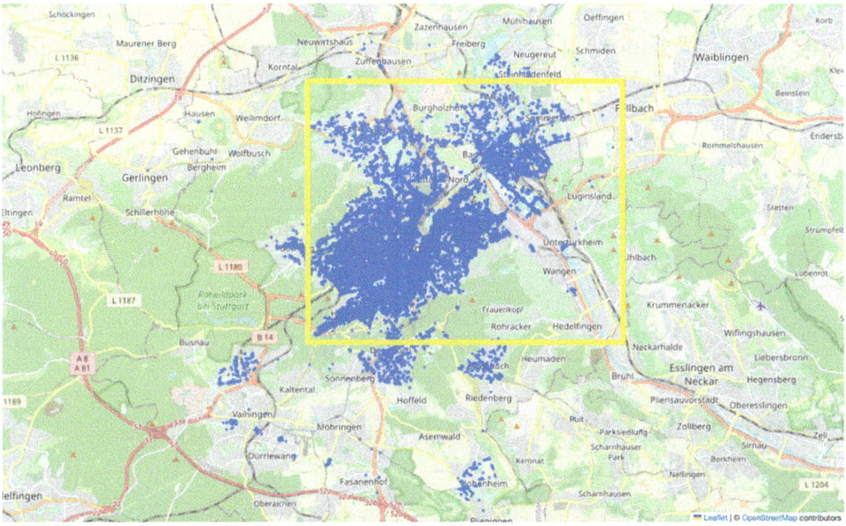

Fig. 1. Startpositions of the considered micromobility trips in Stuttgart (Germany)

3.3 Remove Trips with Unknown Paths

From the remaining 4619 trips, those trips where the path-length differs from the shortest path have to be removed. Due to the fact that for the ride-data only the start- and the end-Positions are known, just the shortest routes between these points are considered. To remove rides with unknown routes, for all 4619 trips the shortest routes were calculated with *SUMO* and compared with the trip-length of the real world data. If there is a deviation of more than 10% in trip-length, the trip is removed from the dataset. After performing this step, 1094 trips remained in the input-dataset. For two vehicles *SUMO* produced incomprehensible SOC-loss results and for another vehicle a routing error occurred, therefore this three rides were excluded from the dataset. Finally, from the 100000 total rides, 1091 trips remained in the input-dataset.

3.4 Filtering Distinct Uphill and Downhill Rides

For investigations on the performance and reliability of the *SUMO* EV energy consumption model [26] a separate consideration of distinct uphill- and downhill rides helps to validate the accuracy in this extreme cases. In the considered real world ride-data no pure uphill and downhill rides can be found, each of the 1091 trips has uphill and downhill sections. To filter distinct uphill- and downhill rides, in the first step two values, the *totalElevationIncrease* and *totalElevationDecrease* were calculated for each trip, by summing up the elevation difference for each timestep in the 3D-SUMO-Simulation. In the next step Eqs. (1) and (2) were used to calculate the *uphillRatio* and the *downhillRatio* for each trip. If the *uphillRatio* is greater than or equal to the set threshold value of 0.8 the trip is considered as uphill ride and if the *downhillRatio* is greater or equal to the set threshold value of 0.8 the trip is considered as downhill ride. After performing this step, 106 distinct uphill rides and 19 distinct downhill rides could be identified.

$$uphillRatio = \frac{totalElevationIncrease}{totalElevationIncrease + |totalElevationDecrease|} \quad (1)$$

$$downhillRatio = \frac{|totalElevationDecrease|}{totalElevationIncrease + |totalElevationDecrease|} \quad (2)$$

4 Setup of the SUMO-Model and Performing the Simulation

In this section the steps to setup the required *SUMO*-model and to perform the simulation are described. Figure 2 shows an overview of the workflow.

4.1 OpenStreetMap Data-Retrieval

In the first step, the selected map area from *OpenStreetMap* shown in Fig. 1 was imported to *SUMO* with the *OSMWebWizard*.

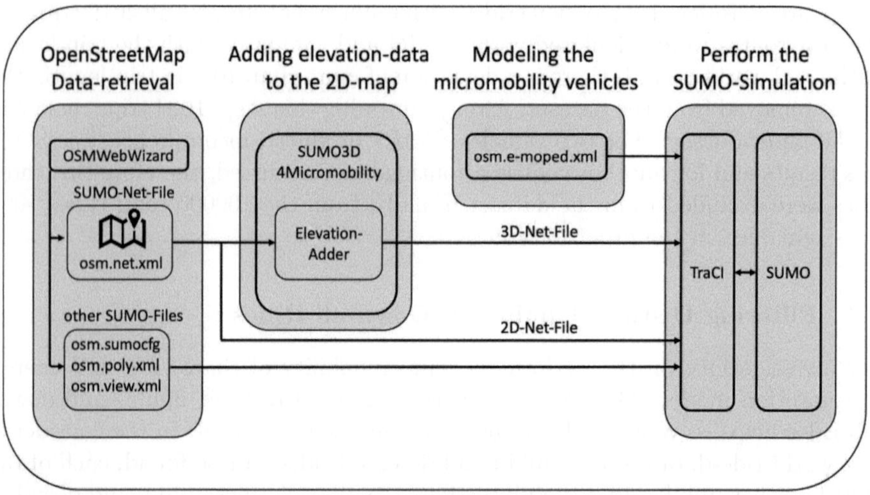

Fig. 2. Workflow to create the SUMO-Model

4.2 Adding Elevation Data to the 2D-Map

In Fig. 3 the topographic map of the selected area from Fig. 1 of Stuttgart is shown, where the different altitude-levels of this area can be seen. To add this elevation-data to the 2D-map (`osm.net.xml` file) the toolset *SUMO3D4MicroMobility* [23] was used. For each of the 43,235 nodes from the `osm.net.xml` file, the 2D-position is separately transferred to the *Open Topo Data* API [17] and the elevation data (z-coordinate) is retrieved. To avoid problems caused by the high number of API calls, the used map area should be kept as small as possible.

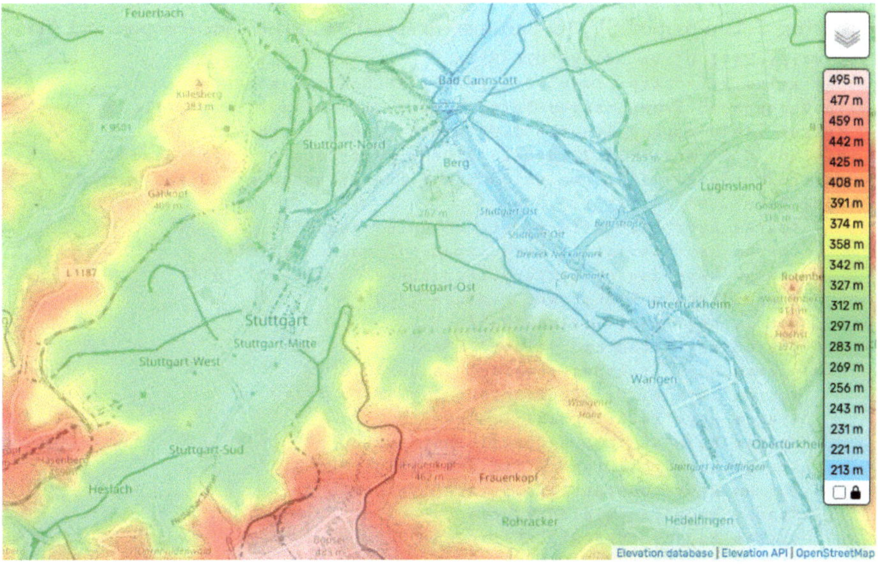

Fig. 3. Topographic-Map [16] of Stuttgart (Germany)

4.3 Modeling the Micromobility Vehicles

In the next step the micromobility vehicles, in this case e-mopeds, need to be modeled in *SUMO*. The properties of the e-moped are specified in XML-format in the file `osm.e-moped.xml`, which is shown in Listing 7.1. The main XML-tag in this file is *<routes>*, where the routes for each vehicle could be defined. The subtag *<vType>* is used to specify vehicle properties. The reason why no routes are defined here is that in this case the routes are not defined in a static way, but are instead generated dynamically with the *SUMO Traffic Control Interface (TraCI)* [20]. The manufacturer of the e-mopeds *emco electroroller GmbH* provides detailed technical information on the webpage [24]. For the used Model *emco NOVA* the following relevant values could be found: 79 kg vehicle weight, 11 kg battery weight, 37 Ah battery capacity and 1700 W engine performance. These values give a total vehicle weight of 90 kg and a battery capacity of 1776 Wh (for the used 48 V system). The passenger weight is assumed as 75 kg. Due to the fact that used e-mopeds are not equipped with recuperation systems, the values for *recuperationEfficiency* and *stoppingThreshold* are set to zero. The values for *frontSurfaceArea* and *airDragCoefficient* were estimated based on values for bicycles and motorcycles [25]. A detailed description of each parameter can be found in the *SUMO* documentation [26]. Due to the lack of data in the literature, assumptions had to be made for the parameters *rotatingMass*, *radialDragCoefficient*, *constantPowerIntake* and *propulsionEfficiency* based on default values for electric cars in the *SUMO* energy consumption model [26]. The complete set of parameters is shown in Listing 7.1.

Listing 7.1. e-moped SUMO-parameters specified in the `osm.e-moped.xml` file

```
<?xml version="1.0" encoding="UTF-8"?>
<routes xmlns:xsi="http://www.w3.org/2001/XMLSchema-instance"
 xsi:noNamespaceSchemaLocation="http://sumo.dlr.de/xsd/routes_file.xsd">
    <vType id="e-moped" length='1.6' width='0.65' height='1.7'
    minGap='0.5' accel='1.2' decel='3' emergencyDecel='7' maxSpeed='12.5'
    desiredMaxSpeed='11.1' emissionClass='Energy/unknown' vClass='moped'
    speedDev='0.1' color="1,0,0">
        <param key="has.battery.device" value="true"/>
        <param key="device.battery.capacity" value="1776"/>
        <param key="device.battery.chargeLevel" value="1776"/>
        <param key="maximumPower" value="1700"/>
        <param key="mass" value="90"/>
        <param key="loading" value="75"/>
        <param key="frontSurfaceArea" value="0.8"/>
        <param key="airDragCoefficient" value="0.7"/>
        <param key="rotatingMass" value="6"/>
        <param key="radialDragCoefficient" value="0.01"/>
        <param key="rollDragCoefficient" value="0.001"/>
        <param key="constantPowerIntake" value="5"/>
        <param key="propulsionEfficiency" value="0.98"/>
        <param key="recuperationEfficiency" value="0"/>
        <param key="stoppingThreshold" value="0.0"/>
    </vType>
</routes>
```

4.4 Performing the Simulation

As shown in Fig. 2, the *SUMO* Simulation was performed with the *SUMO Traffic Control Interface (TraCI)* [20], which brings the advantage that after each simulation step (usually one second) each parameter of the current simulated state can be retrieved and processed. This helps to perform statistical calculation during the runtime of the simulation. The other option would be to perform the simulation in a static way and to process the output files after the simulation is finished, which makes the process more complex. *TraCI* is available in several programming languages; in this case the *Python* [21] version of *TraCI* was used. The *SUMO*-simulations can be performed with or without a graphical user interface (GUI). In Fig. 4 the *SUMO-GUI* of the considered area of Stuttgart is shown. Each red entity in the figure represents an e-moped. To save simulation time, all 1091 e-moped rides are simulated simultaneously because the start time is not relevant for the SOC tracking. The simulation was performed twice, one 3D-SUMO-simulation and one 2D-SUMO-simulation. During each of the two simulations a separately evaluation for all 1091 considered rides, for the 106 uphill rides and for the 19 downhill rides was performed, which lead to six sets of results, shown in Table 1. The simulations were performed with *SUMO*-version 1.20 on a MacBook Air M3 with 16 GB RAM. The computation time was 199.8 s for the 3D-SUMO-simulation and 195.8 s for the 2D-SUMO-simulation.

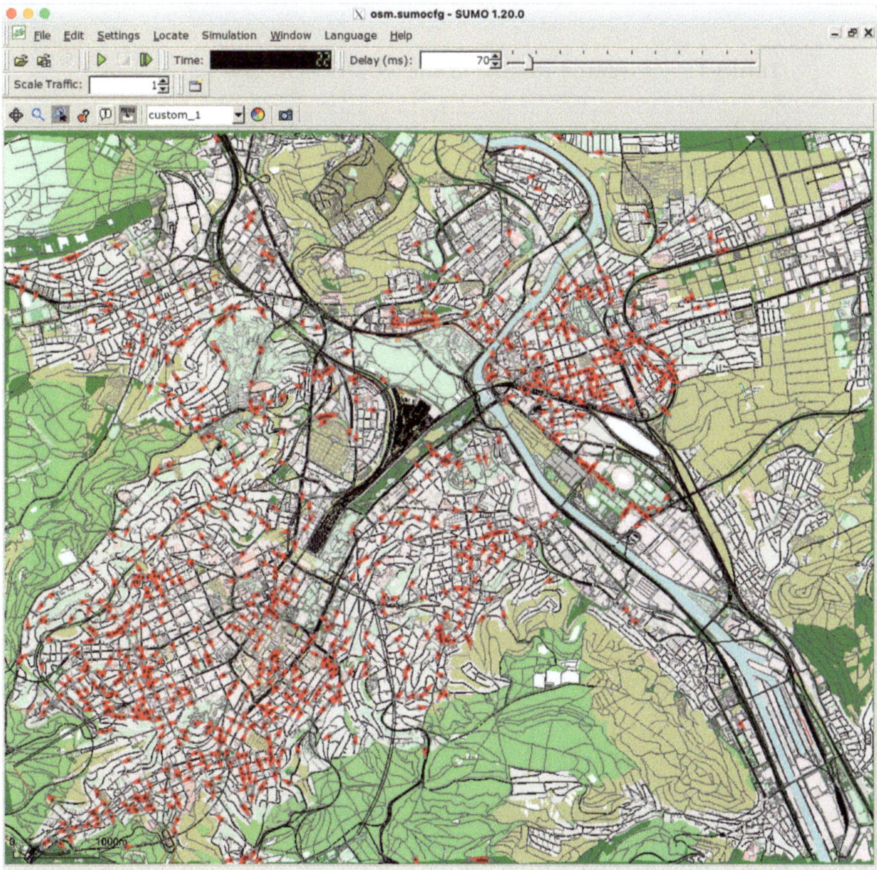

Fig. 4. SUMO Micromobility Simulation in Stuttgart (Germany)

5 Validation

In this section, the *SUMO* SOC-simulation results are presented and discussed. To simplify the results the SOC-loss is calculated as numbers in the interval

[0, 100] instead of percentage. The aggregated values, shown in Table 1, were calculated according Eq. (3) for the expected error value μ, Eq. (4) for the mean relative error (MRE), and Eq. (5) for the variance σ^2. The Number of used data points is represented by m in all of the equations. The expected error value μ gives a hint, whether the simulated SOC-loss values are biased to be too high or too low. The mean relative error (MRE) gives a measure on how precise the simulation result are and the variance σ^2 and standard deviation σ give a measure on how dispersed the simulation result are in relation to the expected value.

Table 1. Aggregated Results of the *SUMO* SOC-loss simulations

	m	μ	MRE	σ^2	σ
full 3D-SUMO-Simulation	1091	0.25	31%	6.99	2.64
full 2D-SUMO-Simulation	1091	−0.84	32%	9.0	3.0
uphill 3D-SUMO-Simulation	106	0.01	30%	22.83	4.78
uphill 2D-SUMO-Simulation	106	−1.91	31%	23.14	4.81
downhill 3D-SUMO-Simulation	19	0.81	33%	1.43	1.2
downhill 2D-SUMO-Simulation	19	2.0	56%	1.61	1.27

$$\mu = \frac{1}{m}\sum_{n=1}^{m}(simulated\_SOC\_loss_n - realWorld\_SOC\_loss_n) \tag{3}$$

$$MRE = \frac{1}{m}\sum_{n=1}^{m}\frac{|\mu_n|}{|realWorld\_SOC\_loss_n|} \tag{4}$$

$$\sigma^2 = \frac{1}{m}\sum_{n=1}^{m}((simulated\_SOC\_loss_n - realWorld\_SOC\_loss_n) - \mu_n)^2 \tag{5}$$

In Fig. 5 the error-distribution-diagram for the full 3D-SUMO-Simulation is shown. A shift towards the positive x-axis (blue solid vertical line) compared to the origin (white dashed vertical line) can be seen, which indicates that the simulated SOC-loss values tend to be too high. In the opposite in Fig. 6 the error-distribution-diagram for the full 2D-SUMO-Simulation is shown, but here a shift towards the negative x-axis (the expected error is represented by the solid vertical line) compared to zero (dashed vertical line) can be seen, which indicates that the simulated SOC-loss values tend to be too low.

The results show that in general the accuracy of the 3D-*SUMO*-Simulation is, as expected, higher than the 2D-*SUMO*-Simulation. The aggregated SOC-loss is, as expected, for the 2D-*SUMO*-Simulation too low, but it is not clear why the aggregated SOC-loss for the 3D-*SUMO*-Simulation is too high. Due to the lack of recuperation systems in micromobility vehicles [5] this observation correspond to the assumption that 2D-simulations are not sufficient for micromobility SOC-simulations.

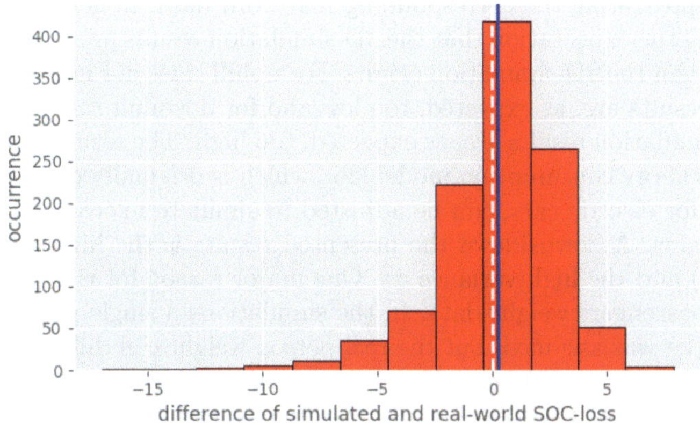

Fig. 5. error-distribution-histogram for the full 3D-SUMO-Simulation

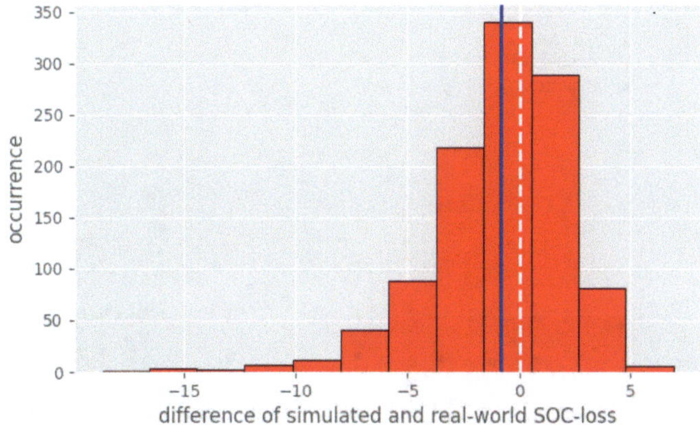

Fig. 6. error-distribution-histogram for the full 2D-SUMO-Simulation

In Figs. 7 and 8 the simulated and real world SOC-loss values are compared in a scatter charts for uphill rides. For a better insight to the close together results, the chart was split into two parts. In Figs. 9 and 10 the corresponding results for downhill rides are shown and are also split into two parts. On the x-axis the average elevation ratio is applied. In Figs. 7 and 8 the values are on a positive axis and correspond the ratio of all increased elevation meters during an uphill ride, divided by the trip-length. In Figs. 9 and 10 the values are on a negative x-axis and correspond the ratio of all decreased elevation meters during a downhill ride, divided by the trip-length. On the y-axis each result for a single micromobility vehicle consists of three dots (at the same x-position), a red dot representing the 3D simulation result, a blue dot representing the 2D simulation result and a green dot representing the corresponding real word data. In general, the results are according the expectation that the 3D-simulation results are closer to the real world data than the 2D-simulation results. For uphill rides in Figs. 7 and 8 the 2D simulation results are, as expected, too low and for downhill rides in Figs. 9 and 10 the 2D simulation results are, as expected, too high. The results show that the *SUMO* EV energy consumption model [26], which is originally designed to track SOC states for electric cars, can be adjusted to simulate micromobility vehicles in hilly terrains. A downside of the presented results is the high mean relative error (MRE) and the high variance σ^2. One major reason for this observation is the lack of passengers weight-data. In the simulations a single passenger with a weight of 75 kg was assumed, but the real person weight can differ strongly from this value and the considered e-moped even allows two passengers, which leads to a higher deviation. Compared to electric cars, the ratio of passenger weight to vehicle weight is much higher for micromobility vehicles due to their low weight (in this case 90 kg) that the passenger weight can even surpass the vehicle weight. For a more detailed validation of the *SUMO* EV energy consumption model [26] additional data for passenger weights are essential.

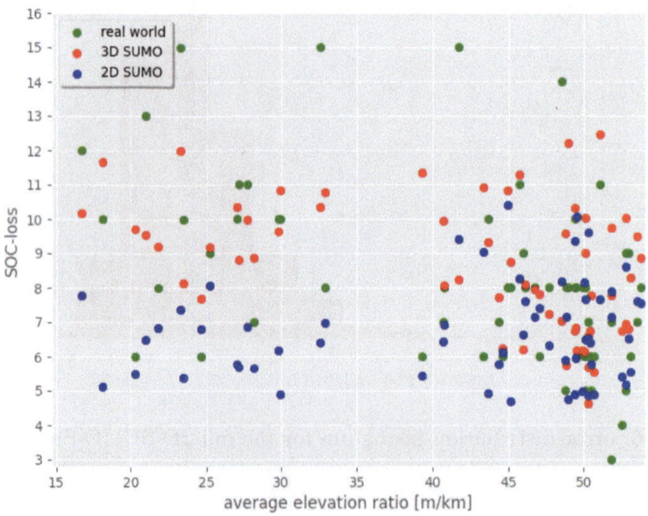

Fig. 7. SOC-loss result comparison for uphill rides (part 1)

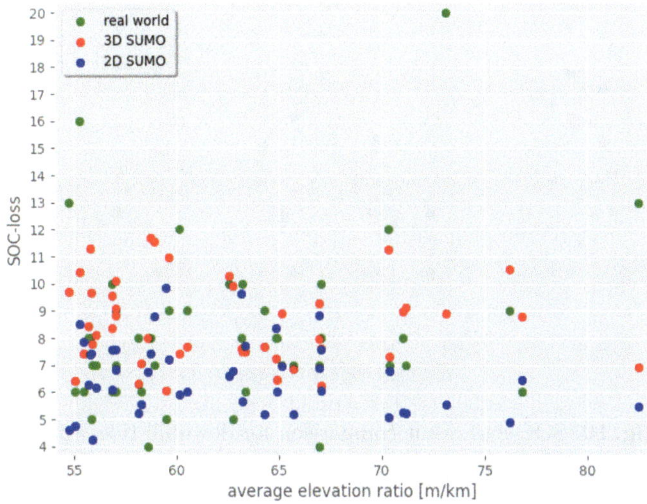

Fig. 8. SOC-loss result comparison for uphill rides (part 2)

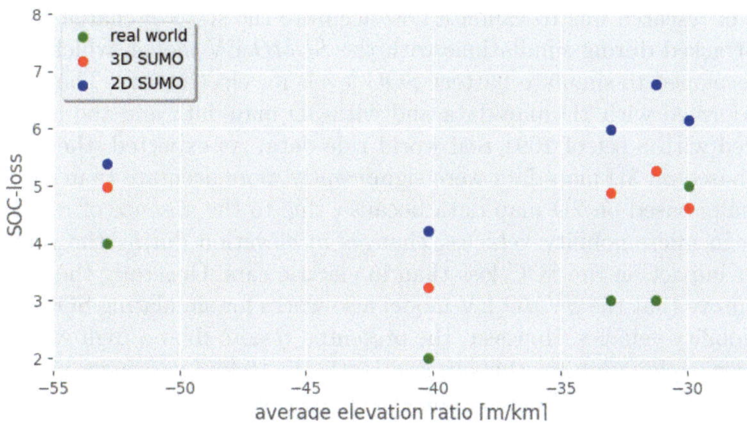

Fig. 9. SOC-loss result comparison for downhill rides (part 1)

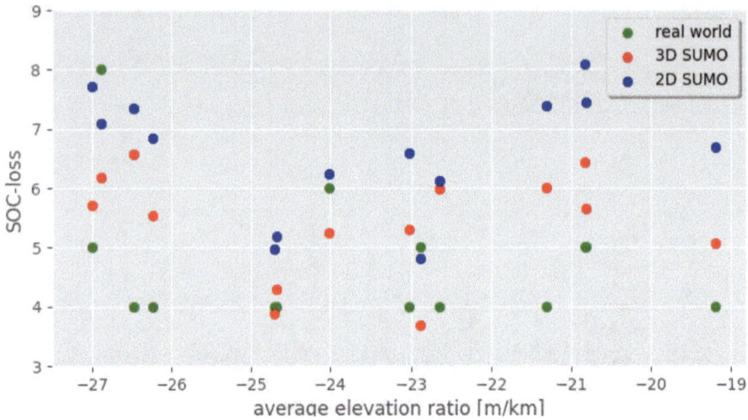

Fig. 10. SOC-loss result comparison for downhill rides (part 2)

6 Conclusion and Future Work

In this work the traffic simulation environment *SUMO* was used to simulate micromobility (e-moped) rides in the hilly terrain of Stuttgart, Germany. The subject of research was to validate how accurate the state of charge (SOC) loss can be tracked during simulations with the *SUMO* EV model, which was originally developed to simulate battery SOC levels for electric cars. The simulation was performed with 2D map-data and with 3D map-data and the results were compared with a set of 1091 real world ride-data. As expected, the simulation results based on 3D map-data were significantly more accurate than the simulation results based on 2D map data because, due to the absence of recuperation systems in micromobility vehicles, changes in elevation during the ride have a stronger impact on the SOC loss than in electric cars. Generally the simulation results prove that the *SUMO* EV model also works for simulating SOC losses for micromobility vehicles. However, the presented results show a high variance and one major explanation for this observation is the lack of passenger weight data. In the presented simulations a vehicle weight of 90 kg was set and a passenger weight of 75 kg was assumed, which shows that the passenger weight has a strong influence on the total weight and highly affects the simulation results. Therefore, further investigations with more detailed real world ride-data including the passenger weight need to be performed to evaluate the limits of accuracy of the *SUMO* EV model in context of micromobiliy vehicles.

References

1. Blomgren, G.E.: The development and future of lithium ion batteries. J. Electrochem. Soc. **164**(1), A5019–A5025 (2017). https://doi.org/10.1149/2.0251701je
2. Fichtner, M.: Recent research and progress in batteries for electric vehicles. Batteries Supercaps **5**(2), e202100224 (2022). https://doi.org/10.1002/batt.202100224

3. Spichartz, P., Bubmann, L., Sourkounis, C.: Comparison of recuperation strategies for electric vehicles regarding energy efficiency. In: IECON 2014 - 40th Annual Conference of the IEEE Industrial Electronics Society, pp. 2984–2990. IEEE, Dallas, TX, USA (2014). https://doi.org/10.1109/IECON.2014.7048934
4. Marčev, D., Kotek, M.: Influence of the road profile in different geographical areas of the Czech R epublic to the operational parameters of the electric vehicle, p. 652.4Kb (2018). https://doi.org/10.15159/AR.18.071
5. Korzilius, O., Borsboom, O., Hofman, T., Salazar, M.: Optimal design of electric micromobility vehicles. In: 2021 IEEE International Intelligent Transportation Systems Conference (ITSC), pp. 1677–1684. IEEE, Indianapolis, IN, USA (2021). https://doi.org/10.1109/ITSC48978.2021.9564429
6. Heumann, M., Kraschewski, T., Brauner, T., Tilch, L., Breitner, M.H.: A spatiotemporal study and location-specific trip pattern categorization of shared e-scooter usage. Sustainability **13**(22), 12527 (2021). https://doi.org/10.3390/su132212527
7. Hu, W., Wang, H., Yan, L.: An actual urban traffic simulation model for predicting and avoiding traffic congestion. In: 17th International IEEE Conference on Intelligent Transportation Systems (ITSC), pp. 2681–2686. IEEE, Qingdao, China (2014). https://doi.org/10.1109/ITSC.2014.6958119
8. Roberg-Orenstein, P., Abbess, C., Wright, C.: Traffic jam simulation. J. Maps **3**(1), 107–121 (2007). https://doi.org/10.1080/jom.2007.9710832
9. Lopez, P.A., et al.: Microscopic traffic simulation using SUMO. In: 2018 21st International Conference on Intelligent Transportation Systems (ITSC), pp. 2575–2582. IEEE, Maui, HI (2018). https://doi.org/10.1109/ITSC.2018.8569938
10. Roosta, A., Kaths, H., Barthauer, M., Erdmann, J., Flötteröd, Y.-P., Behrisch, M.: State of bicycle modeling in SUMO. In: SUMO Conference Proceedings, vol. 4, pp. 55–64 (2023). https://doi.org/10.52825/scp.v4i.215
11. Kaths, H., Roosta, A.: Framework for simulating cyclists in SUMO. In: SUMO Conference Proceedings, vol. 4, pp. 105–113 (2023). https://doi.org/10.52825/scp.v4i.219
12. Codeca, L., Härri, J.: Monaco SUMO traffic (MoST) scenario: a 3D mobility scenario for cooperative ITS. In: Presented at the SUMO 2018- Simulating Autonomous and Intermodal Transport Systems, pp. 43–29. https://doi.org/10.29007/1zt5
13. Sagaama, I., Kchiche, A., Trojet, W., Kamoun, F.: Evaluation of the energy consumption model performance for electric vehicles in SUMO. In: 2019 IEEE/ACM 23rd International Symposium on Distributed Simulation and Real Time Applications (DS-RT), pp. 1–8. IEEE, Cosenza, Italy (2019). https://doi.org/10.1109/DS-RT47707.2019.8958704
14. Koch, L., et al.: Accurate physics-based modeling of electric vehicle energy consumption in the SUMO traffic microsimulator. In: 2021 IEEE International Intelligent Transportation Systems Conference (ITSC), pp. 1650–1657. IEEE, Indianapolis, IN, USA (2021). https://doi.org/10.1109/ITSC48978.2021.9564463
15. Freymann, A., Reichsöllner, E., Ravlija, D., Trautwein, I., Sonntag, M.: Integrating topographical map information in SUMO to simulate realistic micromobility trips in hilly and steep terrains. In: SUMO Conference Proceedings, vol. 5, pp. 235–246 (2024). https://doi.org/10.52825/scp.v5i.1131
16. topographic-map.com. https://en-gb.topographic-map.com/map-vpm5k/Stuttgart. Accessed 18 Feb 2025
17. Open Topo Data. http://www.opentopodata.org. Accessed 18 Feb 2025

18. Schwinger, F., Tanriverdi, B., Jarke, M.: Comparing micromobility with public transportation trips in a data-driven spatio-temporal analysis. Sustainability **14**(14), 8247 (2022). https://doi.org/10.3390/su14148247
19. OSMWebWizard. https://sumo.dlr.de/docs/Tutorials/OSMWebWizard.html. Accessed 18 Feb 2025
20. SUMO-TraCI. https://sumo.dlr.de/docs/TraCI.html. Accessed 26 Feb 2025
21. Python. https://www.python.org. Accessed 26 Feb 2025
22. OpenStreetMap. https://www.openstreetmap.org. Accessed 18 Feb 2025
23. SUMO3D4MicroMobility. https://github.com/keim-hs-esslingen/SUMO3D4MicroMobility. Accessed 18 Feb 2025
24. emco-e-Scooter. https://www.emco-e-scooter.com/elektroroller/e-roller-retro-nova. Accessed 21 Feb 2025
25. auto-wiki. https://automobil-guru.de/auto-wiki/cw-wert-heute-wichtiger-denn-je/. Accessed 07 Apr 2025
26. SUMO-EV-Model. https://sumo.dlr.de/docs/Models/Electric.html. Accessed 26 Feb 2025

Unmasking SSH Attackers: A Study on Brute-Force Attempts and Cryptographic Usage

Bastian Buck(✉) and Tobias Heer

Esslingen University of Applied Sciences, 73728 Esslingen, Germany
{Bastian.Buck,Tobias.Heer}@hs-esslingen.de

Abstract. The SSH protocol is ubiquitous on today's Internet and is mainly used for remote administration of servers. Usernames and associated passwords (or keys) are typically used to access SSH servers. The combination of a common username and a password that is difficult to guess provides extensive access to the systems and is therefore an attractive target for attackers. As real quantum computers approach in time, post-quantum cryptography also becomes more relevant alongside existing password attacks. In this work, we logged SSH brute-force attempts over a period of 7 months using a honeypot in the US to analyze the current attack behavior. Our results show that SSH attackers do not use PQC algorithms and prefer traditional cryptography. Furthermore, we confirm typical attack patterns from previous work, but also show relevant attack days of the year, mainly during holidays, and identify regional irregularities in the origin of IP addresses. In addition, we analyze the attack behavior of the 2024 discovered xz-Utils backdoor.

Keywords: SSH Attacks · SSH Brute-Force · SSH Honeypot · SSH Security · xz-Utils Backdoor

1 Introduction

Administrators use Secure Shell (SSH) worldwide for the administration of ser-vers. The protocol is particularly common for devices with no physical access, e.g. large data centers. In addition to other functionalities such as port-forwarding, SSH usually provides access to the server in the form of a shell, often with high privileges. High privileges refer to access by a user who can obtain administrative access, also known as root privileges, on the device. SSH is typically exposed to the Internet for this purpose. As a result, SSH is a popular target for attacks on the Internet. In addition to secure access options, which primarily consist of username-password or username-key combinations, modern cryptographic primitives are crucial for ensuring secure transmission at the transport layer in SSH. If attackers guess an access method or break cryptographic protocols, the affected server and possibly also the client device are considered

L. Bechtel and T. Heer (Eds.): CCSSS 2025 PTT, pp. 125–139, 2026.
https://doi.org/10.1007/978-3-032-10569-1_8

compromised. Infections with malware or the publication of confidential (customer) data are possible consequences.

However, insights into such attacker activities are rare. Therefore, in this research, we aim to collect and analyze information about attackers and password brute-force behavior from the Internet, as well as cryptographic primitives used. To investigate the behavior, we set up a honeypot in an AWS instance in California, USA. We monitored this instance for a duration of 227 days since July 5, 2024 and used results up to February 16, 2025. We modified the SSH server to avoid detection as a honeypot and to collect additional information.

This work is organized as follows. In Sect. 2, we present related work. Section 3 highlights the structure of the honeypot and the methodology of the analysis. In Sect. 4, we present the results of our analysis. We focus on aspects such as the use of cryptographic primitives, username-password behavior, as well as the origin of the attackers and preferred special days of the year. We conclude the paper in Sect. 5.

2 Related Work

Attacks on SSH servers are not new and have been very common to date. In this work, we evaluate common attack metrics and the cryptography used by attackers. Several works followed similar approaches and are of relevance.

More recent work by Faust [1] from 2018 and Hetzler et al. [2] from 2023 use ready to use honeypot systems such as the open source system Cowrie [3]. Otherwise, the observation times for the studies [2,4–6] are very short at 10 h to 45 days to produce comprehensive results. Bell [7] shows various attack metrics over a long period of time in its web overview, but there has been no update since 2021. Something similar can also be found in the work of Cisco [8]. An alternative with comparable but missing metrics (only IP address, usernames and passwords are logged) shows Netwatch-Team [9] with daily updated values. Cao et al. [10] develop a comprehensive system, including an SSH honeypot. With a runtime of 463 days, these results can be meaningful, but detailed values like the analysis of IP addresses or usernames are missing.

The vast majority of papers evaluate basic metrics such as total attacks, usernames, passwords and IP addresses. In most cases, the root user is attacked, the password 123456 is used and most of the attacking IP addresses are localized in China and the USA. In our work, we are able to confirm these results. In addition, we elaborate on the cryptography used, which so far can only be found in the outdated work of Bell [7]. In addition to the basic metrics, we inspect special days of the year, like holidays, and their characteristics (and therefore update the work of Faust [1]) as well as affiliation to botnet-like behavior. Furthermore, we investigate the attack behavior against the xz-Utils backdoor in the context of SSH.

3 Honeypot and Analysis Methodology

In this Section, we describe the structure of our honeypot, necessary changes to obtain data and the methodology of our analysis. We deliberately did not use an existing honeypot solution such as Cowrie [3], sshesame [11] or ssh-honeypot [12], as these can easily be classified as a honeypot, since these usually use specific and outdated SSH versions, and we wanted to avoid this.

3.1 Honeypot

We built the honeypot ourselves and hosted it on Amazon Web Services (AWS). Our honeypot is located in an EC2 instance in the AWS Northern California region. The operating system is Ubuntu 24.04. The SSH server is a modified and locally compiled version of the well-known OpenSSH project and runs on ports 22 and 23, whereby no distinction is made between these in the analysis. Over the period of the analysis, we modified versions 9.6p1, 9.8p1 and 9.9p1 of the OpenSSH server. As version 9.7p1 does not contain any security patches, we omitted this version. For the OpenSSH honeypot, we used the program code from openssh-portable [13] so that various components of a possible attack are logged. We adapted the configuration of OpenSSH (file `sshd_config`) so that logins to local users are not possible, but a possible authentication on the server is still simulated. We only adapted the cryptographic primitives of the server from version 9.9p1 to the standard ciphers of version 9.6p1. We did not modify the logging, which runs unchanged with the systemd service.

The most important features of our logging include remote IP address, remote port, attempted username and password. To achieve this, we primarily modified or extended debug messages so that they are logged even without debug mode. Other characteristics that we also log are the time, date, characteristics of an attempted attack with the xz-Utils backdoor, and cryptographic primitives that are relevant when establishing a connection for key exchange (KEX), host key, encryption (client->server and server->client), message authentication (MAC), and compression. The cryptographic primitives cannot currently be assigned to the attacking IP addresses, as this would mean significant changes to our program code and we therefore omitted them for this work. Consequently, the data cannot be cross-correlated.

We also included a detection of possible attacks by the xz-Utils packer backdoor found in 2024. The backdoor, summarized under CVE-2024-3094, made it possible to gain direct root access via a specific Ed448 key by integrating xz-Utils into systemd and this into the OpenSSH process of various Linux-based operating systems [14]. Since no studies on the exploitation of this attack are published so far and an attack is trivial, we added this to our work. For the detection of an attack using the xz-Utils backdoor, which could compromise a vulnerable server, we added the program code of [15]. In our case, the OpenSSH honeypot always specifies the same server version 9.6p1, as this was the only version at the time of the xz-Utils backdoor. We adapted the program code accordingly. As a result of the changes, the server is not vulnerable to the xz-Utils backdoor vulnerability, but logs attempts to exploit this vulnerability.

3.2 Analysis Methodology

The logging of OpenSSH is extensive and shows many important as well as unimportant values for us when using systemd, which is why we save them in separate files. These files are archived daily. The logging of the primary characteristics (username, password, remote IP address, remote port, xz-Utils backdoor attempts, date and time) were stored from Jul 05, 2024 to Feb 16, 2025 (227 days). We added the logging of the cryptographic primitives to the honeypot on Dec. 23, 2024 (56 days), so results may be less representative accordingly. We finished the analysis of the cryptographic properties on Feb. 16, 2025.

For our analysis, we implemented several programs in Python which, on the one hand, capture and store components of the log data and, on the other, perform the relevant analyses and generate graphics. To analyze the country of origin of the attacking party, we used the API of the online service IPinfo.io [16]. We also adjusted the corresponding date according to the day of the week and US public holidays. We used the Python project holidays [17] to determine the public US holidays.

4 Results

In this Chapter, we present the results of our study. We collected connection data from July 5, 2024 up to and including February 16, 2025, i.e. a total of 227 days. During the evaluation of the 316,726 logged authentication attempts, we were able to identify various attack patterns, most of them matching our expectations. However, the built-in logging of a potential xz-Utils backdoor attack only recorded our own tests. We were unable to record attacks from other parties. The next parts of this Section are organized as follows. First, we analyze the use of cryptographic primitives by the attacking hosts and compare these with the default settings of common SSH client programs. This allows us to differentiate between natural client behavior and that of an attacker. We then examine the effects of the location of the attacking hosts via the IP addresses. We then evaluate the username and password behavior. By doing so, we discovered possible botnet behavior, which we determined by comparing the behavior of different attacking parties. Finally, we examine the influence of the day of the year.

Since our honeypot runs in the AWS cloud, certain fluctuations in the results compared to other cloud providers or vendors are to be expected. We therefore cannot determine which attackers specifically attack or avoid AWS cloud hosts. Consequently, we also cannot identify attackers who do not attack AWS hosts. Also it cannot be ruled out that attackers recognized our honeypot as such and adapted their behaviour accordingly.

4.1 Cryptographic Primitives Used by Attackers

In this Section, we first analyze the influence of key exchange algorithms. Then we evaluate the host-key behavior and subsequently the used symmetric encryption algorithms and associated MACs. We carried out the logging of cryptographic primitives in a shorter frame from Dec. 23, 2024 up to and including Feb. 16, 2025 (56 days). However, an assignment between cryptographic algorithms and IP addresses is not possible with this implementation.

We adjusted the allowed cryptographic primitives that an OpenSSH server has in its default configuration in version 9.6p1 (e.g., in 9.9p1, "mlkem768x25519-sha256" was added as a KEX). We left this unchanged despite updates to newer versions due to the xz-Utils backdoor, which only persisted in this version. To create a distinction between clients and the attacking hosts in our logging, we show default settings for individual clients in Table 1. It should be noted that clients may prefer newer algorithms such as Ed448, but our honeypot does not accept this. We therefore chose the first preferred primitive.

Table 1. Order of cryptographic primitives provided by common SSH client programs (per first algorithm occurring in results)

Client	KEX	Host-Key	Cipher	MAC
Putty[26]	sntrup761x25519-sha512@openssh.com	Ed25519	chacha20-poly1305@openssh.com	-
OpenSSH (Client)[27]	sntrup761x25519-sha512@openssh.com	Ed25519	chacha20-poly1305@openssh.com	umac-64-etm@openssh.com
Tabby[28]	curve25519-sha256	Ed25519	chacha20-poly1305@openssh.com	hmac-sha2-512-etm@openssh.com
libssh (Library)[29]	curve25519-sha256	Ed25519	chacha20-poly1305@openssh.com	hmac-sha2-256-etm@openssh.com
russh (Rust Library)[30]	curve25519-sha256	Ed25519	chacha20-poly1305@openssh.com	hmac-sha2-512-etm@openssh.com

According to our results, which we present in Table 2, attacking hosts seem to prefer pre-PQC algorithms for key exchange. The only post-quantum cryptography (PQC) algorithm accepted by our honeypot (sntrup761x25519-sha512@openssh.com) was never used. Curve25519 (11,123 occurrences or ~96,6%; standardized by the IETF in [20]) emerges as the preferred KEX algorithm. ECDH [21] with the 3 different curve types (key length 384 and 521 not used at all) and the various Diffie-Hellman groups are rarely used in comparison. The insecure DH group with ID 14 is used 24 times (~0,2%). In comparison, clients such as Putty or OpenSSH use the PQC algorithm, the others and also libraries prefer Curve25519. As Curve25519 and not PQC was predominantly used, these clients can effectively be excluded, which does not mean that they were not reconfigured. We assume that attackers avoid PQC algorithms, at least in our honeypot. One reason for this may be that PQC algorithms such as sntrup768 [18] or mlkem [19] are currently only available as Internet-Drafts from the IETF. Furthermore, PQC algorithms are usually more inefficient than pre-PQC algorithms, which is useless for these types of attacks, because SSH attackers rely on speed. In addition, pre-PQC algorithms are currently secure and seem to be accepted by attackers despite possible "harvest now, decrypt later" methods.

Table 2. Order of the cryptographic primitives provided by the honeypot and number of occurrences. Values in brackets show the occurence of no matching algorithm. In the encryption algorithm section the values in brackets show the differences in the choice of cipher by the server, as both may use different algorithms.

Type and cryptographic algorithm	Number of occurrences
key exchange algorithms (KEX) and (no match)	**11509 (2)**
sntrup761x25519-sha512@openssh.com	-
curve25519-sha256	9518
curve25519-sha256@libssh.org	1605
ecdh-sha2-nistp256	243
ecdh-sha2-nistp384	-
ecdh-sha2-nistp521	-
diffie-hellman-group-exchange-sha256 (4096-bit)	95
diffie-hellman-group16-sha512	-
diffie-hellman-group18-sha512	-
diffie-hellman-group14-sha256	24
host-key algorithms and (no match)	**11512 (25)**
rsa-sha2-512 (3072-bit)	96
rsa-sha2-256 (3072-bit)	6
ecdsa-sha2-nistp256	7167
ssh-ed25519	4218
encryption algorithms (ciphers) client->server (difference server->client)	**11490 (+2)**
chacha20-poly1305@openssh.com	199 (0)
aes128-ctr	1718 (+1)
aes192-ctr	-
aes256-ctr	259 (0)
aes128-gcm@openssh.com	5386 (+1)
aes256-gcm@openssh.com	3928 (0)
message authentication (MAC) + (implicit (by AEAD mode)**)**	**22982 + (19027)**
umac-64-etm@openssh.com	12
umac-128-etm@openssh.com	-
hmac-sha2-256-etm@openssh.com	2812
hmac-sha2-512-etm@openssh.com	-
hmac-sha1-etm@openssh.com	117
umac-64@openssh.com	-
umac-128@openssh.com	-
hmac-sha2-256	894
hmac-sha2-512	66
hmac-sha1	54
compression	**22982**
zlib@openssh.com + none	0 + 22982

The host keys are required to identify the server and are normally rarely renewed. As a host key algorithm, ECDSA with ~62,3% (7,167 occurrences) clearly stands out from Ed25519 [22] keys with ~36,6% (4,218 occurrences), although all clients from Table 1 prefer this key type. RSA host keys are clearly in the minority with a total of 102 occurrences (~0,9%), although the IETF still accepts them in [23]. The algorithm can also be changed in the clients. Despite the usual specification of the Ed25519 algorithm in clients, ECDSA is used more frequently. We therefore assume that the attackers used none of the clients. In addition, Ed25519 keys were not standardized for very long, which could mean that older libraries or clients used by attackers do not yet support them.

Symmetric encryption is required in a total of 11,490 cases, each for client to server and server to client. The values can be found in Table 2 in the third row and can be divided into AEAD modes and counter mode. The latter requires a subsequent MAC, AEAD calculates both functionalities at the same time. In our time period, the GCM [24] mode with AES encryption clearly stands out from the other modes with ~81,1% (9,314 occurrences). AES in counter mode is used in particular with a key length of 128 bits, but no connection with a 192-bit key is established. The AEAD mode chacha20-poly1305@openssh.com preferred by our honeypot and the clients shown is at the bottom of the list with 199 occurrences (~1,7%). As this is still in the form of a Internet-Draft [25] and our clients used it in tests, it cannot be completely ruled out that these occurrences were caused by us. It can be seen that atypical key lengths such as 192 bits are not used by attackers, instead small (128 bits) and then large key lengths (256 bits) are preferred. In general, AEAD modes are more likely to be used by attackers. We suspect that the performance improvement through integrated MAC is the reason for this.

As mentioned, a MAC algorithm is mandatory for non-AEAD modes. It is therefore of interest which algorithms attackers prefer in this case. Of 22,982 occurrences, ~82,8% (19,027 occurrences) were implicitly calculated by an AEAD mode. The remaining ~17,2% are distributed as follows. Our data shows that when using one of the CTR modes, the hmac-sha2-256-etm@openssh.com with 2,812 occurrences (~12,2%) was primarily used as a MAC. Only libssh as a library uses this algorithm by default in the standard configuration. For the insecure algorithms with a small tagsize (e.g. umac-64-...) or SHA1, the number of occurrences is low compared to the algorithms that are considered secure. From the data, we see that attackers tend to favor today's recommended algorithms. Insecure algorithms (SHA1) and comparably unknown algorithms (umac) seem to be used only rarely.

SSH supports the compression of data using zlib, which can save traffic, especially on low-power Internet links. However, we did not observe compression in any of the 22,982 cases, although our server supports it. We assume that compression is not useful in this type of attack and that the attackers do not rely on it.

Our results show that the algorithms used differ greatly from the default settings, particularly for host key and encryption.

4.2 Attack Origins

In this Section, we discuss the relevance of the country of origin of attacking hosts based on the IP address. We examined 316,726 authentication attempts during the observation period. These attempts originated from a total of 5,389 different IP addresses from a total of 118 countries. As mentioned in Sect. 3, we obtained the origin of the respective IP address using IPinfo [16]. We present the results of the evaluation by country in Fig. 1. The highest number of attacking hosts originated from China with 1,228 or 22.8% (rounded). The USA represents half as often with 624 (or 11.6%) attacking hosts, as are South Korean hosts with 340 different IP addresses. In past studies, China is also followed by the USA with the most attacking IP addresses [1,4,5,8], so we can confirm these values. The values then decrease continuously.

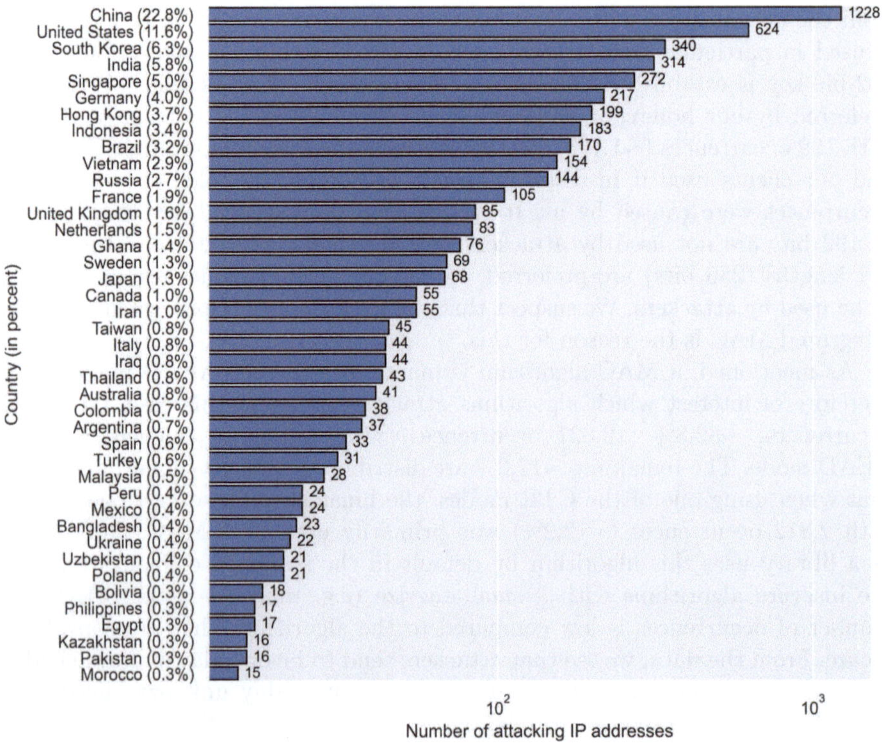

Fig. 1. Countries of the attacking hosts located by the IP address. Only countries with at least 15 occurrences are shown (logarithmic scale)

4.3 Username and Password Behaviour

Out of the 316,726 login attempts, we were able to register 78,054 different passwords and 35,422 different usernames. The length of the passwords ranged from 0 (no password specified) to 130 characters. An overview of the different password lengths and their occurrence shows Fig. 2a. Passwords with 6 characters are clearly at the top with ∼25,3% (80,216 occurrences), whereas 8-character passwords with ∼15,2% (48,259 occurrences) are in second place with almost half as many attempts. The most commonly used character lengths are between 0 and 18 characters. Lengths above this have significantly lower values, but are usually the same passwords if the individual passwords (see Fig. 2b) are considered. For example, 81-character passwords are represented 54 times, but they are always the same password. A comparison shows that 6-character passwords are often attempted several times, which we show later. Nevertheless, the difference between the password lengths remains very similar. In total, there are 13,047 or ~16,7% different 6-character passwords. Attackers therefore prefer lengths of less than or equal to 12 characters. This can be explained by the fact that such attacks become ineffective after this length. In general, insecure passwords assigned by administrators seem to be within this range.

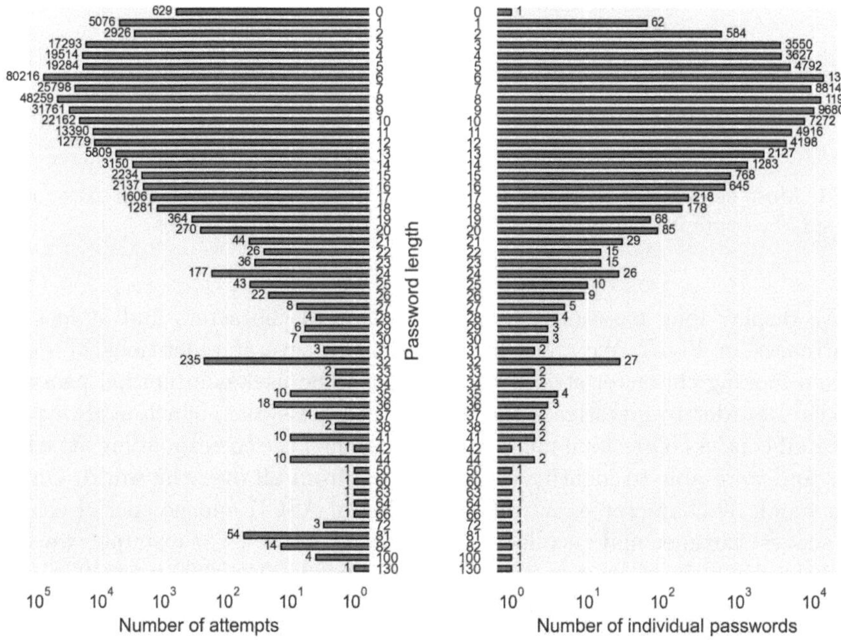

(a) Most used password lengths by brute force attempts

(b) Number of individual passwords by password length

Fig. 2. Analysis of password lengths in brute-force attacks (logarithmic scale)

The choice of password is mainly limited to simple passwords that are known to be insecure, such as 123456 (represented 34,778 thousand times in total), see Fig. 5 below. This 6-character password accounts for 11% of all recorded passwords, followed by the password 111111 (6,290 times or 2%) and 123 (5,349 occurrences or 1.7% of all attempts). Passwords that appear to be random only occur with a reduced number of attempts. The simplicity of the passwords used makes it clear that the attackers are targeting poorly configured machines and can therefore more easily add them to a botnet or compromise them. By using the same passwords very often, attackers could also check temporary accounts that are only available for a short period of time.

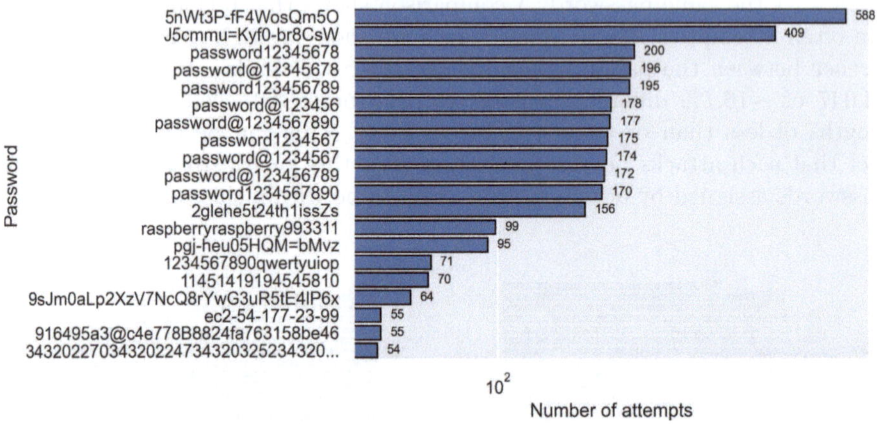

Fig. 3. Most used passwords with length of 15 or more chars and with 20 or more attempts by brute force attempts. (20 most used) (logarithmic scale)

We display long passwords with more than 15 characters and at least 20 occurrences in Fig. 3. We were able to identify several repetitions of partly random-looking character strings that appear to be useless in normal password attacks. In order to investigate the 81-character password, which is always the same and consists of decimal numbers, we examined the corresponding attacking hosts and were able to identify various servers from all over the world. On the other hand, 32-character passwords consisting of ASCII and no special characters suggest hexadecimal encoded MD5 or SHA1 hashes. For example, we were able to register the character string "d41d8cd98f00b204e9800998ecf8427e" several times, which corresponds to the MD5 hash of null (no value). More of these values can also be found in public lists. By analyzing random strings such as "5nWt3P-fF4WosQm5O" or "J5cmmu=Kyf0-br8CsW" that occur several times and always together, we were able to register botnet behavior. According to our findings, attacking hosts with such password attempts always use the same passwords in exactly the same number of occurrence for corresponding attacks on our honeypot. Below we show the behavior with the number of attempts.

```
‘‘toor": 17, ‘‘12345": 13, ‘‘1234": 13, ‘‘test": 13
```

The values differ from our previous findings in the fact that the password "toor" is used more often and, apart from the random character strings, the length of the passwords is very short (up to 5 characters). The passwords are also more or less trivial to guess. As a further indication, by analyzing the corresponding IP addresses, we were able to identify mainly IoT devices such as network cameras and unpatched routers in private ISP areas from all over the world. This clearly supports the assumption that these attempts are caused by botnets. In addition, the only usernames used are pi and contador, with the username pi only appearing with the first random string. We were able to register similar behavior with the password "broadguam1" with 2,464 occurrences or ~0,8%. The password occurs exclusively with the username root and is used exclusively by IP addresses located in Russia. The attacking servers primarily only use this single password without trying any others.

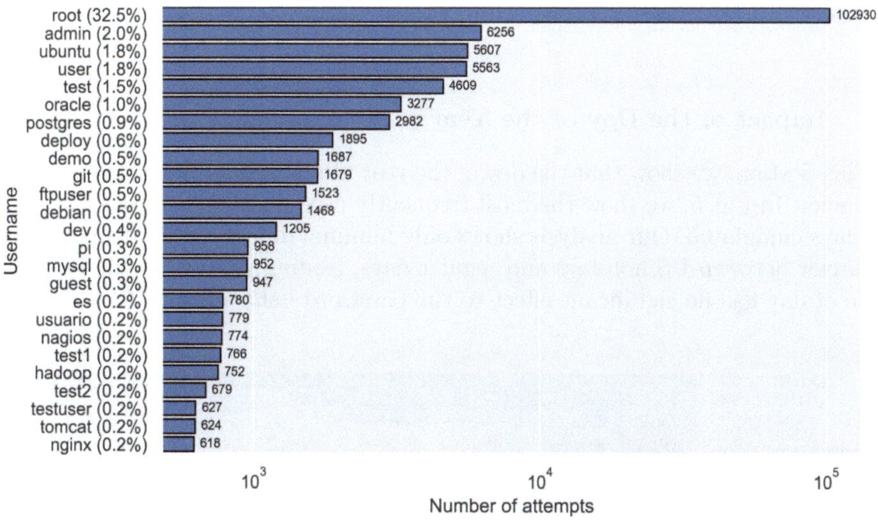

Fig. 4. Most used usernames by brute force attempts (20 most used) (logarithmic scale)

When analyzing the 35,422 different usernames used, we were able to identify the username root as the most frequently attacked user with 32.5% or a total of 102,930 occurrences, see Fig. 4. This can be explained by the fact that the user is always present on Linux systems and the corresponding system privileges can cause great damage if compromised. The other most frequently used usernames are admin (2%) and ubuntu (1.8%). The usernames are often associated with common Linux users such as database users (mysql, postgres, oracle), test users (ftpuser, test, guest) or system users (root, ubuntu, pi, nginx, tomcat). Furthermore, by analyzing the combination of username and password in Table 3, we were able to determine that, with the exception of the root user, the username is often also used as the password (admin:admin (239 occurrences), ubuntu:ubuntu (301 occurrences)).

Table 3. The 5 most attempted usernames and 3 most frequently used password attempts (the second most attempted password of root is null (no password)).

Username (rounded percent of occurence)	Passwords (number of occurence) in combination with the username
root (**32.5%**)	broadguam1 (**2464**), (**506**), 1234 (**469**)
admin (**2.0%**)	admin (**239**), 1234 (**233**), 123456 (**190**)
ubuntu (**1.8%**)	ubuntu (**301**), 123456 (**177**), 12345678 (**99**)
user (**1.5%**)	user (**217**), 123456 (**140**), 111111 (**135**)
test (**1.0%**)	test (**306**), 123456 (**175**), test123 (**147**)

4.4 Impact of the Day of the Year

In this Section, we show that the day of the year also has an influence on attacker behavior. In Fig. 5, we show the most frequently used passwords in the period of all days cumulated. Our analysis shows only minimal differences in the password behavior between US holidays and regular days, leading us to conclude that the type of day has no significant effect to the password behavior.

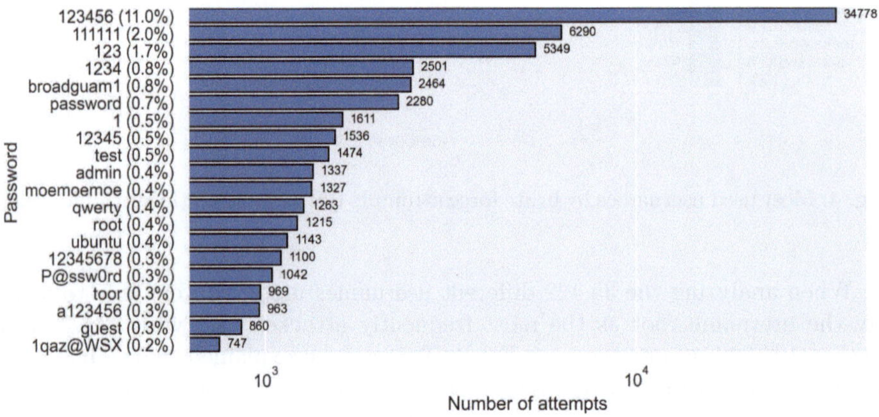

Fig. 5. Analysis of passwords using days of the year: Most used passwords by brute force attempts (20 most used) (logarithmic scale)

In contrast to the password behavior, we found clear irregularities in the number of attempts for the type of day. For example, we detected by far the most attacks on our honeypot before and at Christmas, as well as between the Christmas holidays and New Year's Eve and New Year's Day, see Fig. 6c (each point a day in the time period). This can be explained by the usual vacation periods and a lack of specialist staff on these days. The day with the most attacks is Dec. 31, 2024 (New Year's Eve) with 15,532 individual attacks, followed by

Jan. 1, 2025 (New Year's Day) with 14,765 attacks. With a few exceptions (Oct. 03–04, 2024), the values with the most attacks per day in the usual vacation period mentioned are mainly in December (see Fig. 6b). In Fig. 6a, we show the weekdays in relation to the US holidays (bottom). A significantly higher value can also be seen here, with the fewest attacks occurring on Wednesdays.

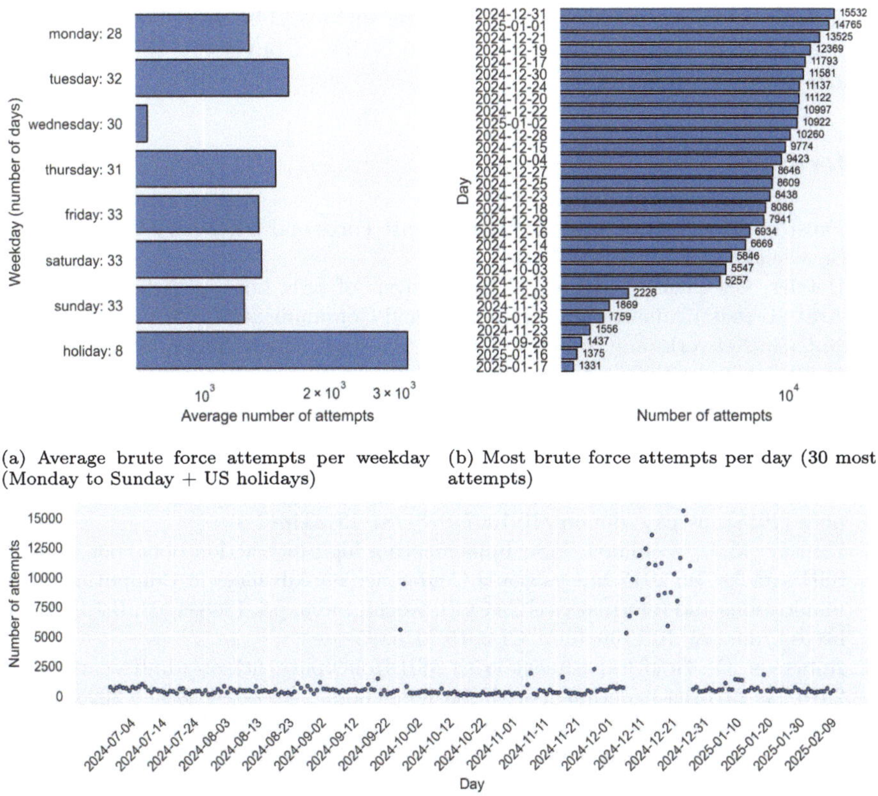

(a) Average brute force attempts per weekday (Monday to Sunday + US holidays)

(b) Most brute force attempts per day (30 most attempts)

(c) Brute force attempts per day over the entire period (timeline; every dot one day)

Fig. 6. Impact of the day in relation to attack behavior (6a and 6b logarithmic scale)

Since our honeypot is located in an American AWS data center, we cannot ensure that the values at other locations will not deviate.

5 Conclusion

In this work, we analyzed the attack behavior of SSH attackers over a period of 7 months using a honeypot in the US. We show that international holidays stand out as preferred times for attacks. Here we were able to record a significant increase of up to 15 times the number of attacks. The attack behavior has changed little compared to previous work. The username root remains by far the most popular, as does the 6-character password 123456, as well as the combination username=password and the countries of the attacking hosts (preferably China and the USA). It strongly suggests that the same attack structures and long random passwords are similar to botnet behavior. We were also able to analyze the attack behavior of the xz-Utils backdoor, but so far we did not detect any such attacks. Furthermore, attackers prefer pre-PQC algorithms despite the availability and long persistence of PQC algorithms. The most commonly used cryptographic primitives are also known to be fast. Conversely, this means that attacks are more performant.

References

1. Faust, J.: Distributed Analysis of SSH Brute Force and Dictionary Based Attacks. St. Cloud State University (2018)
2. Hetzler, C., Chen, Z., Khan, T.M.: Analysis of SSH honeypot effectiveness. In: Arai, K. (eds.) Advances in Information and Communication. FICC 2023. Lecture Notes in Networks and Systems, vol. 652. Springer, Cham (2023). https://doi.org/10.1007/978-3-031-28073-3_51
3. Cowrie Project: cowrie. https://github.com/cowrie/cowrie. Accessed 28 Feb 2025
4. Sadasivam, G.K., Hota, C., Anand, B.: Honeynet data analysis and distributed SSH brute-force attacks. In: Chakraverty, S., Goel, A., Misra, S. (eds.) Towards Extensible and Adaptable Methods in Computing, pp. 107–118. Springer, Singapore (2018). https://doi.org/10.1007/978-981-13-2348-5_9
5. Zemene, M.S., Avadhani, P.S.: Implementing high interaction honeypot to study SSH attacks. In: 2015 International Conference on Advances in Computing, Communications and Informatics (ICACCI), Kochi, India, pp. 1898–1903. IEEE (2015). https://doi.org/10.1109/ICACCI.2015.7275895
6. Roberson, D.: Brief Experiment With SSH Honeypots. https://dmfrsecurity.com/2016/12/29/brief-experiment-with-ssh-honeypots/. Accessed 28 Feb 2025
7. Bell, S.: Secure Honey. https://securehoney.net/. Accessed 28 Feb 2025
8. Cisco Security: Observations of Login Activity in an SSH Honeypot. https://sec.cloudapps.cisco.com/security/center/resources/ssh_honeypot.html. Accessed 28 Feb 2025
9. Netwatch-Team: Daily-Attack-Summary. https://github.com/NetWatch-team/Daily-Attack-Summary. Accessed 28 Feb 2025
10. Cao, P.M., et al.: CAUDIT: continuous auditing of ssh servers to mitigate brute-force attacks. In: 16th USENIX Symposium on Networked Systems Design and Implementation (NSDI 2019), Boston, MA. USENIX Association (2019)
11. Jakab, K.: sshesame. https://github.com/jaksi/sshesame. Accessed 28 Feb 2025
12. Roberson, D.: ssh-honeypot. https://github.com/droberson/ssh-honeypot. Accessed 28 Feb 2025
13. The OpenSSH Project: OpenSSH-portable. https://github.com/openssh/openssh-portable. Accessed 28 Feb 2025
14. Collin, L.: XZ Utils backdoor. https://tukaani.org/xz-backdoor/. Accessed 28 Feb 2025
15. Weems, A.: xzbot. https://github.com/amlweems/xzbot. Accessed 28 Feb 2025
16. IPinfo. https://ipinfo.io/. Accessed 28 Feb 2025

17. Open World Holidays Framework: holidays. https://github.com/vacanza/holidays/. Accessed 28 Feb 2025
18. Friedl, M., Mojzis, J., Josefsson, S.: Secure Shell (SSH) Key Exchange Method Using Hybrid Streamlined NTRU Prime sntrup761 and X25519 with SHA-512: sntrup761x25519-sha512 (Internet-Draft). Internet Engineering Task Force (2024)
19. Kampanakis, P., Stebila, D., Hansen, T.: PQ/T Hybrid Key Exchange in SSH (Internet-Draft). Internet Engineering Task Force (2024)
20. Adamantiadis, A., Josefsson, S., Baushke, M.D.: Secure Shell (SSH) Key Exchange Method Using Curve25519 and Curve448 (RFC 8731) (2020). https://www.rfc-editor.org/info/rfc8731
21. Stebila, D., Green, J.: Elliptic Curve Algorithm Integration in the Secure Shell Transport Layer (RFC 5656) (2009). https://www.rfc-editor.org/info/rfc5656
22. Harris, B., Velvindron, L.: Ed25519 and Ed448 Public Key Algorithms for the Secure Shell (SSH) Protocol (RFC 8709) (2020). https://www.rfc-editor.org/info/rfc8709
23. Bider, Denis: Use of RSA Keys with SHA-256 and SHA-512 in the Secure Shell (SSH) Protocol (RFC 8332) (2018). https://www.rfc-editor.org/info/rfc8332
24. Igoe, K., Solinas, J.: AES Galois Counter Mode for the Secure Shell Transport Layer Protocol (RFC 5647) (2009). https://www.rfc-editor.org/info/rfc5647
25. Miller, D., Josefsson, S.: Secure Shell (SSH) authenticated encryption cipher: chacha20-poly1305 (Internet-Draft). Internet Engineering Task Force (2025)
26. Putty User Manual. https://the.earth.li/~sgtatham/putty/0.83/htmldoc/. Accessed 28 Feb 2025
27. ssh_config. https://man.openbsd.org/ssh_config. Accessed 28 Feb 2025
28. Eugene: tabby - algorithms. https://github.com/Eugeny/tabby/blob/master/tabby-ssh/src/algorithms.ts. Accessed 28 Feb 2025
29. libssh Features. https://www.libssh.org/features/. Accessed 28 Feb 2025
30. Eugene: russh. https://github.com/Eugeny/russh. Accessed 28 Feb 2025

Network Automation with Flow-Based Programming: A Case Study with Node-RED

Lukas Bechtel[1,2](✉), Julius Ruppert[2], René Hummen[2], and Tobias Heer[1,2]

[1] University of Applied Sciences Esslingen, Esslingen am Neckar, Germany
[2] Belden Inc., Neckartenzlingen, Germany
{tobias.heer,lukas.bechtel}@hs-esslingen.de,
{julius.ruppert,rene.hummen}@belden.com

Abstract. Industrial networks are becoming increasingly complex due to rising connectivity demands, real-time requirements, and cross-domain integration challenges. These changes require efficient and adaptive configuration and management solutions. State-of-the-art tools depend on manual configurations or rigid rule-based automation, limiting scalability and responsiveness. This paper presents a Flow-Based Programming (FBP) approach using Node-RED to enable flexible, event-driven network automation. By integrating Information Technology (IT) and Operational Technology (OT) components, our framework enhances both security and operational safety, reduces manual intervention, and ensures consistent policy enforcement. We demonstrate its effectiveness through two industrial use cases—automated port lockdown for secure access control and automated software updates for Automated Guided Vehicles (AGVs), showcasing its potential to streamline network management and reduce operational downtime.

Keywords: Flow-based Programming · Node-RED · Industry 4.0 · Network Automation · Industrial Automation · Network Security

1 Introduction

Industrial networks are transitioning from rigid, hierarchical designs toward highly connected, software-controlled systems. This transformation is driven by the demands of Industry 4.0 for real-time responsiveness, security, and flexible reconfiguration. Modern production systems must ensure seamless communication between industrial end devices, networking infrastructure, and IT services. However, achieving this level of automation while maintaining security and reliability is a complex challenge.

Industrial network environments consist of three primary categories of devices: A) Industrial End Devices: These include all kinds of operational technology (OT) devices responsible for executing industrial processes, such as programmable logic controllers (PLCs), sensors, and actuators. B) Industrial-Grade

L. Bechtel and T. Heer (Eds.): CCSSS 2025 PTT, pp. 140–154, 2026.
https://doi.org/10.1007/978-3-032-10569-1_9

Network Equipment: Switches, routers, firewalls, and other networking components ensure real-time communication between industrial end devices. C) IT Services: Systems for access control (e.g., Radio-Frequency Identification (RFID)-based keycards), security surveillance, and centralized data storage, which interact with the industrial infrastructure.

IT, OT, and infrastructure systems are often operated in silos, resulting in fragmented workflows, increased manual overhead, and a broader attack surface. Manual network configuration adjustments introduce inconsistencies and increase the attack surface. Consider a scenario where a service engineer visits a production site to adjust machine parameters. To complete this task, multiple manual steps are required:

1. The IT department activates the service engineer's keycard to allow physical access to the cabinet.
2. The application engineer manually enables network ports on relevant switches.
3. The service engineer connects to the machine and modifies the parameters.

These steps are necessary for ensuring physical and logical access control in high-security environments. However, because they are managed independently—often across different teams or systems—they are error-prone and inefficient. Potentially, after the visit, either the key card is not deactivated or unused network ports are not disabled, both of which increase the attack surface for hackers.

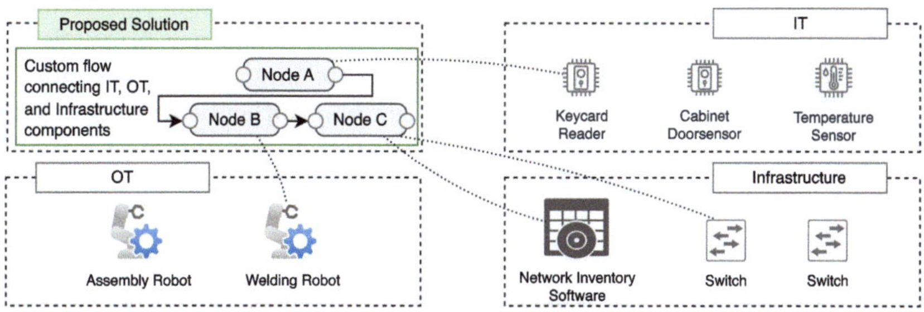

Fig. 1. Proposed solution connects components from IT, OT, and Infrastructure.

This paper proposes an FBP-based automation framework to eliminate manual interventions and integrate OT and IT operations. We leverage Node-RED, a flow-based programming (FBP) environment, to enable event-driven network automation. Figure 1 shows the proposed solution to connect IT, OT, and Infrastructure components with custom flows. By abstracting low-level device interactions through reusable components, we provide a visual programming approach that allows engineers without deep programming knowledge to define automation flows. For example, our system can dynamically enable and disable network ports based on external triggers such as RFID authentication or environmental sensors, e.g., door sensors in machine cabinets. While many input sources, such as RFID access systems and cabinet door sensors, already exist in IT systems, they are rarely integrated with network infrastructure or OT workflows due to heterogeneous protocols and missing standardized interfaces.

This paper proposes a unifying Flow-Based Programming (FBP) approach using Node-RED to orchestrate event-driven automation across IT, OT, and network infrastructure. Our method uses protocol adapters and abstraction layers to harmonize inputs from diverse systems, enabling automation logic that is both modular and portable across deployment scenarios. The remainder of this paper is organized as follows: First, we provide an overview of the fundamental concepts of FBP and its components. Next, we present our proposed design, detailing the abstraction mechanisms and interface structures used to achieve network independence. This is followed by implementing and validating our design through two use cases. Finally, we conclude the paper with a discussion of future research directions.

2 Background

FBP is a software paradigm in which applications are modeled as networks of independent processing components ("nodes") that communicate exclusively through asynchronous message-passing over well-defined connections ("wires"). Instead of controlling execution order explicitly, the system's behavior is driven by the flow of data between nodes. Each node processes input messages, transforms them according to its logic, and emits results downstream. This decoupling of logic, data, and control enables modularity and concurrency properties particularly well-suited to network automation, where inputs may originate from diverse and asynchronous sources such as sensors, authentication systems, or network events.

2.1 Data-Centric Design

In FBP, each node operates independently and processes structured messages received through input ports. These messages are passed along predefined "wires" that connect the output ports of upstream nodes to the input ports of downstream ones. This enables engineers to express processing logic as a series of modular transformations, similar to a data pipeline. Because control is implicitly defined by message arrival, rather than hard-coded sequences, workflows remain robust to changes in timing or data source availability. This separation allows for reuse, testing, and independent development of individual components.

For example, an industrial automation system can use FBP to dynamically adjust network configurations based on sensor inputs or operational events. If a sensor publishes a value update, an FBP workflow can trigger an automated switch configuration update, ensuring seamless integration without manual intervention. This design improves consistency and reduces programming errors such as logic duplication, invalid state transitions, or unintended side effects. It also scales naturally across devices, as flows operate on message data rather than device-specific state.

2.2 Asynchronous Execution

FBP supports asynchronous execution, making it ideal for handling concurrent network automation tasks in dynamic network environments. Each node operates independently and responds to messages as they arrive. For instance, door sensors in different factory zones can simultaneously trigger switch configuration updates, and these actions are processed in parallel due to the decoupled nature of flow execution. Because flows are triggered by message arrivals and not a central scheduler, unrelated automation tasks can proceed without blocking each other. This architecture avoids execution bottlenecks common in sequential control logic, as long as flows are scoped appropriately and do not overload shared system resources.

Moreover, integrating asynchronous execution with event-driven triggers enhances automation responsiveness. FBP enables concurrent running flows, ensuring that high-priority automation tasks do not interfere with routine monitoring or background processes. For example, a critical event, such as a failed network link, can trigger an immediate re-routing mechanism while other ongoing configurations continue without delay. This design is particularly useful in environments requiring rapid failover, dynamic access control, or automated security policy enforcement.

2.3 Visual Programming

A key advantage of FBP is its integration with visual programming environments like Node-RED [9]. These platforms provide a graphical interface where automation workflows are defined using interconnected nodes. This approach reduces complexity and lowers the entry barrier for network engineers who may not have extensive programming expertise. Engineers can construct automation logic through an intuitive drag-and-drop interface by leveraging reusable function blocks.

For example, a typical Node-RED workflow for access-based network automation may involve: 1) An RFID authentication module detects personnel entry. 2) A database query node retrieves user permissions and network access rights. 3) A network management node dynamically enables or disables specific switch ports. Such workflows allow adaptive, event-driven network automation, reducing manual intervention. The visual structure of flows makes dependencies and logic explicit, helping engineers to identify misconfigurations early and trace unexpected behavior during debugging.

3 Design

The design of our network automation system leverages the modularity and message-driven execution model of FBP to enable flexible, scalable workflows across heterogeneous infrastructure. We start the design section with a general overview and more detailed requirements. Then, we present the three main components of the design: event-based triggers, topology independence, and component reusability.

3.1 Overview

The proposed framework addresses three critical requirements to ensure automation is adaptable and portable: (1) event-based triggers, (2) independence from physical network topology, and (3) reusability of automation components.

First, **event-based execution** allows the automation framework to respond dynamically to changes in network conditions. Rather than relying on static, pre-deployed rules, the system reacts dynamically to real-time triggers such as sensor updates or scheduled changes. This enables more responsive automation workflows, although some static baseline configurations may still exist for fail-safe defaults.

Second, **topology independence** means that flows are driven by abstract identifiers (e.g., machine labels) and retrieve device information dynamically from external inventory systems, rather than encoding physical layout into automation logic. Many industrial environments require very similar interactions but have varying topologies for their specific purpose. The system must support flexible interactions with network elements while avoiding rigid dependencies on specific topologies.

Third, **instance independence and component reusability** are fundamental to enabling scalable automation. The system ensures that configurations can be applied across different infrastructures by decoupling network automation logic from specific device instances. Component reusability further simplifies adaptation by allowing pre-defined function blocks to handle a range of tasks without modification.

The following sections detail the specific implementation strategies for achieving these design goals.

3.2 Trigger-Based Execution

Message-based execution in FBP tools, such as Node-RED, requires specific triggers to initialize the flow of network management tasks. The list of available triggers includes *event-driven*, *threshold-based*, or *time-based* triggers. Node-RED offers many internal triggers and allows connectors for OT protocols to also define triggers. Two commonly used protocols in industrial environments are MQTT and OPC UA: MQTT is a lightweight publish/subscribe messaging protocol often used for sensor data. At the same time, OPC UA (Open Platform Communications Unified Architecture) is a machine-to-machine or device-to-controller communication protocol designed for secure, standardized data exchange in industrial automation. Each trigger must be initialized with an initial configuration stored in a database. Figure 2 visualizes this initialization of the *SNMP Trap* or *MQTT Subscription* on the top left.

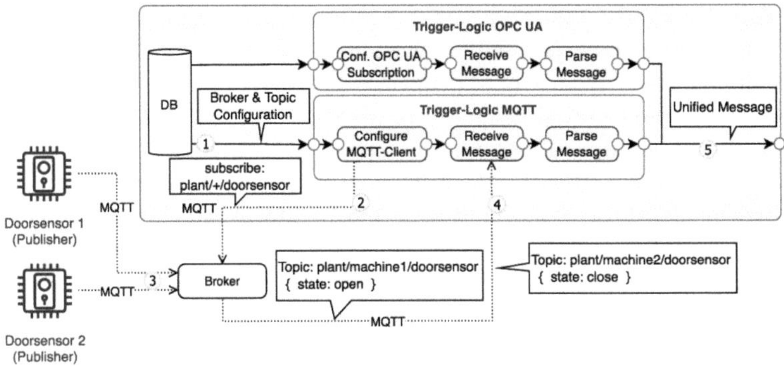

Fig. 2. Unifying different trigger technologies to start the same automation flow.

In realistic deployments, one machine may have a door sensor that publishes messages via MQTT, while another may expose sensor values through an OPC UA server. However, the user does not want two independent flows for each system but rather to reuse the logic. Therefore, in our concept, we combine different implementations of triggers to harmonize the execution of the same network management tasks. The protocol-specific triggers are configured as subscriptions to either a specific NodeID on an OPC UA client or a specific MQTT topic on a broker. Figure 2 shows this aggregation of different trigger instances, e.g., an *OPC UA Subscription* or *MQTT Subscription*, into the same uniform message to initialize the flow. For example, every cabinet has its own MQTT topic to publish the state of the door. The trigger logic can subscribe to multiple machines simultaneously with wildcards and uses the topic to differentiate the machines later. The trigger logic extracts the cabinet ID or name from the MQTT topic and passes it to the workflow. In OPC UA, the subscriber in the trigger logic receives the data directly from the end devices, so differentiation occurs, e.g., via the IP address. Depending on the implementation, every protocol can have a different payload. In this example, we present a small JSON-encoded payload containing the state, whereas OPC UA typically has raw values for each subscribed variable. The protocol-specific parsing enables a unification of the relevant data.

3.3 Topology Independence

Topology independence refers to the decoupling of automation logic from fixed network layouts. Instead of hardcoding switch addresses or port mappings, our flows retrieve relevant device lists based on machine context or metadata from external inventory systems. This is particularly important in industrial environments where network topologies can be complex or follow given patterns but differ slightly in dimension or addressing. The following design principles enable topology independence.

External Topology Source: The FBP tool connects the process environment with the infrastructure environment. Hence, it does not store data but pulls the required information from the appropriate tools. As Fig. 3 shows, the network inventory data is stored in the external software *NW-Inventory*, where the FBP component *getDevices* pulls the data from. The FBP environment requires the information and authentication information on the network inventory API, initialized by the database *DB*. This database contains all relevant tools to which the different flows must connect, such as Network Access Control (NAC), NW-Inventory, or SCADA dashboards for visualization. We require the network inventory software to follow standardized interfaces, i.e., we propose the tool to implement the *IETF Network Topology* model [2]. The component *getDevices* pulls the information on a set of devices, identified by the parameter handed over from the trigger. The trigger logic, as detailed in Sect. 3.2, derives the label of a machine from, e.g., the MQTT topic. The *IETF Network Topology* model can store a large topology consisting of sub-topologies, each identified with a name. If everything is configured correctly, the label of the machine equals the name of the sub-topology to filter for. Alternatively, topologies can be filtered by, e.g., manufacturer, supported feature, or device state, such as power supply state.

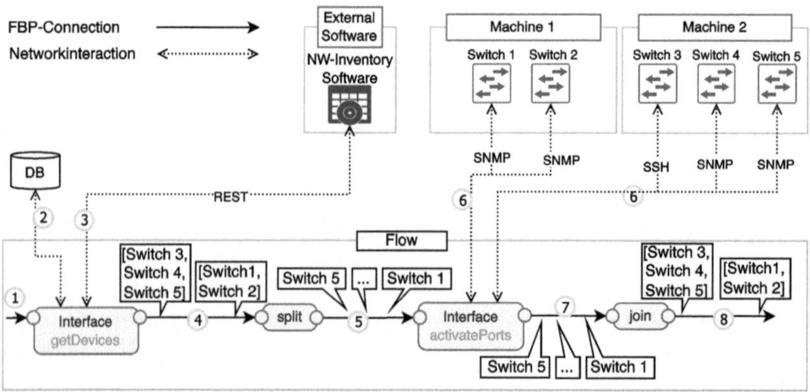

Fig. 3. External storage of devices and execution of configuration on a per-device level with the *aligned* and *join* functionality.

Device-Centric Execution: The network inventory software returns a set of devices per request. However, the design of the FBP flows is independent of the topology, i.e., on the number of devices and their specific layout. To handle cases where a machine or site maps to multiple devices, we use Node-RED's *aligned* and *join* nodes. The *aligned* node decomposes a device list into individual configuration messages, allowing per-device execution. The *join* node then reassembles results or synchronizes processing steps. The single message entering the split results in individual messages per device between the *aligned* and *join* components. Figure 3 visualizes sequential processing of the node *activatePorts* for illustrative clarity. While some flows may execute sequentially (e.g., for ordered configuration), Node-RED supports parallel execution when device-specific operations do not depend on shared state or ordering constraints. Specifically, if the flow runs for triggers of different machines, each machine returns a set of devices of varying sizes. The split and join resolve this difference and enable a uniform execution of the desired functionality for each switch after another. With this concept, the dimension of a network does not impact the implementation of individual functionalities in the components.

3.4 Instance Independence and Component Reusability

Instance independence defines the decoupling of configuration logic from specific network device instances. In traditional network automation systems, scripts and configurations are often tied to particular devices, making them difficult to reuse or adapt to different environments. Our design introduces a harmonized interface for every specific functionality and addresses the challenges through the following strategies.

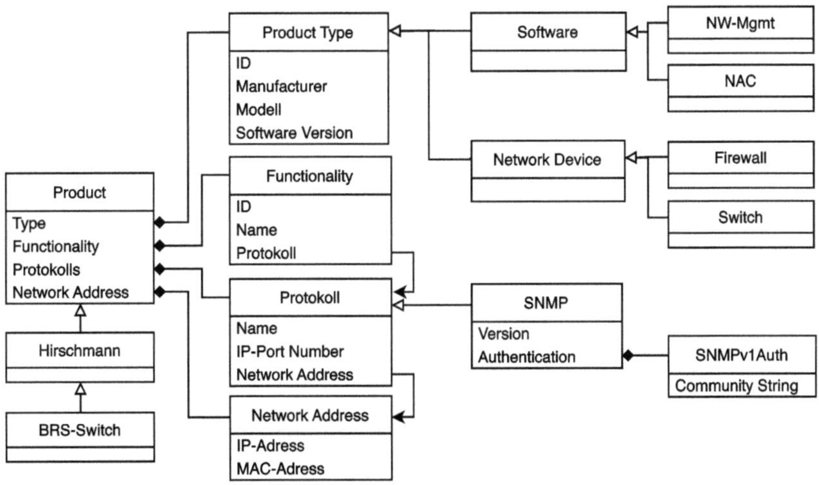

Fig. 4. Generic device model covering product type, functionality, addressing, and protocols for communication.

Structured Device Descriptions: Each network device is described using a structured format that includes essential information such as IP addresses, supported protocols (e.g., SNMP or NETCONF), and available functions. This abstraction layer allows the management logic to interact with devices based on their capabilities rather than their specific identities. As Fig. 4 visualizes, the generic device model includes the set of functionalities, network protocols with authentication, and addressing for every device. The structure is the same for every device. Once the node *getDevices* receives data on switches from the NW-Inventory software, it parses the data and fills the given structure. With that, only the *getDevices* node must be able to handle different interfaces from the external software, and all following nodes can rely on the unified structure.

Generic FBP Components: We design the components within the FBP environment to perform generic functions, such as activating a network port or retrieving device status. Therefore, we develop a single interface for the interaction with devices in the network, as shown in Fig. 5. Depending on device properties, a conditional structure, e.g., *switch-case*, selects the appropriate implementation for that device. This branching resembles a basic form of state machine, enabling extensibility without changing the overall flow. For example, certain features are configurable via standardized YANG modules via NETCONF, so all products use the same implementation. Other features require interaction with the command line and operating system-specific commands. This second *switch-case* can use the vendor-specific product, or even versions to execute the correct implementation. The FBP component receives the generic device model, i.e., *Switch 1*, together with optional parameters on the input port on the left. If a device does not support the requested feature or an error occurs during execution, the node returns the message via a dedicated "error" or "not supported" port. This allows follow-up handling, such as skipping that device, logging a warning, or triggering remediation.

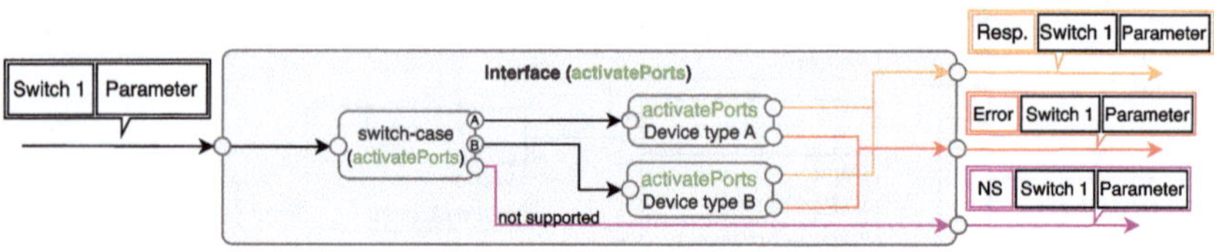

Fig. 5. Example FBP component differentiating functionality and device type.

4 Applicability of FBP in Network Automation

For the applicability of the presented approach to automate the network, the components themselves must have no coupling with the use case. Additionally, the availability of components defines the set of enabled workflows an engineer can create. We propose establishing an app store providing a library of implemented functionality for the second requirement. For the first requirement, we demonstrate the applicability with two use cases. In the paper, we present the workflow in an abstracted form, but open-source the detailed Node-RED code on GitHub[1].

4.1 Automated Port Lockdown to Prevent Unattended Access

The port lockdown scenario ensures security by dynamically restricting access to network ports based on predefined triggers. In Fig. 6, we use a door sensor as a trigger, assuming the cabinet is locked with the key of authorized personnel. Similarly, other sensors, such as a smart card reader, can trigger the flow.

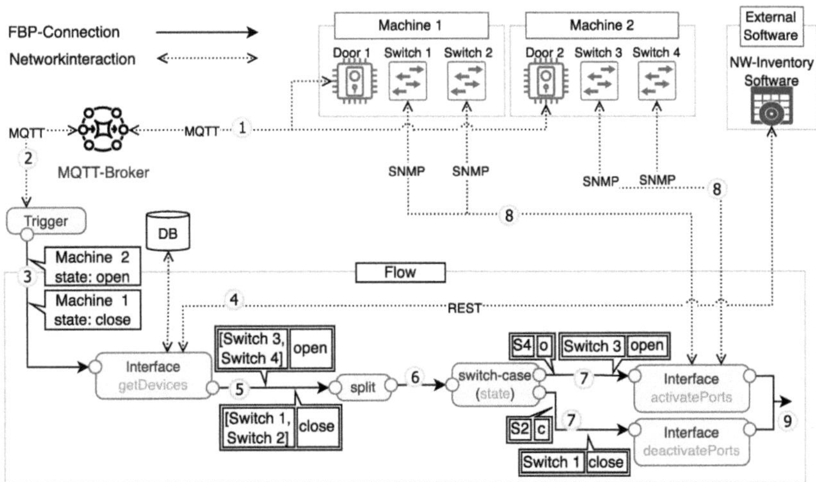

Fig. 6. FBP automation to shutdown network ports while the cabinet is locked.

Unlocking the door results in a publish on the MQTT broker, and a subscription by the trigger node. Based on the published topic and payload, the trigger extracts the machine label and state of the door. With the machine label, *getDevices* collects the relevant switches and passes the door state parameter with the list of switches. The *aligned* node only splits the list of switches and passes each switch individually with the parameter along the flow. Depending on the door state, the flow calls either the *activatePorts* or *deactivatePorts* node. In this example, we abstract the information on which ports to activate and deactivate. One strategy is the activation of all deactivated ports and the deactivation of all unused ports. This reduces the attack surface by ensuring that only known connections are allowed. However, it does not eliminate threats from devices already connected before the cabinet is locked, such as a malicious device left behind by a service engineer. In the available implementation, the flow maintains a list of active ports per cabinet, stored upon unlock. When locking the cabinet again,

[1] https://github.com/hs-esslingen-it-security/hses-network-automation-nodered.

the system compares this list to the currently active ports. It disables any that were not explicitly used, ensuring consistent access control without relying on static port mappings.

This automated workflow enhances security by reducing the response time to potential threats, minimizing human intervention, and ensuring that security policies are enforced consistently across the industrial network.

4.2 Automated Software Update During Charging of AGV

The AGV (Automated Guided Vehicle) upgrade workflow ensures seamless software and configuration updates while maintaining operational continuity, as illustrated in Fig. 7. Every time an AGV enters the charging station, the system knows the AGV will accept software and configuration upgrades, which may require reboots. Only a parked AGV can handle this potential equipment outage.

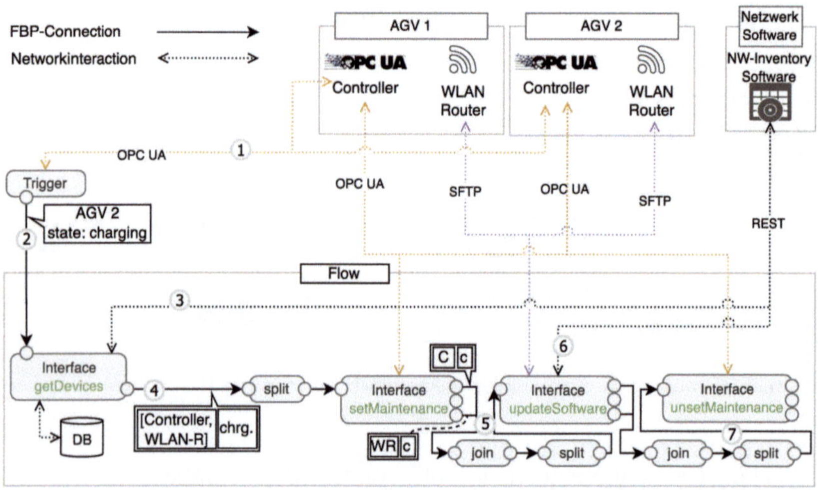

Fig. 7. FBP automation to update software on AGV router if while charging.

For each AGV, the system configures a trigger on the OPC UA server for the charging state. Once an AGV starts to charge, e.g., *AGV 2*, the flow collects all network components associated with the corresponding AGV. Unlike the previous example, the list of devices does not just contain network equipment but a combination of end devices and network equipment. In this flow, the execution order is important, but it is challenging to know which device supports which node in advance. The update flow uses the *not supported* output to determine which devices support maintenance mode, and *split/join* to coordinate execution. However, in a more robust design, such sequencing should ideally be part of the flow logic itself rather than relying on protocol behavior or assumptions about device capabilities.

As a first step, the flow enables the maintenance mode on the controller. This step ensures that the AGV does not accept new tasks during the update. This configuration of the maintenance mode is only available on the controller, but not the router. Still, as the controller is in maintenance mode, the software can update the router safely. We use the joins as synchronization points in the program flow. This synchronization ensures that the next step does not upgrade the router without enabling maintenance mode, as all devices from the initial array only join if no error occurs. For example, while retrieving the set of devices on the AGV, it could have started again, leading to a failure to set the maintenance mode. The join node waits for all responses to ensure maintenance mode is set where supported. However, requiring all devices to succeed may be overly strict. Only after all devices have passed the *setMaintenance* correctly, the upgrade is executed if the maintenance mode is enabled.

The flow retrieves the latest software version from the inventory and transfers it to the router using the *SFTP* protocol. While this example focuses on the router, the same mechanism can be extended to other devices as long as their capabilities are known and appropriately abstracted. For example, it can also upgrade the software on the controller or update configuration files.

After completing all upgrades and the next join, the flow disables the maintenance mode again. With this step, the AGV is able to accept new requests again and can participate in the operational service.

5 Related Work

Network automation has been extensively explored through various commercial and open-source tools. While these solutions have improved configuration management and orchestration, they often lack real-time adaptability and vendor independence.

Tools such as Ansible [11], SaltStack [17], Progress Chef [10], and CFEngine [8] automate configuration management using an "infrastructure as code" model. These systems define and enforce static configurations, ensuring consistency but lacking real-time responsiveness. Similarly, commercial tools like ManageEngine [19] and SolarWinds [13] integrate automation with proprietary network devices but are often constrained by vendor lock-in. Our FBP-based approach differs by enabling dynamic, event-driven automation. Instead of enforcing predefined configurations, it adjusts network states in real time based on triggers, enhancing flexibility and operational efficiency in industrial settings. Additionally, our framework is vendor-agnostic, ensuring compatibility across diverse infrastructures.

Modern network automation incorporates event-driven architectures, as seen in StackStorm [14], Ansible Automation Platform [12], NetBox [7], and Zenoss [18]. StackStorm and Ansible Automation Platform process predefined event-driven workflows but require extensive scripting. NetBox and Zenoss focus on network inventory and monitoring, offering visibility but lacking automation capabilities that actively modify network states. Our approach improves on these by leveraging Node-RED for visual programming, making automation more accessible. Unlike scripting-heavy solutions, our framework allows engineers to design automation workflows via an intuitive interface. Additionally, our solution bridges the gap between passive monitoring and active network management by integrating real-time monitoring with automation workflows.

Tabaa et al. [15] explore industrial communication using Modbus and Node-RED, demonstrating its suitability for distributed automation. Toc and Korodi [16] proposed an OPC UA wrapper using Node-RED for the water industry, highlighting its applicability in industrial environments. Furthermore, studies on programmable network automation emphasize the role of modern workflows in transitioning to intent-based networking. The OpenStack Mistral Workflow Service [5] has also been used for orchestrating automated network tasks. Additionally, NAPALM [3] provides a vendor-agnostic abstraction layer for network automation. Machine learning techniques have been integrated into network automation, particularly in Open RAN environments, as explored by Hamdan et al. [6]. Self-healing mechanisms in IoT systems have been explored to enhance reliability and resilience. For instance, Amit et al. [1] propose a framework that enables IoT devices to autonomously detect and recover from malfunctions or cyber-attacks using machine learning techniques. Additionally, Dias et al. [4] introduce SHEN (Self-Healing Extensions for Node-RED), providing nodes that enable the implementation of self-healing strategies within the Node-RED visual framework.

Our FBP-based approach builds upon these concepts by integrating dynamic, real-time automation workflows while ensuring interoperability with industrial communication protocols and network management frameworks. Our approach facilitates flexible and efficient network automation in industrial environments by combining the benefits of event-driven automation, modularity, and visual programming.

6 Conclusion

This paper presents a flow-based approach to network automation using Node-RED, addressing the integration challenges between IT, OT, and network infrastructure in industrial environments. By leveraging the modular and graphical capabilities of Node-RED, we demonstrated how event-driven automation can reduce complexity, enhance reusability, and improve network management efficiency. Our proposed framework integrates industrial OT and IT components, enabling seamless automation workflows that dynamically adapt to changing network conditions.

Through two use cases, automated port lockdown and AGV software updates, we demonstrate how automation can reduce manual steps like physical port reconfiguration and improve safety through consistent, event-driven enforcement. The approach abstracts topology and decouples logic from specific device instances. While it requires vendor-specific adapters to interpret device capabilities, the automation logic remains portable and scalable across infrastructures.

By replacing manual workflows, such as those required during on-site service visits, with unified, trigger-based flows, our framework reduces misconfiguration risk and enhances both operational safety and security.

Future work will explore further integration with additional industrial protocols, enhancing automation robustness, and evaluating real-time performance in large-scale deployments. Continuing to refine and expand this approach, we aim to establish FBP as a foundational technique for flexible and intelligent industrial network automation.

Acknowledgement. This work has been funded by the Deutsche Forschungsgemeinschaft (DFG, German Research Foundation) – Project-ID 528745080 - FIP 68. Additionally, this research was supported by the project "FHP: Qualifizierung und Entwicklung des professoralen Personals der Hochschule Esslingen für zukunftsweisende Themen" (FKZ: 03FHP115) as part of the Federal States Program "FH-Personal", funded by the BMBF and MWK Baden-Württemberg. The authors alone are responsible for the content of the paper.

References

1. Amit, G., Shabtai, A., Elovici, Y.: A self-healing mechanism for internet of things devices. IEEE Secur. Priv. **19**(1), 44–53 (2020)
2. Clemm, A., Medved, J., Varga, R., Bahadur, N., Ananthakrishnan, H., Liu, X.: A YANG Data Model for Network Topologies. RFC 8345 (2018)
3. Contributors, N.: NAPALM: Network Automation and Programmability Abstraction Layer with Multivendor support (2025). https://napalm.readthedocs.io/. Accessed 4 Mar 2025
4. Dias, J.P., Restivo, A., Ferreira, H.S.: Empowering visual internet-of-things mashups with self-healing capabilities, pp. 44–51 (2021)
5. OpenInfra Foundation: Mistral Workflow Service (2025). https://docs.openstack.org/mistral/latest/. Accessed 4 Mar 2025
6. Hamdan, M.Q., et al.: Recent advances in machine learning for network automation in the o-ran. Sensors **23**(21) (2023). https://doi.org/10.3390/s23218792. https://www.mdpi.com/1424-8220/23/21/8792
7. NetBox Labs, Inc.: Netbox: Network source of truth (2025). https://netbox.dev/. Accessed 4 Mar 2025
8. Northern.tech AS: Cfengine infrastructure automation (2025). https://cfengine.com. Accessed 4 Mar 2025
9. OpenJS Foundation: Node-red - low-code programming for event-driven applications (2025). https://nodered.org. Accessed 4 Mar 2025
10. Progress Software Corporation: Progress chef (2025). https://www.chef.io/. Accessed 4 Mar 2025
11. Red Hat, Inc.: Ansible automation (2025). https://www.ansible.com/. Accessed 4 Mar 2025
12. Red Hat, Inc.: Red hat ansible automation platform (2025). https://www.redhat.com/en/technologies/management/ansible. Accessed 4 Mar 2025
13. SolarWinds: Solarwinds network automation manager (2025). https://www.solarwinds.com/. Accessed 4 Mar 2025

14. StackStorm: Stackstorm (2025). https://stackstorm.com/. Accessed 4 Mar 2025
15. Tabaa, M., Chouri, B., Saadaoui, S., Alami, K.: Industrial communication based on modbus and node-red. Procedia Comput. Sci. **130**, 583–588 (2018)
16. Toc, S.I., Korodi, A.: Modbus-OPC UA wrapper using node-red and IoT-2040 with application in the water industry. In: 2018 IEEE 16th International Symposium on Intelligent Systems and Informatics (SISY), pp. 000099–000104 (2018). https://doi.org/10.1109/SISY.2018.8524749
17. VMware, Inc.: Saltstack automation (2025). https://www.saltproject.io/. Accessed 4 Mar 2025
18. Zenoss, Inc.: Zenoss network monitoring (2025). https://www.zenoss.com/. Accessed 4 Mar 2025
19. Zoho Corporation Pvt. Ltd.: Manageengine network configuration automation (2025). https://www.manageengine.com/. Accessed 4 Mar 2025

Weight Initialization of Ensemble Forecast Output Statistics Models for Probabilistic Wind-Speed Forecasting

Götz Grimmer[1(✉)], Steffen Schober[1], and Corinna Möhrlen[2]

[1] Institute for Intelligent Systems, University of Applied Sciences Esslingen, Esslingen am Neckar, Germany
{Goetz.Grimmer,Steffen.Schober}@hs-esslingen.de
[2] WEPROG GmbH, Böblingen, Germany
com@weprog.com

Abstract. This study investigates optimal initialization strategies for Ensemble Model Output Statistics (EMOS) in weather forecasting, with a focus on multi-scheme ensemble systems that address physical process uncertainties. While previous research has primarily focused on loss function refinement for probabilistic forecast calibration, our work examines the critical role of parameter initialization in training effectiveness. Drawing inspiration from neural network weight initialization research as source of familiar domains, we evaluate truncated normal, beta and gamma probability distributions for initializing EMOS parameters. We find that common neural network initialization techniques like He-initialization are unsuitable for EMOS due to the fundamental constraints of positive weights for ensemble members and spread estimation. Through systematic evaluation using different formulations of the continuous rank probability score (CRPS) across time windows 25, 30, 35, and 40 days, we demonstrate that sampling from a beta distribution produces superior initialization results compared to truncated normal and gamma distributions. Interestingly, the mixture model approach did not outperform alternative methodologies due to differences in training methodologies or the properties of the geographical domain. We employed the methods on WEPROG's Multi-Scheme Ensemble Prediction System (MSEPS) for a test site at Stötten, Germany. Our findings contribute to the advancement of ensemble post-processing techniques by providing evidence-based initialization strategies that enhance the calibration of probabilistic weather forecasts irrespective of the objective function employed.

Keywords: Machine Learning · Post-Processing · Ensemble Forecast · EMOS · weight-initialization

1 Introduction

Today, weather forecasting relies heavily on sophisticated ensemble forecasts, which are used to predict atmospheric behavior. Each ensemble member sim-

L. Bechtel and T. Heer (Eds.): CCSSS 2025 PTT, pp. 155–170, 2026.
https://doi.org/10.1007/978-3-032-10569-1_10

ulates the dynamical and physical characteristics of the atmosphere, collectively approximating its true state. This approach was first proposed by Epstein [9]. The uncertainty inherent in weather forecasts is quantified through ensembles, with each prediction derived from a statistical process perpetuating properties of a physical process by its parameters or initialization. The forecasting process begins with an initial condition sampled from real atmospheric observations. Over a specified time interval, this initial state evolves into a probabilistic distribution representing the forecast's uncertainty. The manner in which this distribution is transformed into a probabilistic forecast depends on the design of the ensemble members and their respective initial conditions. A notable early method was introduced by Leith [17], which incorporates random Gaussian noise into the initial state to account for uncertainties. In further work of e.g. Bessa et al. [4] they use singular vector (SV), breeding, multi-model, and multi-scheme approaches. Interpretation of ensemble forecasts typically involves analyzing both the mean value and the dispersion within the ensemble, as these metrics provide insight into forecast uncertainty. In an ideal scenario, a perfect model would be initialized with a representative sample of atmospheric states. This would result in an accurate representation of the forecast uncertainty through its output distribution. However, models are subject to two primary sources of error:

- The finite resolution in time, space, and measurement values limits the precision of computations.
- The physical processes represented in the model are simplifications of real-world phenomena, often parameterized using approximations.

The multi-scheme approach used in this paper deals with the second source of error. The ensemble is built by exchanging parametrizations schemes for the fast physical processes at the earths surface. If the ensemble is calibrated correctly, the ensemble members describe the uncertainty analogue to the simplifications of the physical processes. Hence, for applications at the earths surface, the uncertainty is time invariant. All these mentioned approaches, along with MSEPS, encounter the following two issues:

- Bias: When all ensemble members deviate significantly from the true state, despite being internally consistent.
- Dispersion: Either overestimating or underestimating the actual uncertainty of the forecast.

Wilks [26] outlines an approach to address bias and dispersion: Ensemble Model Output Statistics (EMOS) presented by Gneiting et al. [12]. This method employs a historical archive of forecasts to statistically correct (not the physical processes) both the bias and dispersion of ensemble predictions. These advancements have improved the calibration of probabilistic forecasts. Subsequent research has enhanced EMOS through the development of more sophisticated loss functions and the application of mixture models, as demonstrated in studies e.g. Baran and Lerch [2], Lerch and Thorarinsdottir [24], Schulz and Lerch [18].

In addition to refining loss functions by accurately modelling data distributions, model initialization plays a crucial role in training effectiveness. Training via gradient descent entails optimizing parameters to find the global minimum of a non-convex objective function. Recent studies from Bishop [6], Narkhede et al. [21,22] have emphasized identifying optimal initialization strategies, particularly with advancements in deep learning and neural network architectures. A significant challenge lies in how architectural choices influence initialization approaches Narkhede et al. [22]. A key aspect involves symmetry breaking through randomized weight sampling, which prevents parameter redundancy. Our study investigates the impact of truncated-normal, beta and gamma distribution sampling distribution for initialization strategies on EMOS post-processing for ensemble forecasts. We draw insights from existing neural network weight initialization research and adapt these methodologies for integration into the EMOS framework. Following this introduction, in Sect. 2 we establish the mathematical framework underpinning our analysis. In Sect. 3 we present the source of data and clearing, in Sect. 4 we present how we train, which optimizer we use and the framework. The outcome of our experiments are presented in Sect. 5 of our different initialization strategies. Finally, we sum up our results and present an outlook of our work in Sect. 6.

2 Methodology

In this section we define the key concepts, present the theoretical models, and develop the mathematical tools necessary for our subsequent investigation.

Table of Symbols

Symbol	Description/Usage
F	Define a distribution
y	Target variable in CRPS
y_t	Target variable in CRPS, t denotes a time point
x	Denote an input variable for CRPS
x_t	Denote an input variable for CRPS, t denotes a time point
X	Used to denote a set of features
$\mathbb{E}_F$	Expectation under distribution F
$\mathcal{N}[\mu_t, \sigma_t]$	Normal Gaussian distribution with location μ and scale σ for time point t, estimated through EMOS
s_t^2	Ensemble variance at time point t
$\overline{x}_t$	Ensemble mean at time point t
μ_t	EMOS predicts mean for time point t
σ_t^2	EMOS predicts standard deviation for time point t
m	Amount of ensemble members
$a, b_1 \dots b_m, c, d$	Parameters for EMOS: a bias of μ_t estimation, $b_1 \dots b_2$ weights of μ_t estimation, c bias of σ_t estimation, d weight of σ_t estimation

m, v	Affine functions for log-normal CRPS values μ and σ
$\mathcal{N}^0(\mu, \sigma, a, b)$	Truncated normal distribution: lower limit a, upper limit b
Φ	CDF of standard Gaussian distribution
φ	PDF of standard Gaussian distribution
$\mathcal{LN}(\mu, \sigma)$	Log-Normal Gaussian distribution with location μ and scale σ
$\tilde{X}_t$	Median of X at time point t
θ	Regime switching wind speed in $\frac{m}{s}$
$h(a)$	Activation function for given value a
n_l	Number of input connections at layer l
w_l	Variance of weights of neurons at layer l
$\Gamma(\alpha, \beta)$	Gamma distributions with shape α and scale β

2.1 Continuous Ranked Probability Score (CRPS)

The CRPS Eq. 1 assesses the quality of a predicted probability distribution F in encompassing the observed outcome y. Lower CRPS values indicate superior performance. Hence, F has a low bias **and** small spread. More precisely, the area between the cumulative distribution function (CDF) of F and the two intervals of the step function are equal.

$$\text{CRPS}[F, y] = \int_{-\infty}^{\infty} \left[F(x) - \mathbb{1}(y \leq x)\right]^2 dx \tag{1}$$

The CRPS score penalizes both distributions that are imprecise in their location (i.e. those with high dispersion around the observation) and those that are overly diffuse (i.e. those with low concentration near the observed value). An optimal CRPS score reflects a balance between a precise focus on the observed outcome and a sufficient concentration. Importantly, CRPS is a strictly proper scoring rule with a unique distribution F that retrieves a minimal CRPS cf. Hersbach [19], Matheson and Winkler [14]. An alternative formulation of CRPS, proposed in Gneiting and Raftery [11], provides a computationally tractable expression:

$$\text{CRPS}[F, y] = \mathbb{E}_F|X - y| - \frac{1}{2}\mathbb{E}_F|X - X'| \tag{2}$$

where $\mathbb{E}_F$ describes the expectation under forecast distribution F, and X, X' are independent sampled under F. Equation 2 is the basis for different closed-form CRPS solutions under distribution F.

2.2 Ensemble Model Output Statistics (EMOS)

EMOS proposed by Gneiting et al. [12] is a post-processing technique that corrects the forecast bias and the spread of the ensemble using a regression algorithm.

$$
\begin{aligned}
y &\sim \mathcal{N}[\mu_t, \sigma_t] \\
\mu_t &= a + b_1 x_{t,1} + b_2 x_{t,2} + \cdots + b_m x_{t,m} \\
\sigma_t^2 &= c + d s_t^2 \\
s_t^2 &= \frac{1}{m} \sum_{k=1}^{m} (x_{t,k} - \overline{x}_t)^2 \\
\overline{x}_t &= \frac{1}{m} \sum_{k=1}^{m} x_{t,k}
\end{aligned}
\tag{3}
$$

The Eq. 3 assumes a normal Gaussian distribution. Parameters a, b_m, c and d can be estimated with an appropriate loss function. The location parameters are defined for $b_m \geq 0, a \in \mathbb{R}$ and scale parameters $c, d \geq 0$. The constraint $b_m \in \mathbb{R}_0^+$ improve the capability of interpreting the influence of each ensemble member. If $\lim\limits_{b_m \to 0}$ the corresponding ensemble member has no impact on the result.

$$
\begin{aligned}
\mathrm{CRPS}\big[\mathcal{N}(\mu, \sigma), y_t\big] = &\sigma \left\{ \frac{y_t - \mu_t}{\sigma_t} \left[2\Phi_{\mathrm{CRPS}}(y_t, \mu_t, \sigma_t) - 1 \right] \right. \\
&\left. + 2\varphi_{\mathrm{CRPS}}(y_t, \mu_t, \sigma_t) - \frac{1}{\sqrt{\pi}} \right\}
\end{aligned}
\tag{4}
$$

$$
\Phi_{\mathrm{CRPS}}(y_t, \mu_t, \sigma_t) = \Phi\left(\frac{y_t - \mu_t}{\sigma_t} \right) \tag{5}
$$

$$
\varphi_{\mathrm{CRPS}}(y_t, \mu_t, \sigma_t) = \varphi\left(\frac{y_t - \mu_t}{\sigma_t} \right) \tag{6}
$$

The closed form of CRPS in Eq. 4 depends on the CDF and PDF of the standard Gaussian distribution with $\mu = 0$ and $\sigma = 1$. Equation 6 denotes the PDF and Eq. 5 denotes the CDF of the given normal distribution $\mathcal{N}(0, 1)$. Additional work of Thorarinsdottir and Gneiting [25] introduced a truncated normal (TN) distribution 9 representing the property of positive wind speeds. The CRPS was further improved by Baran and Lerch [2] with a log-normal (LN) distribution 10 to consider a larger variability of wind speeds. In comparison, LN describes high speeds better than TN due to its long tail. Therefore, both CRPS functions lead to a wind speed regime-switching approach 11, derived by similar work in Lerch and Thorarinsdottir [18]. LN is parametrized using the affine functions m and v:

$$\begin{aligned} m &= e^{\mu+\sigma^2/\mu} \\ v &= e^{2\mu+\sigma^2}(e^{(\sigma^2)}-1) \\ \mu &= \log\left(\frac{m^2}{\sqrt{v+m^2}}\right) \\ \sigma &= \sqrt{\log\left(1+\frac{v}{m^2}\right)} \end{aligned} \tag{7}$$

with an adapted EMOS:

$$\begin{aligned} m_t &= a + b_1 X_{t,1} + b_2 x_{t,2} + \cdots + b_m x_{t,m} \\ v_t^2 &= c + d s_t^2 \end{aligned} \tag{8}$$

$$\begin{aligned} \text{CRPS}\left[\mathcal{N}^0(\mu,\sigma,a,b),y_t\right] =& \sigma_t\left[\Phi\left(\frac{\mu_t}{\sigma_t}\right)\right]^{-2} \\ & \cdot \left[\frac{y_t-\mu_t}{\sigma_t}\Phi\left(\frac{\mu_t}{\sigma_t}\right)\right. \\ & \cdot \left(2\Phi\left(\frac{y_t-\mu_t}{\sigma_t}\right)+\Phi(\mu_t\sigma_t)-2\right) \\ & + 2\varphi\left(\frac{y_t-\mu_t}{\sigma_t}\right)\Phi\left(\frac{\mu_t}{\sigma_t}\right) \\ & \left. - \frac{1}{\sqrt{\pi}}\Phi\left(\frac{\sqrt{2}\mu_t}{\sigma_t}\right)\right] \end{aligned} \tag{9}$$

$$\begin{aligned} \text{CRPS}\left[\mathcal{LN}(\mu,\sigma),y_t\right] =& y_t\left[2\Phi\left(\frac{\log y_t-\mu_t}{\sigma_t}\right)-1\right] \\ & - 2e^{\mu_t+\frac{\sigma_t^2}{2}}\left[\Phi\left(\frac{\log y_t-\mu_t}{\sigma_t}-\sigma_t\right)\right. \\ & \left. + \Phi\left(\frac{\sigma_t}{\sqrt{2}}\right)-1\right] \end{aligned} \tag{10}$$

The TN-CRPS is truncated at 0 ($a = 0$) due to the non-existence of negative wind speeds. TN and LN distributions use the PDF and CDF function properties of $\mathcal{N}(0,1)$.

$$H = \begin{cases} \text{CRPS}\left[\mathcal{N}^0(\mu,\sigma,a,b),y_t\right], \text{ if } \tilde{X}_t \leq \theta \\ \text{CRPS}\left[\mathcal{LN}(\mu,\sigma),y_t\right], \quad \text{ if } \tilde{X}_t > \theta \end{cases} \tag{11}$$

If in Eq. 11 the median wind ensemble forecast speed $\tilde{X}_t$ at time t surpasses the wind speed θ, the data is used to train an LN-CRPS model; otherwise, the data is used for a TN-CRPS model.

2.3 Weight Initialization

By Narkhede et al. [22], a comprehensive review of several weight initialization methods is provided. It is essential to evaluate which method is most suitable for our testing purposes, as these methods are primarily designed for neural networks.

The methods discussed involve sampling from random distributions that are scaled in specific ways to maintain the parameter variance of both the input and output layers. An alternative approach focuses on ensuring that the gradients of the output layer exhibit a desired value or variance. The chosen scaling and distribution depend heavily on the neural network's architecture and activation function.

Since our model does not employ a neural network in the EMOS framework, we adapt the aforementioned methods. Specifically, we reformulate the EMOS, cf. Eq. 3, into a one-layer, two-node neural network structure cf. Bishop [5]:

$$\mu_t = a + \sum_{i=1}^{m} b_i x_{t,1} \tag{12}$$

$$\sigma_t^2 = c + \sum_{i=1}^{1} d_i s_t^2 \tag{13}$$

In our context, the input wind speed is always ≥ 0, effectively acting like a Rectified Linear Unit (ReLU) function, $h(a) = \max(0, a)$. The properties of truncated normal and log normal distributions require a positive μ and σ, hence we assume positive values for μ and σ in TN-CRPS and LN-CRPS. These assumptions are necessary to compare the weight initialization strategy described by He et al. [13], which aligns the most closely with our problem. The authors propose a simple initialization method based on the number of input connections, n_l, in a layer index by l:

$$\frac{1}{2} n_l \text{Var}[w_l] = 1, \quad \forall l \rightarrow \sigma_l = \sqrt{\left(\frac{1}{n_l}\right)} \tag{14}$$

This approach, known as *He-initialization*, is derived from the convolutional neural network layer under the assumption that each layer uses a ReLU activation function, cf. Eq. 15.

$$\mathbf{y}_l = W_l \mathbf{x}_l + \mathbf{b}_l \tag{15}$$

They assume that the weights w_l and x_l are independent and identically distributed (i.i.d.) leading to $Var[y_l] = n_l Var[w_l]\mathbb{E}[x_l^2]$. Due to the usage of ReLU as an activation function, the assumption is false for $\mathbb{E}[x_l^2]$; the authors argued with the i.i.d. property of the $l-1$ layer and reformulated to $Var[y_l] = n_l \frac{1}{2} Var[w_l] Var[y_{l-1}]$. In the EMOS discussion from Gneiting et al. [12], they used only positive weights, arguing for better convergence and interpretable results.

Despite *He-initialization*, we have not found a weight initialization scheme that meets all of our requirements. However, after reviewing the literature Drago and Ridella [22], Duch and Korczak [21], Narkhede et al. [7,8], we observe that the work can be reduced to sampling from either a normal or uniform distribution, with additional parameterization strategies. Considering these points, we will adopt the following three distributions to construct a hyperparameter search space for their parameters:

- Truncated Normal: Regarding the widely utilized normal distribution for initialization, the truncated normal distribution serves as the closest alternative, allowing for the constraint of sampling positive values
- Beta: Generates distributions with extended tails approaching zero and one. Although confined within the interval $[0, 1]$, normalization ensures that the weights remain small.
- Gamma: A distribution characterized by a long tail can be advantageous when the model benefits from having a select few weights with large values.

3 Data

The available data cover the period from 2019 to March 2023. Measurements are obtained from WINSENT at Stötten, which utilizes a met mast to measure wind speed and direction at a height of 97 m. Data are recorded at 10-min intervals.

The Multi-Scheme Ensemble Prediction System (MSEP) provides wind speed predictions at a height of 100 m above ground. It generates an hourly forecast with a 48-h ahead prediction horizon and updates every 6 h. Post-processing EMOS is applied to the 6-h to 12-h forecast window.

3.1 Data Cleaning

The WEPROG data did not require pre-processing, as the MSEP quality assurance procedures did not produce implausible values. However, the WINSENT data presented several challenges:

- One wind speed value is significantly erroneous and had to be removed.
- Eliminate gaps in the time series data.
- Remove constant consecutive wind speeds.

3.2 WINSENT

The South German wind energy research cluster, Windenergie Forschungscluster (WindForS), is currently developing a globally unique research platform in the districts of Stötten and Kuchalb, situated in complex mountainous terrain. Both projects and their subsequent operations are coordinated and managed by the Center for Solar Energy and Hydrogen Research Baden-Württemberg (ZSW).

The research test site is located on an unforested, exposed plateau downstream of a steep escarpment. This terrain feature generates higher wind speeds, increased turbulence, and oblique flow conditions. In addition, seasonal vegetation changes along the Swabian Alb escarpment influence the characteristics of the wind flow.

3.3 WEPROG

The predictions for Stötten are produced by WEPROG's MSEPS, a 75-member ensemble model. Each ensemble member employs different formulations of specific physical processes, particularly those related to fast meteorological phenomena, such as fronts and surface friction. These variations are essential to accurately simulate dynamic atmospheric conditions described by Möhrlen and Jørgensen [20].

3.4 Rolling Window

The EMOS method is calculated using a rolling window, which is continuously updated to capture seasonal variations, model dynamics, and broader meteorological trends such as climate change. The existing literature Gneiting et al. [27] Thorarinsdottir and Gneiting [12] Wilson et al. [25] extensively discusses this topic, leading to the following conclusions: Shorter training windows enhance adaptability to changes but tend to be under-dispersive, whereas longer training periods mitigate variability but may compromise skill. The optimal window typically ranges from 30 to 45 days. Specifically, Gneiting et al. [12] identified 40 days as optimal, while Thorarinsdottir and Gneiting [25] suggested a broader range of 35 to 70 days, emphasizing its dependence on local stations. Furthermore, Baran and Lerch [2] used training windows of 20 and 43 days for different ensemble forecast models. In general, previous research highlights a considerable range of viable training periods.

For TN, LN, and TN-LN mixture models, we employ four distinct training window lengths: 25, 30, 35, and 40 days. The research test site on an exposed plateau with steep slopes. The dynamical influence of changes due to seasons has larger impact; we have to consider in rolling window width to a lower end.

4 Experiments

4.1 Model Selection

Based on chapter Sect. 2 we prepared four different models:

- EMOS with TN-CRPS
- EMOS with LN-CRPS
- Mixture EMOS based on TN- and LN-CRPS
- EMOS with standard Gaussian CRPS

Each model has the following degrees of freedom:

- Rolling period window
- Weight scheme initialization approach with parameters

The weight scheme initialization includes truncated normal $\mathcal{N}^0(\mu, \sigma)$, beta $\mathcal{B}(\alpha, \beta)$, and gamma $\Gamma(a, \lambda)$ distributions. The rolling period window is selected for each weight scheme.

4.2 Model Optimization

The validation dataset consists of data 12 h after the training period window, corresponding to the optimal prediction horizon identified by MSEPS. No additional preprocessing is applied as both numerical relationships and magnitudes are fundamental to the assumptions underlying the EMOS equation formulation.

All functions and tests are implemented in Python using PyTorch cf. Paszke et al. [23] and PyTorch Lightning cf. Falcon et al. [10] for gradient descent optimization. Hyperparameter tuning and rolling window adaptation are performed using the Optuna library cf. Akiba et al. [1], leveraging the Parzen-Tree Estimator (TPE) cf. Bergstra et al. [3]. The TPE is a hybrid non-parametric approach that combines recursive space partitioning with kernel density estimation. Hierarchically segment the feature space using decision tree principles while applying kernel smoothing functions at the terminal nodes. Unlike fixed-bandwidth kernel methods, TPE dynamically adjusts its resolution based on local data density, enabling more accurate estimations in regions with complex distributions.

Optimization is carried out using Adaptive Moment Estimation (Adam) cf. Kingma and Ba [16], chosen for its robustness, adaptability across diverse problem domains, and minimal need for extensive hyperparameter tuning. Adam updates each parameter using an exponentially decaying average of past gradients, enhancing convergence stability and efficiency.

4.3 Hyperprameter Search Space Estimation

First, we determine the appropriate search space for the sampling distributions and the learning rate for each model. Initial results yield high learning rates (e.g. 0.8), leading to poor estimation of weight initialization parameters, an issue we initially acknowledged but underestimated in severity.

Training runs exhibit substantial initial errors and need to converge within a limited number of epochs, necessitating high learning rates. Based on our experiments, we select a learning rate of 0.01 and adopt the following strategy: The EMOS system, particularly the CRPS TN and LN functions, is highly sensitive to initialization parameters. Without proper initialization, convergence requires both adaptive learning rate strategies and an increased number of optimization steps.

Once a suitable initialization scheme is established, learning rate adaptation can be introduced. It is crucial to avoid estimating both simultaneously, as this may lead to instability and suboptimal performance.

4.4 Implementation

The loss functions are evaluated against the implementation provided by the authors in a later version of the R package Jordan et al. [15]. A total of 250 different configurations are trained based on the empirical distribution function (EDF):

$$\hat{F}_n(t) = \frac{1}{n+1} \sum_{i=1}^{n} \mathbf{1}_A$$

n represents the number of samples, and $\mathbf{1}_A$ is an indicator function that defines the probability of a value being less than or equal to a given objective. As the number of sampled points from the search space increases, the EDF represents the improvement of the search.

During hyperparameter search, each sample cycle selects a rolling window from the training dataset at random. Each hyperparameter trial involves training a model for 500 epochs. The training systems employ early stopping with a minimum improvement threshold of 0.01, measured against the best results obtained during training. The patience values for early stopping are set to 100 epochs, avoiding premature stopping.

5 Results

Calibration and statistical post-processing are tools to increase the reliability of forecasting results. While it will always be possible to find optimal training periods for the EMOS for some specific condition, such methods only add value if they are robust and can be generally applied. We therefore defined three general objectives as our success criteria:

- Overall performance: One distribution with a limited parametrization shows similar results over all periods.
- Low dispersion in parameter: The parametrization itself lacks variability.
- Single dominant value: The parameterset does not result in multiple equal clusters.

We characterize each CRPS variant with respect to its a) distribution, b) the parameter set for initialization, c) its behaviour during the hyperparameter search, and d) evaluate how the EDF behaves. Figure 1 shows the EDF with CRPS in the range zero to one for the truncated normal, beta, and gamma distributions over 25, 30, 35, and 40 day training periods. In all graphical representations, the orange-delineated beta distribution consistently shows more samples with low CRPS compared to the competing distributions. During hyperparameter optimization, configurations of the beta distribution appear to yield more favorable outcomes. This observation is supported by the higher frequency of lower CRPS scores associated with these configurations. Nonetheless, the beta distribution does not invariably surpass other distributions in performance.

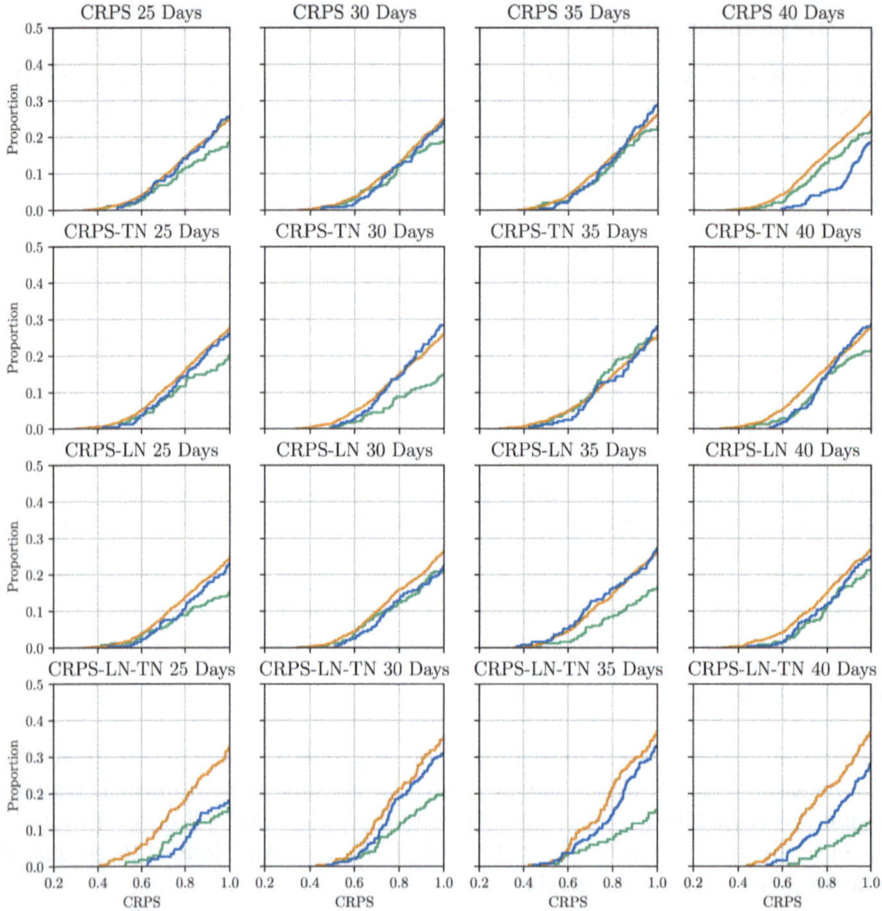

Fig. 1. Hyperparameter EDF of (orange) beta, (blue) truncated normal, (green) gamma distribution; comparing the periods 25, 30, 35, 40 with CRPS, CRPS-TN, CRPS-LN and mixture.

In Fig. 2, we compare the results for each period between all distributions and CRPS types, considering only the 20 best results. We observe that the performance of EMOS systems initialized with a beta distribution shows a pattern of being more favourable. Results of the gamma distribution of the mixture model in period 40 are excluded due to overall poor performance. We encountered issues when sampling from the hyperparameter search space and suspect that the search space needs to be adjusted, especially for the mixture model.

Analysis of the sampling distributions illustrated in Fig. 3 reveals the absence of a statistically significant concentration within any particular region of the parameter space. This observation suggests two potential interpretations:

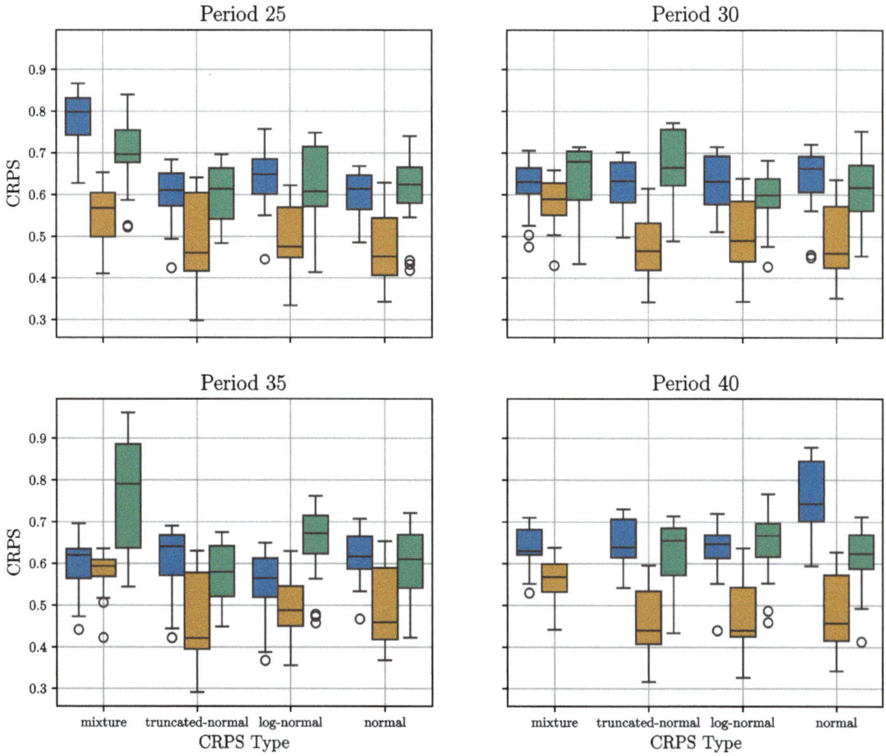

Fig. 2. Overview of all CRPS types (without mixture-LN-TN gamma distribution, due bad results); (orange) beta, (blue) truncated normal, (green) gamma distribution

- The beta distribution demonstrates considerable robustness in this context due to its intrinsic mathematical properties, rendering the specific parameterization relatively inconsequential for obtaining statistically sound results.
- Additional experimental iterations are required to delineate the region of interest with sufficient statistical power and precision.

We predominantly advocate for the second argument, as our data demonstrates a continuous decline in the variability of results. We recommend the exploration of more expansive parametrization spaces than the hyperparameter training process in subsequent research endeavors.

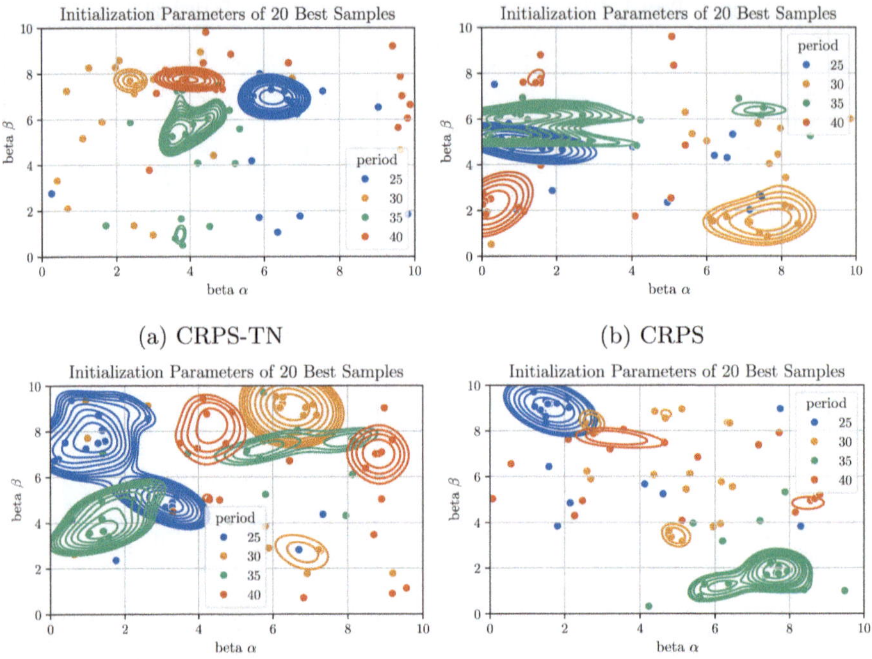

(a) CRPS-TN

(b) CRPS

(c) CRPS-LN

(d) CRPS mixture-LN-TN

Fig. 3. CRPS-LN|TN|LN-TN parametrization of 20 best samples of periods 25, 30, 35, 40

6 Conclusion

In this study, we aimed to explore different initialization schemes for EMOS. Due to the impact of the objective function used for training, we employed several CRPS functions to examine their effects and to compare how they differ or behave similarly. While this question has been exhaustively researched in Narkhede et al. [21,22] for neural networks, we attempted to apply the *He-initialization*. However, we encountered challenges due to the assumptions made for the structure of neural networks, which cannot be directly applied to EMOS. The foundation of all these initialization schemes is a normal distribution, which is modified based on the properties of activation functions, the number of layers, or connections. Alternative methods must be explored for our problem, given the fundamental constraints of EMOS, such as positive weights for ensemble members and spread estimation by Gneiting et al. [12]. Among the potential solutions we researched is sampling from strictly positive distributions for the initialization parameters. In our study, we examined the effects of truncated normal, beta, and gamma distributions across 25, 30, 35, 40 days period rolling windows. The results indicate that the beta distribution is the most suitable for sampling initial weights. The choice of objective function and training periods did not significantly affect the results comparing the performance of each sampling strategy. A surprising outcome is the mixture model proposed by Lerch and Thorarinsdottir [18] did not demonstrate superior performance compared to the alternative methods examined. This observed effect likely arises from the variation in training methodologies used or the relatively unusual geographical domain where wind forecast corrections are applied. These contextual factors should be considered when evaluating the transferability of our findings to other meteorological settings.

Acknowledgments. The authors acknowledge support by the state of Baden-Württemberg through bwHPC providing computational resources to perform the measurements. We also thank WEPROG for supplying the forecasts and the WinForS Consortium and WINSENT Testfield Coordinator ZSW Baden-Württemberg, Germany for providing us measurement data. This work is financially supported by the Deutsche Bundesstiftung Umwelt (DBU) under grant number 37549/01. We gratefully acknowledge their generous funding, which has been instrumental in the successful completion of this research project.

References

1. Akiba, T., Sano, S., Yanase, T., Ohta, T., Koyama, M.: Optuna: a next-generation hyperparameter optimization framework. In: Proceedings of the 25th ACM SIGKDD International Conference on Knowledge Discovery and Data Mining (2019)
2. Baran, S., Lerch, S.: Log-normal distribution based ensemble model output statistics models for probabilistic wind-speed forecasting **141**(691), 2289–2299 (2018). ISSN 0035-9009, 1477-870X. https://doi.org/10.1002/qj.2521
3. Bergstra, J., Bardenet, R., Bengio, Y., Kégl, B.: Algorithms for hyper-parameter optimization. In: Shawe-Taylor, J., Zemel, R., Bartlett, P., Pereira, F., Weinberger, K. (eds.) Advances in Neural Information Processing Systems, vol. 24, Curran Associates, Inc. (2011)
4. Bessa, R.J., et al.: Towards improved understanding of the applicability of uncertainty forecasts in the electric power industry. Energies **10**(9) (2017). ISSN 1996-1073. https://doi.org/10.3390/en10091402
5. Bishop, C.M.: Pattern Recognition and Machine Learning. Information Science and Statistics. Springer (2006). ISBN 978-0-387-31073-2 and Statistics, Springer (2006), ISBN 978-0-387-31073-2
6. Bishop, C.M.: Deep Learning: Foundations and Concepts. Springer (2024). ISBN 978-3-031-45468-4
7. Drago, G., Ridella, S.: Statistically controlled activation weight initialization (SCAWI) **3**(4), 627–631 (1992). ISSN 10459227. https://doi.org/10.1109/72.143378
8. Duch, W., Korczak, J.: Optimization and global minimization methods suitable for neural networks **2**, 163–212 (1998)
9. Epstein, E.S.: Stochastic dynamic prediction **21**(6), 739 (1969). ISSN 1600-0870. https://doi.org/10.3402/tellusa.v21i6.10143
10. Falcon, W., et al.: PyTorchLightning/pytorch-lightning: 0.7.6 release (2020). https://doi.org/10.5281/ZENODO.3828935

11. Gneiting, T., Raftery, A.E.: Strictly Proper Scoring Rules, Prediction, and Estimation **102**(477), 359–378 (2007). ISSN 0162-1459, 1537-274X. https://doi.org/10.1198/016214506000001437
12. Gneiting, T., Raftery, A.E., Westveld, A.H., Goldman, T.: Calibrated probabilistic forecasting using ensemble model output statistics and minimum CRPS estimation **133**(5), 1098–1118 (2005). ISSN 1520-0493, 0027-0644. https://doi.org/10.1175/MWR2904.1
13. He, K., Zhang, X., Ren, S., Sun, J.: Delving deep into rectifiers: surpassing human-level performance on imagenet classification. In: Proceedings of the IEEE International Conference on Computer Vision, pp. 1026–1034
14. Hersbach, H.: Decomposition of the Continuous Ranked Probability Score for Ensemble Prediction Systems **15**(5), 559–570 (2000). ISSN 0882-8156, 1520-0434. https://doi.org/10.1175/1520-0434(2000)015⟨0559:DOTCRP⟩2.0.CO;2
15. Jordan, A., Krüger, F., Lerch, S.: Evaluating Probabilistic Forecasts with **scoringRules90**(12) (2019). ISSN 1548-7660. https://doi.org/10.18637/jss.v090.i12
16. Kingma, D.P., Ba, J.: Adam: A Method for Stochastic Optimization (2014). https://doi.org/10.48550/ARXIV.1412.6980
17. Leith, C.E.: Theoretical Skill of Monte Carlo Forecasts **102**(6), 409–418 (1974). 10.1175/1520-0493(1974)102¡0409:TSOMCF¿2.0.CO;2
18. Lerch, S., Thorarinsdottir, T.L.: Comparison of non-homogeneous regression models for probabilistic wind speed forecasting **65**(1), 21206 (2013). ISSN 1600-0870. https://doi.org/10.3402/tellusa.v65i0.21206
19. Matheson, J.E., Winkler, R.L.: Scoring Rules for Continuous Probability Distributions **22**(10), 1087–1096 (1976). ISSN 0025-1909, 1526-5501. https://doi.org/10.1287/mnsc.22.10.1087
20. Möhrlen, C., Jørgensen, J.U.: The role of ensemble forecasting in integrating renewables into power systems: from theory to real-time applications. In: Du, P., Baldick, R., Tuohy, A. (eds.) Integration of Large-Scale Renewable Energy into Bulk Power Systems. PEPS, pp. 79–134. Springer, Cham (2017). https://doi.org/10.1007/978-3-319-55581-2_3
21. Narkhede, M., Mahajan, S., Bartakke, P.: Data-driven weight initialization strategy for convolutional neural networks **18**(1), 1 (2015). ISSN 1864-5909, 1864-5917. https://doi.org/10.1007/s12065-024-00985-w
22. Narkhede, M.V., Bartakke, P.P., Sutaone, M.S.: A review on weight initialization strategies for neural networks. Artif. Intell. Rev. **55**(1), 291–322 (2021). https://doi.org/10.1007/s10462-021-10033-z
23. Paszke, A., et al.: Automatic differentiation in PyTorch (2017)
24. Schulz, B., Lerch, S.: Machine Learning Methods for Postprocessing Ensemble Forecasts of Wind Gusts: A Systematic Comparison **150**(1), 235–257 (2022). ISSN 0027-0644, 1520-0493. https://doi.org/10.1175/MWR-D-21-0150.1
25. Thorarinsdottir, T.L., Gneiting, T.: Probabilistic Forecasts of Wind Speed: Ensemble Model Output Statistics by using Heteroscedastic Censored Regression **173**(2), 371–388 (2010). ISSN 0964-1998, 1467-985X. https://doi.org/10.1111/j.1467-985X.2009.00616.x
26. Wilks, D.S.: Statistical Methods in the Atmospheric Sciences. Elsevier, 4th edn. (2019). ISBN 978-0-12-815823-4
27. Wilson, L.J., Beauregard, S., Raftery, A.E., Verret, R.: Calibrated Surface Temperature Forecasts from the Canadian Ensemble Prediction System Using Bayesian Model Averaging **135**(4), 1364–1385 (2007). ISSN 1520-0493, 0027-0644. https://doi.org/10.1175/MWR3347.1

Improving Anonymization of Mobility Trajectories with Map-Matching

Di Hu(✉) and Gabriele Gühring

Esslingen University of Applied Sciences, Flandernstraße 101, 73732 Esslingen, Germany
{di.hu,gabriele.guehring}@hs-esslingen.de

Abstract. With increasing importance of digitalization and requirements of data collection and mining in the mobility sector, the demand on privacy protection of mobility trajectories is also growing. Mobility trajectories offer important insights which could be applied for traffic simulations and planning. However, they also allow one to understand the behavior of individual users. These serve as potential vulnerable attack points, as the data may allow conclusions to be drawn about personal situations.

Anonymization methods are therefore required for the use of these privacy-sensitive data. One of the central challenges is on the one hand to undermine the traceability to specific individuals and on the other hand to keep the overall usability of data as much as possible. This can be ensured by generation of anonymized synthetic data with a Local Differential Privacy mechanism and the use of publicly available geographical maps that display among others streets, railroad lines and pedestrian zones.

In this paper, a map matching algorithm is applied to synthetic trajectories created with a Local Differential Privacy mechanism. This way, anonymization as well as a high level of utility for the synthetic mobility trajectories is achieved.

Keywords: Anonymization · Local Differential Privacy · Synthesized Trajectories · Map-Matching · Topsøe Distance

1 Introduction

The rapid digitalization impacts the mobility world significantly, in which the data collection and mining are becoming ever more important since it can be used to generate surplus value for both public and private stakeholders. The collection and analysis of mobility data can not only provide valuable insights into the behavior and needs of users, but also poses as potential data protection weak points. Information about travel time, frequency of travel, travel routes and transportation modes can allow conclusions to be made about personal and private information about certain users, see [21]. It therefore poses a challenge

L. Bechtel and T. Heer (Eds.): CCSSS 2025 PTT, pp. 171–182, 2026.
https://doi.org/10.1007/978-3-032-10569-1_11

for data collection and publication in compliance with different governmental data i.e. in Europe, the General Data Protection Regulation (GDPR) [15].

Another challenge may also occur during the data processing. Often the data is collected unchanged from users throughout an edge device, such as smartphone or in-vehicle infotainment system. The data will then be collected by a central instance and being processed by a so-called data curator which requires that this data curator can be trusted to handle and protect the data from unauthorized access.

Therefore suitable anonymization algorithms are necessary which modify the data in such a way that it is no longer possible to track down certain individual persons without compromising the data quality too much. One of the most important anonymization methods is Differential Privacy (DP), [2]. In this case the data is anonymized by adding noise to the raw data by a central party. Recently, different approaches have been proposed to perform DP locally so that the data is already anonymized before it is transmitted to the curator [1]. One such approach is the concept of Local Differential Privacy (LDP) which is particularly effect when user information should not be disclosed to third parties. Noise is added before the data is transmitted to the data curator on users' device. The LDPTrace framework proposed in [1], is such an approach which can be applied to mobility data by adding noise to the trajectories with the help of LDP.

We use the work in [1], apply it to two different mobility datasets as described in Sect. 4.1 and show that overall the utility metric can be improved by applying a map matching algorithm, see [22], to the anonymously created synthesized trajectories. Our results hold for different utility budgets ε and different grid regions of San Francisco and Esslingen.

2 Related Works

Compared to privacy preservation methods, e.g. k-anonymity [13], l-diversity [10] and t-closeness [7]) that require assumptions on some specific attack and background knowledge, differential privacy (DP) is independent of background data. It has, therefore, been becoming a standard in the field of data anonymization, [4] and [2]. While DP is based on the assumption that a data curator can be trusted, LDP is based on the assumption that the data curator is untrusted, [5] and [20]. However, as LDP is more difficult with trajectory data, many approaches use the generation of synthetic trajectories based on features of the original data with the inclusion of noise instead of adding noise to individual points of the trajectories [1,4–6]. In [1] the length, transition matrix and start and end points are used as features of a trajectory in order to add noise to them. However, these syntethetic trajectories very often do not fit real maps or roads [12].

Therefore post-processing methods are required for synthetic trajectories. Map-matching is one of the possibilities to post-process synthetic trajectories. Different map-matching approaches are introduced and compared in [12], such as commercial map-matching services like Google and Mapbox, whereas open-source map-matching services like OSRM and Valhalla are also introduced. A comprehensive research of OSRM-based map-matching is described in [16]. The challenge is that it is usually not possible to verify that the results of a map matching algorithm are actually correct, since there is generally no ground truth for a given track. Though many advances concerning the accuracy of map-matching were made in the past, further research is still to be done to improve the matching to the road network [19]. However, in this work we use map-matching in order to improve the utility metrics of the LDP algorithm LDP-Trace [1]. Therefore, the ground truth is always given with the original recorded trajectory datasets. For our analysis we use of the most examined datasets concerning trajectory anonymization is the San Francisco Cabspotting dataset, [11] consisting of mobility data from approximately 500 taxis in San Francisco, USA, as well as our own dataset, consisting of SUMO simulated GPS coordinates in the city of Esslingen.

3 Preliminaries

3.1 Differential Privacy and Local Differential Privacy

Differential Privacy (DP) ensures that the results of queries to a database remain essentially the same, regardless of whether an individual users data is included in the database or not. ε-DP can be formally defined as follows [2]:

Definition 1. An algorithm $\mathcal{A}$ fulfills ε-DP if for all data sets D_1 and D_2, which differ only in one element, and for all $S \subseteq Range(\mathcal{A})$

$$P[\mathcal{A}(D_1) \in S] \leq e^{\varepsilon} P[\mathcal{A}(D_2) \in S]. \quad (1)$$

Applied to mobility data and trajectories in particular, this means that the data sets may only differ in a single trajectory. In order to ensure DP on the basis of the user (user-level privacy), the data sets D_1 and D_2 would have to differ in a single person, i.e. in all trajectories of the person concerned. The parameter ε determines the amount of added noise and can be considered as a privacy budget. A lower value of ε leads to more noise and thus to more privacy, but also most of the time to less useful results.

DP has two fundamental properties [2]. The first is the composition theorem, which can be divided into two types:

- **Sequential Composition**: If multiple ε_i-DP mechanisms are applied sequentially to the same data set, the ε_i values of the individual queries add up to achieve ε-DP, where $\varepsilon = \sum_i \varepsilon_i$.
- **Parallel Composition**: If multiple ε_i-DP queries are applied to disjoint subsets of a data set, the ε value of the entire operation remains equal to the largest ε_i value of the individual queries.

In addition, **Post-processing immunity** applies, i.e. that DP is maintained even after the output has been processed by another algorithm.

In [1], the concept of LDP is used for trajectories. ε-LDP differs from ε-DP in how the input data x is perturbed with an algorithm ε before it is sent to an unreliable input aggregator [1].

Definition 2. An algorithm $\mathcal{A}$ fulfills ε-LDP with $\varepsilon \geq 0$, if for each input x_1, x_2 and each output y

$$P[\mathcal{A}(x_1) = y] \leq e^{\varepsilon} P[\mathcal{A}(x_2) = y] \tag{2}$$

As in DP, ε represents a metric for the privacy budget. LDP protects the privacy of users by sending the input $\hat{x}_{\varepsilon}$ to the aggregator locally falsified with the privacy budget ε instead of the true value x. This means that privacy remains protected even with malicious data curators. In addition, the basic mechanisms of ε-DP apply, namely composition theorems and postprocessing immunity [1] in which an enhanced map-matching framework able to process larger amount of GPS data is proposed.

3.2 Optimized Unary Encoding with Differential Privacy

The concept of LDP can be implemented with a so-called LDP protocol, which still allows the estimation of the frequencies of any value x i.e. the length of a trajectory or the location in a grid. For LDP the so-called Optimized Unary Encoding (OUE) might be used, see [18].

OUE is a special version of Unary Encoding (UE) that has been optimized with respect to variance and selectable parameters p and q [18]. The following three main phases are run through during OUE [18] and [1]:

- **Encoding**: An original value x is first encoded into a binary bit vector of length d, where d is the number of possible values of x. Thereby only the x-th bit is set to 1, i.e. $V[i] = 1(\iff i = x)$
- **Perturbation**: Perturbation is applied to the encoded vector V to protect privacy. The perturbation is defined as follows, where ε represents the privacy budget and $\hat{V}$ the perturbed vector:

$$P[\hat{V}[i] = 1] = \begin{cases} \frac{1}{2}, & \text{if } V[i] = 1 \\ \frac{1}{e^{\varepsilon}+1}, & \text{if } V[i] = 0 \end{cases} \tag{3}$$

  The central data curator estimates with these noisy vectors $\hat{V}$ the probability distributions for each component as in Eq. 5.
- **Aggregation**: In the aggregation phase, to obtain an unbiased estimate of the actual value from the perturbed vectors, the data is aggregated and adjusted using the following rule

$$\tilde{g}(x) = \frac{\hat{g}(x) - nq}{p - q}, \quad p = \frac{1}{2}, \quad q = \frac{1}{e^{\varepsilon} + 1} \tag{4}$$

where p and q are the parameters of the OUE. The variable n is the number of perturbed vectors $\hat{V}$ and $\hat{g}(x)$ is the number of vectors $\hat{V}$ in which every x-th bit has the value 1, such that $\hat{g}(x) = |\{\hat{V}|\hat{V}[x] = 1\}|$. It should be noted that the privacy budget ε used in each OUE adjustment process has to remain the same for all data in the corresponding process in order to allow proper estimations. The mean value and the variance of the OUE are then

$$E[\tilde{g}(x)] = f_x, \quad Var[\tilde{g}(x)] = n\frac{4e^{\varepsilon}}{(e^{\varepsilon}-1)^2}, \tag{5}$$

where f_x is the frequency of the value x and ε is again the budget for privacy. The adjusted estimate $\tilde{g}$ is unbiased, see [18].

In [1] the LDP framework LDPTrace for mobility trajectories is described. It starts with a spatial discretization of user trajectories into predefined rectangular grid regions. The key components x that are transmitted with a privacy budget ε to a central data curator via OUE include transitions between rectangular grid regions, start/end points and trajectory lengths.

In [1] synthesized trajectories are estimated from probability distributions obtained with the help of these transmitted and perturbed data.

3.3 Map-Matching Algorithm

Since GPS data is mainly used for collecting position data, it may be associated with two different kinds of errors. Firstly, the measurement errors may occur when the measured position deviates from its real position. Secondly, sampling errors may occur which results in loss of information between recorded points [12].

Furthermore, the perturbed trajectories generated with the LDPTrace Algorithm presented in [1] do not correspond to the real map either since its randomly generated waypoints deviate from the real map, leading to a higher utility loss, since the generated routes cannot be crossed over on the real map as shown in Fig. 1. With map-matching algorithm the perturbed trajectory can be fit into the street data, which means that utility loss can be reduced since the trajectory corresponds more to reality as shown in Fig. 2.

Currently, there are several map-matching services, such as Google API and MapBox. However, since these services are commercial in nature, larger request counts necessary for processing a larger amount of trajectory can result in a cost explosion [12].

There are also open-source approaches which allow setting up a local map-matching server, such as OSRM, and Valhalla. The advantage of both map-matching engines is that they are based on OpenStreetMap data which also serves as the basis for traffic simulation, which will be introduced in Sect. 4.1. Also, OSRM possesses a higher routing performance while it demands higher RAM usage at the same time. However, since the map-matching is performed on a system with high RAM capacity, this disadvantage is not of significance for our work. Furthermore, the possibility of multi-modal map-matching [12] is of relevance. We therefore opted to set up a local OSRM server because of its higher performance and multi-modal map-matching ability, which is crucial for this application and future works.

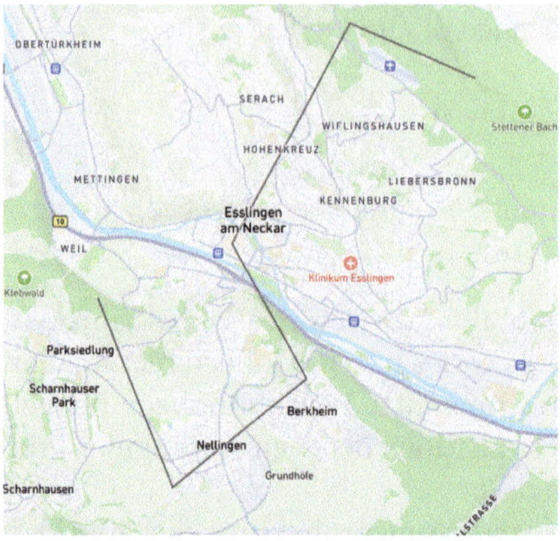

Fig. 1. Example of a synthesized trajectory generated from LDPTrace

Fig. 2. Post-Processed example synthesized trajectory with map matching

Since map-matching only incorporates information which is already available to any user or attacker, such as the nearest street or the nearest POI, this does not change the size of the privacy budget ε. It simply makes publicly available information transparent. Even if map matching were not used to calculate the utility metric, map-matching could still be used during an attack at any time. Therefore, map-matching does not compromise privacy, and thus, the value of the parameter ε remains unchanged.

4 Evaluation

4.1 Experimental Setup and Datasets

The experiments were performed in a Windows 11 based machine with an Intel Core i7-1370P CPU, 64 GiB RAM and 1.76 TiB storage.

The implementation of the synthesized trajectories is based on [1] with modifications from [3]. A local map-matching engine based on OSRM [9] was also established on the environment to process the synthetic trajectories.

For the evaluation we use the following trajectory data sets:

San Francisco Cabspotting: The dataset contains mobility data in form of GPS coordinates of approximately 500 taxis in San Francisco, USA, collected in the San Francisco Bay Area [11]. The data collection dates back to 2008.
Esslingen SUMO Simulation: The dataset contains mobility data in the form of SUMO-simulated GPS coordinates of approximately 1000 motorists in the city of Esslingen.

To evaluate the results of the San Francisco Cabspotting dataset, the trajectories of the taxi data are derived by the occupancy of taxi cabs, which means that all unoccupied trips are removed. Additionally, trajectories outside of the specified ranges of San Francisco City Center are removed. The exact area is listed in Table 1.

In the Esslingen SUMO Simulation dataset, the trajectories are extracted by a SUMO-based traffic simulation which contains motorist road users with different modalities. Alike the San Francisco Cabspotting dataset, the trajectories are restricted to a defined area which covers the central city of Esslingen and so a sample of 1,468 trajectories was taken.

Furthermore, out of these trajectories a synthesized San Francisco Cabspotting and a synthesized Esslingen SUMO Simulation dataset will be both post-processed with the locally deployed OSRM map matching engine so that the synthesized trajectories correspond to real road geometries [22].

Table 1. Information on the two datasets used for evaluation

Dataset	Size	Area (Longitude/Latitude)			
		Longitude		Latitude	
		min.	max.	min.	max.
San Francisco Cabspotting	562,202	−122.5	−122.34	37.6	37.83
Esslingen SUMO Simulation	1,468	9.265	9.374	48.702	48.772

4.2 Results

The distribution of data points in both synthetic datasets and synthetic-map matched datasets are analyzed on grids with a different size. A grid granularity $N = 6, 13$ is selected for the San Francisco Cabspotting dataset, whereas $N = 4, 7$ is selected for the Esslingen SUMO Simulation dataset. For the evaluation different privacy budgets $\varepsilon = 1.0, 1.5, 2.0, 3.0$ are selected for both datasets, see Table 2. We evaluate the utility of the synthesized trajectories with the Topsøe Distance d_{Topsoe}

$$d_{\text{Topsøe}}(P,Q) = \sum_{i,j} = \left(P_{ij} \ln \frac{2P_{i,j}}{P_{i,j} + Q_{i,j}}\right) + \left(Q_{ij} \ln \frac{2Q_{i,j}}{P_{i,j} + Q_{i,j}}\right) \tag{6}$$

where P and Q are the probability distributions for the data points of the respective grids before and after synthesization. Topsøe Distance is a measure used in information theory which quantifies the difference between two probability distributions [14].

Another metric used for evaluating divergence is Jensen-Shannon-Divergence d_{JS}, which is half of the Topsøe Distance d_{Topsoe}, see [17].

$$d_{JS}(P,Q) = \frac{1}{2} \sum_{i,j} = \left(P_{ij} \ln \frac{2P_{i,j}}{P_{i,j} + Q_{i,j}}\right) + \left(Q_{ij} \ln \frac{2Q_{i,j}}{P_{i,j} + Q_{i,j}}\right) \tag{6}$$

The minimum and maximum range of Jensen-Shannon-Divergence is discussed in [8], meaning that the range of Jensen-Shannon-Divergence is bounded by the following for two discrete possibility distributions:

$$0 \leq d_{JS}(P,Q) \leq 1 \tag{7}$$

Since the Jensen-Shannon Divergence is half of the Topsøe Distance, the bound on the Topsøe Distance would then be

$$0 \leq d_{\text{Topsøe}}(P,Q) \leq 2 \tag{9}$$

The result of Topsøe Distance is summarized in Table 2. It can be seen that the Topsøe Distance decreases with the map-matching algorithm applied to the synthetic generated dataset depending on the respective grid used. This effect becomes smaller for finer-grained grid structures but leads to a significant amount of improvement for coarser grid structures. The application of map-matching algorithm therefore improves the accuracy of synthetic trajectories. Additionally, the Topsøe Distance can be evaluated across whole grid structure and there shows a similar result, as is illustrated in Fig. 3 for the case of a N=4×4 grid.

Table 2. Topsøe Distances for Esslingen and Cabspotting datasets, synthetic and synthetic map-matched.

Dataset	Grid	Synthetic				Synthetic map-matched			
		$\varepsilon = 1.0$	$\varepsilon = 1.5$	$\varepsilon = 2.0$	$\varepsilon = 3.0$	$\varepsilon = 1.0$	$\varepsilon = 1.5$	$\varepsilon = 2.0$	$\varepsilon = 3.0$
Cabspotting	6 × 6	1.147	1.13	1.125	1.112	1.132	1.115	1.109	1.094
	13 × 13	1.33	1.325	1.323	1.323	1.325	1.32	1.317	1.317
Esslingen	4 × 4	1.116	1.136	1.092	1.092	1.091	1.075	1.046	1.05
	7 × 7	1.27	1.289	1.284	1.282	1.258	1.269	1.265	1.256

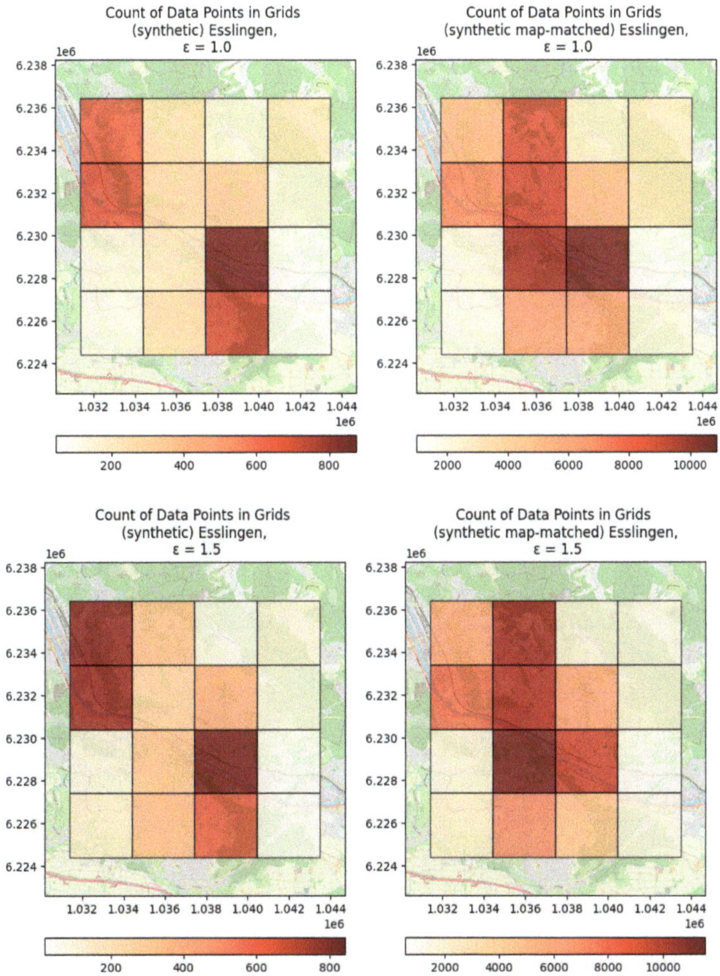

Fig. 3. Heat map of Data Points from synthesized trajectories Esslingen, Grid size $N = 4 \times 4$ for different εs with (right) and without (left) map matching

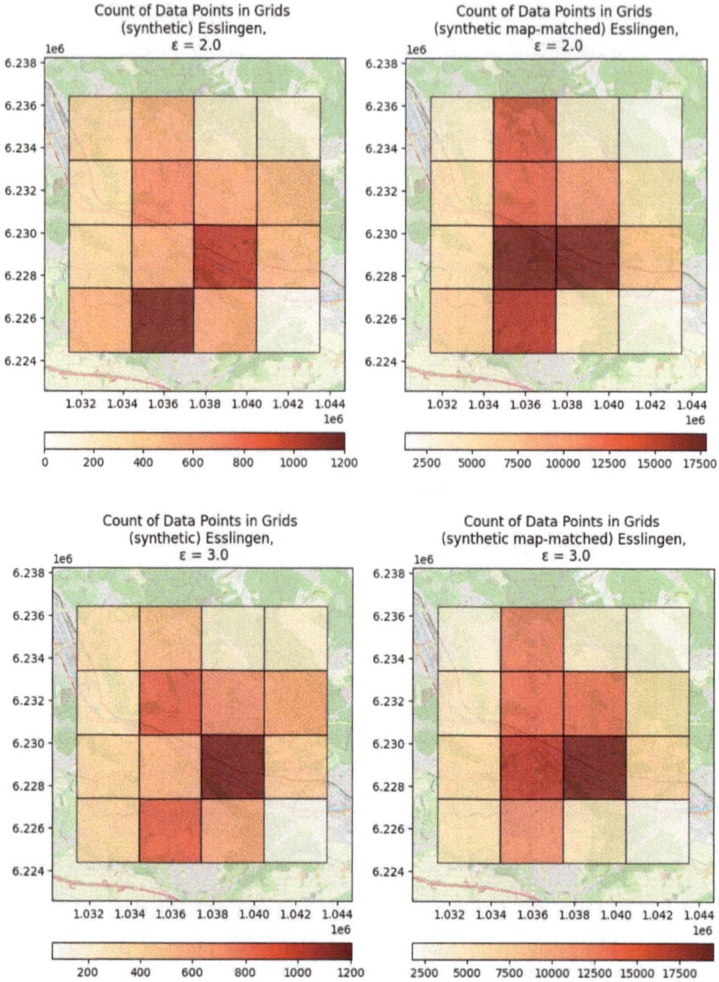

Fig. 3. (*continued*)

5 Conclusions

In this paper, we improve the utility metrics based on a Local Differential Privacy framework combined with a map-matching algorithm. This combination increases the utility of synthetic anonymized trajectories throughout all selected datasets, grid sizes, and privacy budgets ε, where the Topsøe Distance is used as a utility metric.

The application of map-matching algorithm is therefore relevant in practice for many use cases, as it allows to reconstruct more realistic synthetic trajectories and still ensures user privacy. Further research should be done on other utility metrics as for example TripCountError or ODFFlowErrors and also on different grid or tessellation sizes, as in [5].

For research in this paper only trajectories with car drivers are taken into consideration. Further research should also be done with trajectories describing other modalities (e.g. pedestrians, buses and mass). It is also planned to consider the multimodality of individual trajectories in map-matching by utilizing the multi-modality capability of the routing engine OSRM.

References

1. Du, Y., et al.: Ldptrace: locally differentially private trajectory synthesis. Proc. VLDB Endow. **16**(8), 1897–1909 (2023). https://doi.org/10.14778/3594512.3594520
2. Dwork, C., Roth, A.: The algorithmic foundations of differential privacy **9**(3–4), 211–407 (2014)
3. Efremidis, A., Walter, P., Hu, D., Gühring, G.: Anonymization of mobility data and its meta information using local differential privacy in combination with bidirectional graphs (2025, preprint)
4. Kapp, A., Hansmeyer, J., Mihaljević, H.: Generative models for synthetic urban mobility data: a systematic literature review. ACM Comput. Surv. **56**(93), 1–37 (2023). https://doi.org/10.1145/3610224
5. Kapp, A., Nuñez von Voigt, S., Mihaljević, H., Tschorsch, F.: Towards mobility reports with user-level privacy. J. Location Based Serv. **17**(2), 95–121 (2023)
6. Kim, J.W., Jang, B.: Privacy-preserving generation and publication of synthetic trajectory microdata: a comprehensive survey **230**(103951), 1–23. https://doi.org/10.1016/j.jnca.2024.103951
7. Li, N., Li, T., Venkatasubramanian, S.: t-closeness: privacy beyond k-anonymity and l-diversity. In: 2007 IEEE 23rd International Conference on Data Engineering, pp. 106–115. IEEE (2006)
8. Lin, J.: Divergence measures based on the shannon entropy. IEEE Trans. Inf. Theory **37**(1), 145–151 (1991). https://doi.org/10.1109/18.61115
9. Luxen, D., Vetter, C.: Real-time routing with openstreetmap data. In: Proceedings of the 19th ACM SIGSPATIAL International Conference on Advances in Geographic Information Systems, GIS 2011, pp. 513–516. ACM, New York (2011). https://doi.org/10.1145/2093973.2094062
10. Machanavajjhala, A., Kifer, D., Gehrke, J., Venkitasubramaniam, M.: l-diversity: privacy beyond k-anonymity. ACM Trans. Knowl. Discov. Data **1**(1), 3–37 (2007). https://doi.org/10.1145/1217299.1217302
11. Piorkowski, M., Sarafijanovic-Djukic, N., Grossglauser, M.: Crawdad EPFL/mobility (2022). https://doi.org/10.15783/C7J010
12. Saki, S., Hagen, T.: A practical guide to an open-source map-matching approach for big GPS data. SN Comput. Sci. **3**(5) (2022)
13. Sweeney, L.: K-anonymity: a model for protecting privacy. Internat. J. Uncertain. Fuzziness Knowl.-Based Syst. **10**(5), 557–570 (2020). https://doi.org/10.1142/S0218488502001648
14. Topsoe, F.: Some inequalities for information divergence and related measures of discrimination. IEEE Trans. Inf. Theory **46**(4), 1602–1609 (2000). https://doi.org/10.1109/18.850703

15. European Union: General data protection regulation (GDPR). Official Journal of the European Union (2018). https://gdpr-info.eu/
16. Vander Laan, Z., Franz, M., Marković, N.: Scalable framework for enhancing raw GPS trajectory data: application to trip analytics for transportation planning. J. Big Data Anal. Transp. **3**(2), 119–139 (2021). https://doi.org/10.1007/s42421-021-00040-5
17. Wang, H., Gao, C., Wu, Y., Jin, D., Yao, L., Li, Y.: Pategail: a privacy-preserving mobility trajectory generator with imitation learning. In: Proceedings of the Thirty-Seventh AAAI Conference on Artificial Intelligence and Thirty-Fifth Conference on Innovative Applications of Artificial Intelligence and Thirteenth Symposium on Educational Advances in Artificial Intelligence, pp. 14539–14547. No. 1631, AAAI Press (2023). https://doi.org/10.1609/aaai.v37i12.26700
18. Wang, T., Blocki, J., Li, N., Jha, S.: Locally differentially private protocols for frequency estimation. In: Proceedings of the 26th USENIX Conference on Security Symposium, SEC 2017, pp. 729–745. USENIX Association, USA (2017)
19. Wöltche, A.: Open source map matching with Markov decision processes: a new method and a detailed benchmark with existing approaches. Trans. GIS **27**(7), 1959–1991 (2023). https://doi.org/10.1111/tgis.13107
20. Xiong, X., Liu, S., Li, D., Cai, Z., Xiaoguang, N.: A comprehensive survey on local differential privacy. Secur. Commun. Netw. **1**, 1–29 (2020). https://doi.org/10.1155/2020/8829523
21. Xu, F., Tu, Z., Li, Y., Zhang, P., Fu, X., Jin, D.: Trajectory recovery from ash: user privacy is not preserved in aggregated mobility data. In: Proceedings of the 26th International Conference on World Wide Web, WWW 2017, pp. 1241–1250. International World Wide Web Conferences Steering Committee, Republic and Canton of Geneva, CHE (2017). https://doi.org/10.1145/3038912.3052620
22. Yang, C., Gidofalvi, G.: Fast map matching, an algorithm integrating hidden Markov model with precomputation. Int. J. Geogr. Inf. Sci. **32**(3), 547–570 (2018). https://doi.org/10.1080/13658816.2017.1400548

Author Index

B
Bechtel, Lukas 53, 140
Buck, Bastian 125

C
Coskunyürek, Enes 1

E
Enzweiler, Markus 1

F
Freymann, Andreas 109

G
Grimmer, Götz 155
Gühring, Gabriele 171

H
Heer, Tobias 13, 53, 74, 125, 140
Hu, Di 171
Hummen, René 140

K
Kandemir, Tolgahan 1
Kaniewski, Sabrina 74
Knauer, Maike 1
Krüger, Clemens 92

L
Lohmiller, Nils 13, 74

M
Möhrlen, Corinna 155
Moriya, Bhavinkumar 92
Müller, Samuel 53

P
Popperl, Lukas 53

R
Ravlija, Damir 37, 109
Reichsöllner, Emanuel 109
Röhner, Ruben 37
Ruppert, Julius 140

S
Schober, Steffen 155
Schoop, Dominik 92
Schramm, Markus 74
Sonntag, Mirko 37, 109

T
Trautwein, Ingo 37

W
Weise, Henning 13

L. Bechtel and T. Heer (Eds.): CCSSS 2025 PTT, p. 183, 2026.
https://doi.org/10.1007/978-3-032-10569-1

MIX
Papier aus verantwortungsvollen Quellen
Paper from responsible sources
FSC® C105338

If you have any concerns about our products, you can contact us on
ProductSafety@springernature.com

In case Publisher is established outside the EU, the EU authorized representative is:
Springer Nature Customer Service Center GmbH
Europaplatz 3, 69115 Heidelberg, Germany

Printed by Libri Plureos GmbH
in Hamburg, Germany